OXFORD CLASSICAL & PHILOSOPHICAL MONOGRAPHS

NOTE

The works published in this series are concerned with subjects falling within the scope of the Faculty of Literae Humaniores, viz. Greek and Latin Language and Literature, Ancient History, and Philosophy

Philosophical

CONSENT, FREEDOM AND POLITICAL OBLIGATION, by J. P. Plamenatz (*Out of print*)

MORALITY AND FREEDOM IN THE PHILOSOPHY OF IMMANUEL KANT, by W. T. Jones (*Out of print*)

AN EXAMINATION OF THE DEDUCTIVE LOGIC OF JOHN STUART MILL, by Reginald Jackson (*Out of print*)

REASON AND CONDUCT IN HUME'S TREATISE, by Rachael M. Kydd (*Out of print*)

THE MORAL SENSE, by D. Daiches Raphael (*Out of print*)

KNOWLEDGE AND THE GOOD IN PLATO'S REPUBLIC, by H. W. B. Joseph (*Out of print*)

THE NATURE OF HISTORICAL EXPLANATION, by Patrick Gardiner

JOHN LOCKE AND THE WAY OF IDEAS, by John W. Yolton

Classical (including History)

THE STOICHEDON STYLE IN GREEK INSCRIPTIONS, by R. P. Austin (*Out of print*)

THE COINAGE OF DAMASTION, by J. M. F. May

AINOS: ITS HISTORY AND COINAGE 474–341 B.C., by J. M. F. May (*Out of print*)

TRAJAN'S PARTHIAN WAR, by F. A. Lepper

GALEN ON JEWS AND CHRISTIANS, by R. Walzer

THE RHODIAN PERAEA AND ISLANDS, by P. M. Fraser and G. E. Bean

MARGINALIA SCAENICA, by John Jackson

LAWS AND EXPLANATION IN HISTORY, by William Dray

EURIPIDES: HYPSIPYLE. Edited by G. W. Bond

THE PARTICIPLE
IN CICERO

BY

ERIC LAUGHTON

Firth Professor of Latin in the
University of Sheffield

OXFORD UNIVERSITY PRESS
1964

Oxford University Press, Amen House, London E.C.4

GLASGOW   NEW YORK   TORONTO   MELBOURNE   WELLINGTON
BOMBAY   CALCUTTA   MADRAS   KARACHI   LAHORE   DACCA
CAPE TOWN   SALISBURY   NAIROBI   IBADAN   ACCRA
KUALA LUMPUR   HONG KONG

PRINTED IN GREAT BRITAIN

PREFACE

THIS study was begun many years ago. Shortly after the Second
World War, I had prepared the first draft of an essay on the
development of a Roman historical prose style, and sent it to
the late Hugh Last, whose interest in his former pupils none of
them is likely to forget. With characteristic kindness he put the
manuscript into the hands of Professor Fraenkel, who invited
me to visit him for a discussion. At this, the first of many meetings, Professor Fraenkel had no difficulty in demonstrating to
me that the material available was far too meagre for the kind
of research I had in mind. Instead, he turned my attention to
a different topic, the investigation of a particular feature in one
prose writer of Rome—and that the greatest—the volume of
whose surviving writings promises to the investigator, if it does
not guarantee, reliable results. Many stylistic studies of Cicero
have suffered from the fact that they have been based on a
sample of his work; the complete survey on which the present
study rests will, I hope, strengthen the validity of its conclusions.
For myself, nothing could have been more educative and re-
warding than the task of reading all that Cicero wrote.

The participle was chosen because I had become specially
interested in its use as an element of subordination in the
sentence; this stylistic concern will be evident enough to the
reader. But the progress of the work and the accumulation of
examples inevitably widened the scope of the inquiry. Since
Cicero was not only an individual writer but also a representative of the educated Romans of his day, a detailed study of his
usage could be expected to give a clearer picture of the syntax
of the Latin participle in general; and I hope that, in fact, some
new light may have been thrown on this field. Primarily, however, the participle attracted my attention not for its own sake,
but as a technical element in the perfecting of a Latin prose style
which reached its culmination in Cicero. As for Cicero's own

contribution to the development of participial usages, the remains of Latin prose from the generation preceding him are
too scanty to permit anything but a tentative assessment. The
evidence of Early Latin is instructive, for it enables us to see
in what respects and to what extent, between the first half of
the second century B.C. and Cicero's day, participles had been
brought into more frequent and varied use; and sometimes a
comparison of Cicero's earlier with his later work discloses
developments which can reasonably be attributed to Cicero
himself.

The value of a book of this kind lies largely in its collection
of examples. In the case of many of the constructions illustrated
it would have been easy to multiply the quotations from Cicero.
But any gain in completeness would have been offset by need-
less weariness and discouragement for the reader. In the selection
of examples I have tried to strike a balance between the
demands of cogency and of readability.

I hope and believe that this work has derived some benefit
from its long incubation. It has certainly benefited immeasur-
ably from the encouragement, criticism, and advice of Eduard
Fraenkel, generously given at every stage of its progress from
first drafts to proof-sheets. My debt to him goes far beyond the
places in the following pages where it is explicit. He has suggested numerous improvements and saved me from numerous
errors; for any that remain I must be held entirely responsible.

I wish also to acknowledge assistance from the University of
Sheffield Research Fund.

E. L.

Sheffield
February 1964

CONTENTS

CONTENTS ix

ABBREVIATIONS

Kühner–Stegmann	*Ausführliche Grammatik der lateinischen Sprache*, 2nd edn. Band II, Satzlehre, Teil 1.
Malcovati[2]	H. Malcovati, *Oratorum Romanorum fragmenta*, 2nd edn. Torino, 1955.
Nägelsbach	C. F. Nägelsbach, *Lateinische Stilistik*, 9th edn., revised by I. Müller. Nürnberg, 1905.
Peter	H. Peter, *Historicorum Romanorum reliquiae*, vol. i. Leipzig, 1914.
Ribbeck	O. Ribbeck, *Scaenicae Romanorum poesis fragmenta*, 3rd edn., 1898. vol. ii, Comicorum fragmenta.
Stolz–Leumann	*Lateinische Grammatik*, 5th edn., 1928. (Laut- und Formenlehre.)
Schmalz–Hofmann	*Lateinische Grammatik*, 5th edn., 1928. (Syntax und Stilistik.)
Tammelin	E. J. Tammelin, *De participiis priscae Latinitatis quaestiones syntacticae.* Helsingfors, 1889.
Wackernagel, I	J. Wackernagel, *Vorlesungen über Syntax*, Erste Reihe. Basel, 1926.
A.L.L.	*Archiv für lateinische Lexicographie.*
R.É.L.	*Revue des études latines.*

In quoting the works of Latin authors, the system of abbreviations adopted by the *Thesaurus* is followed with slight modifications.

I

THE PREDICATIVE PARTICIPLE

In attempting to describe the various functions of the Latin participle, one is faced at the outset by the difficulty of finding a sufficiently clear and appropriate nomenclature. An adjective can be adequately described as either attributive or predicative; it either expresses a permanent, or quasi-permanent, characteristic of the noun to which it belongs (*libera civitas*), or it may be asserted—or form part of what is asserted—of a noun, and thus belong closely to the verbal predicate (*civitatem tradidit liberam*— 'in a free condition', 'when it was free'). Sometimes an adjective is an essential part of the predicate, because it completes a verbal phrase which, without it, would be either meaningless or insufficiently precise (*civitatem liberam esse voluit, civitatem liberam reddidit*). Since participles are verbal adjectives, they can be described in the same way, and most authorities class all non-attributive uses of the participle as predicative. There is a need, however, to distinguish between the first and second types of predicative use just mentioned. The first type, comparatively infrequent in the case of adjectives, is by far the most characteristic use of the participium coniunctum in Latin, and includes the vast number of instances in which a participle takes the place of a temporal, causal, concessive, conditional, or modal clause. The second type of predicative use is, where adjectives are concerned, much commoner than the first; with participles, on the other hand, it is relatively restricted both in scope and in interest.

C. E. Bennett tries to make the necessary distinction by giving the name 'appositive' to the first type[1] (where the participle expresses time, circumstances, cause, &c.), and reserving the

---

[1] *Syntax of Early Latin*, i. 429 ff. Tammelin had earlier used the term in the same way, but his definition of it (p. 5) is not clear, and he admits (p. 49) that there is a close affinity between appositive and predicative function.

term 'predicative' for the second type. Unfortunately, he tends to include under 'predicative' all participles which carry special emphasis in a sentence. Thus, whilst he classes *ad nos veniunt flentes* among 'appositive' instances, he regards *flens abiit* as 'predicative'. Clearly both these participles are of the same type, in that both belong closely to the verbal predicate. Emphasis is too arbitrary and accidental a feature to be invoked as a criterion in drawing a distinction involving syntactical function. Possibly Bennett was led into this mistake by the fact that predicative adjectives of the first type (*civitatem tradidit liberam*) can generally only be revealed as such, when they are removed from their normal attributive position, either immediately before or immediately after the noun. The result is that they are frequently found in one of the emphatic positions of the sentence; and, indeed, in this type of predication an emphasis on the adjective is often (though not always) appropriate. But emphasis is not the essential factor which differentiates the predicative adjective from the attributive. Another objection to Bennett's nomenclature is that the word 'appositive' is for some more naturally associated with attributive than with predicative function.[1]

It seems to me that the best solution is to find a special description not for the great mass of predicative participles of the first type, but for the comparatively small proportion which complete the verbal predicate. To such participles I propose to give the name 'completive', always remembering that they are, none the less, predicative. Since the completive participles, in their contribution to sentence-structure, are of relatively little interest, I shall discuss them briefly in a note appended to the present chapter.

A. PAST PARTICIPLE

There is reason to believe that the form which came to be used in Latin as the past participle passive was originally neither a participle nor necessarily passive in meaning. Its formal similarity to the Greek verbal adjective ending in -τός suggests that in

---

[1] Thus, Schmalz–Hofmann, 605, gives to a paragraph on the present participle the heading: 'Attributiver (appositiver) und praedikativer Gebrauch'.

its prehistory it had a similar function, i.e. that it was purely adjectival and lacked the verbal force of the developed participle. This view is confirmed by the existence of a number of forms derived from verbs which are not passive, e.g. *cenatus, potus, pransus, iuratus, praeteritus*. Some such forms, like *tacitus* and *quietus*, do not imply past time.[1] It is significant that a large number of past participles in Plautus are used purely as adjectives: e.g. Most. 1115 *nam* elixus *esse quam* assus *soleo suavior*; Rud. 269 f. *ergo aequius vos erat* candidatas *venire* hostiatasque. Similarly, the frequency in Plautus of the ante-classical construction *aliquid effectum reddere (dare)*, in which the participle has the force of a predicative adjective (Type 2), points in the same direction: e.g. Pseud. 223 f. *nisi quidem hodie tu omnia* facis effecta *haec ut loquor*; ibid. 386 *qui imperata* effecta reddat (cf. ibid. 530); Mil. 208 *quidquid est,* incoctum[2] *non expromet,* bene coctum dabit. Cf. Most. 786 *quod me miseras,* adfero *omne* impetratum; Pseud. 163 *haec, quom ego a foro revortar, facite ut* offendam parata.

However, the basic predicative use of the past participle, as it appears in classical Latin, was already established in Plautus, and was further developed by Terence. If one surveys the *Rhetorica ad Herennium* and the fragments of Sisenna, one finds that it was being quite freely exploited when Cicero began to write, and in the course of his writing there is no perceptible tendency (such as we shall observe in his treatment of the present participle) either to increase its frequency or materially to enlarge its scope. In this basic use the past participle expresses an event anterior to the action of the main verb, and therefore it can take the place of a temporal clause. By acquiring the appropriate 'colour' from its context, it may also represent a causal, concessive, or conditional clause. This 'colour' may be heightened and made unmistakable by the addition, to the main clause or to the participle, of an adverb such as *praesertim* or *tamen*.

Remembering that more Latin sentences will contain a subject than a direct object, and that a direct object is much commoner

---

[1] Tammelin, 35 f.; Wackernagel, i. 287 ff.; Stolz–Leumann, 340.

[2] The prevalence in early Latin of adjectival past participles with the negative prefix *in-* gives further support to this view of the past participle's pedigree.

than an indirect, we shall expect to find the past participle used mostly in the nominative and accusative cases. This is, in fact, what we do find in Cicero, throughout his writing, but the relative incidence of the nominative, the accusative, and the other oblique cases shows a disparity much too great to be explained simply by the intrinsic difference between the cases in their opportunities for use in the sentence. A rough count, which claims no absolute accuracy, but which, since it covered a total of some 1,400 examples, can be regarded as sufficiently reliable, yielded the following figures: nominative (or subject-accusative) 75 per cent., accusative 22 per cent., dative 1·5 per cent., ablative 1·5 per cent. The handful of genitive examples, in relation to the total, were statistically insignificant. These proportions remain virtually constant throughout Cicero's literary career. It seems clear that the first and most natural predicative use of the past participle was to qualify the subject, and that it remained so for Cicero; it seems equally clear that he deliberately restricted its use with the oblique cases other than the accusative.

This apparent restriction, however, takes on a different aspect, if we consider the use of the predicative past participle in pre-Ciceronian Latin. In Plautus I have found no instances in cases other than nominative or accusative,[1] none in Terence, none even in the *Rhetorica ad Herennium*. The examples, therefore, about fifty in number, in which Cicero uses the participle in the genitive, dative, or ablative, though they form less than 4 per cent. of the total, may indicate, if not innovation (since his earliest writing is represented), at least development on the part of Cicero. It will be convenient, at this point, to quote a selection of these passages: (genitive) Mur. 34 *cuius expulsi et eiecti vita tanti aestimata est ut morte eius nuntiata denique bellum confectum arbitrarentur*; (dative) S. Rosc. 27 *hospitique oppresso iam desperatoque ab omnibus opitulata est*; Sull. 91 *quid enim erat mali quod huic spoliato fama, honore, fortunis deesse videretur?*; (ablative) Verr. II. 1. 130 *qua potestate iste permissa sic abusus est ut . . . cognovistis*; nat. deor. 2. 93 *posse ex iis* (sc. *formis litterarum*) *in terram excussis annales Enni, ut deinceps legi possint, effici.*

---

[1] Except Rud. 621 *vi victo*, a subject-dative after *licet*.

(1) Past participle expressing mental or emotional motivation, compulsion, or hindrance

Among participles qualifying the subject there is one type which bulks so large—it is the most prevalent of all predicative uses in Cicero—that it deserves special notice. In this the past participle expresses the motivation, compulsion, or hindrance, generally mental or emotional, which has influenced the subject's action. Participles frequently used in this manner are *adductus, inductus, commotus, impulsus, doctus, coactus, victus, impeditus*. Examples are rare in Plautus; I have noticed only *vi coactus* (Bacch. 271), *vi victo* (Rud. 621), and *domo doctus* (Merc. 354, Poen. 216, Truc. 453).[1] In Terence, however, the use has become relatively frequent: *coactus* Andr. 73, 275, 632; Haut. 446; Ad. 69. *impulsus* Haut. 389; Hec. 484. *victus* Hec. 168, 244, 589. The fragments of Sisenna include several examples of such participles: fr. 43 (Peter) *praemio libertatis inductus magno*; 46 *indulgitate victus*; 50 *sublatus laetitia atque impotentia commotus animi*; 79 *formidine oppressus*; 98 *neque metu neque calamitatis necessitudine inductum*. In the *Rhetorica ad Herennium* more than 40 per cent. of the predicative past participles are of this type. Many of the Ciceronian instances are simple phrases of the inherited kind, such as Verr. II. 2. 10 *hoc commoti dolore*; ibid. 98 *benignitate aut ambitione adductus*; ibid. 150 *metu coacti*; fin. 1. 48 *voluptate victi*, &c. More expansive treatment, which appears already in Cicero's earliest works, may be illustrated by the following selection: invent. 2. 106 *et confirmare se et hoc peccato doctum et beneficio eorum, qui sibi ignoverint, confirmatum omni tempore a tali ratione afuturum*; S. Rosc. 29 *hoc consilio atque adeo hac amentia impulsi . . . eum iugulandum vobis tradiderunt*; Verr. II. 3. 6 *et in hoc homine saepe a me quaeris, Hortensi, quibus inimicitiis aut qua iniuria adductus ad accusandum descenderim*; de orat. 1. 36 *non prudentium consiliis compulsum potius quam disertorum oratione delenitum se oppidis moenibusque saepsisse*; off. 1. 71 *et iis qui aut valetudinis imbecillitate aut aliqua graviore causa impediti a re publica recesserunt*. Cf. Verr. II. 2. 118; Phil. 6. 2.

---

[1] Tammelin (p. 40) quotes also Asin. 822 *percitum*; Trin. 658 *vi Veneris vinctus*.

(2) Qualifying the object

When it qualifies the object (normally direct object) of a finite verb, the predicative past participle expresses anterior action experienced or suffered by the object, either from the subject of the verb or from some other person or agency. When the participle refers to an agent other than the subject, this agent (or instrument) is usually expressed in the ablative. If no such ablative is present, the presumption is that the participle refers to action on the part of the subject, and therefore provides a substitute for a past participle active. Examples of the first type from early Latin are: Plaut. Merc. 973 *adulescenti amanti amicam eripere emptam argento suo*; Ter. Hec. 21 ff. *ita poetam restitui in locum | prope iam remotum iniuria advorsarium | ab studio atque ab labore atque arte musica*; Ad. 875 *ita eos meo labore eductos maximo hic fecit suos.* The second type is illustrated by Plaut. Epid. 561 *filiam quam ex te suscepi . . . eductam perdidi* and Ter. Andr. 824 *ut beneficium verbis initum dudum nunc re comprobes.*

These principles, if we can so describe something which was doubtless quite unconscious, are borne out by Cicero's practice. A sample of 130 passages gave the following result: participles whose agent is the subject of the finite verb, unspecified or (occasionally, for emphasis) specified—63 (49%); participles whose agent is other than the subject, specified—42 (32%), unspecified—25 (19%). I add a few illustrations of each type:

AGENT = SUBJECT: Verr. II. 1. 12 *videat quid de illis respondeat quos in eorum locum subditos domi suae reservavit*; Manil. 22 *rerum omnium quas et a maioribus acceperat et ipse bello superiore ex tota Asia direptas in suum regnum congesserat*; Brut. 53 *qui potentissimum regem clarissimi regis filium expulerit civitatemque perpetuo dominatu liberatam magistratibus annuis legibus iudiciisque devinxerit.* This is the normal usage. When the subject-agent is specified, it is intended to carry emphasis: e.g. Quinct. 74 *unus fuit . . . qui . . . cupidissime contenderet ut per se adflictum atque eversum propinquum suum . . . communi luce privaret.*

AGENT OTHER THAN SUBJECT (SPECIFIED): dom. 112 *hanc deam quisquam violare audeat . . . a fure sublatam, a sacrilego conlocatam?*; Sest. 16 *hanc taetram immanemque beluam, vinctam auspiciis, adligatam more maiorum, constrictam legum sacratarum catenis, solvit subito lege curiata consul* (where the specification is exploited for the rhetorical purpose of a tricolon with expanding members); fam. 6. 22. 2 *quae didicisti quaeque ab adulescentia pulcherrime a sapientissimis viris tradita memoria et scientia comprehendisti.*

AGENT OTHER THAN SUBJECT (UNSPECIFIED): In the instances (19 per cent. of the sample taken) in which the participle, without specification, refers to an agent other than the subject, the context is generally sufficient to make the reference clear: e.g. Sest. 58 *hic* (sc. Tigranes) *et ipse per se vehemens fuit et acerrimum hostem huius imperi Mithridatem, pulsum Ponto, opibus suis regnoque defendit*; de orat. 3. 124 *nam neque tam est acris acies in naturis hominum et ingeniis, ut res tantas quisquam nisi monstratas possit videre.* But in many such passages the reference is also made practically explicit by a contrast in sense between the participle and the finite verb, which manifestly excludes the possibility of the subject as agent. We shall have occasion later to observe Cicero's taste for using participles in antithetic phrases. Here it is sufficient to notice how this stylistic device can serve the purpose of clarity: Brut. 54 *qui post decemviralem invidiam plebem in patres* incitatam *legibus et contionibus suis* mitigaverit (cf. de orat. 1. 202); Marcell. 2 *ergo et mihi meae pristinae vitae consuetudinem, C. Caesar,* interclusam aperuisti; Phil. 2. 85 *unde diadema? non enim* abiectum sustuleras, *sed attuleras domo* (cf. Sest. 87; Att. 3. 15. 7; leg. 2. 38).

(3) Representing clauses other than temporal

In its commonest predicative use the past participle takes the place of a temporal clause. In an appropriate context, however, its basic temporal force could easily acquire a causal, conditional, or concessive character.

(a) Causal

The idea of causality lies close to that of mere anteriority. Sometimes it is inherent in the meaning of the participle itself, as in many of the examples given in section 1 above (p. 5); sometimes it is sufficiently indicated by the context: e.g. Verr.

I. 10 *quae tanta facultas dicendi aut copia, quae istius vitam tot vitiis flagitiisque convictam, iam pridem omnium voluntate iudicioque damnatam, aliqua ex parte possit defendere?* ; Sest. 83 *non dubito quin . . aliquando statua huic ob rem publicam interfecto in foro statueretur.* But when Cicero, especially in his later work, wishes to emphasize the idea of causality, the force of the participle is made explicit by the addition of *praesertim* : Sest. 88 *sed quamquam dolor animi . . . fortissimum virum hortabatur vi vim, oblatam praesertim saepius, ut frangeret et refutaret* ; rep. 2. 4 *concedamus enim famae hominum, praesertim non inveteratae solum sed etiam sapienter a maioribus proditae* ; fin. 4. 1 *quare istam quoque aggredere, tractatam praesertim et ab aliis et a te ipso saepe.* Cf. Sest. 43 ; prov. 39 ; Marcell. 20.

(b) Conditional

A participle with conditional force is most easily recognized when the finite verb is in the subjunctive, and clearly represents a conditional apodosis : off. 3. 52 *quae tibi plus* prodessent cognita *quam tritici vilitas* ; Brut. 118 *idem* traducti *a disputando ad dicendum inopes* reperiantur (cf. ibid. 121). Occasionally the conditional character is made explicit by a corresponding conditional clause : fin. 5. 42 *si vicerunt efferunt se laetitia, victi debilitantur animosque demittunt* ; de orat. 3. 20 *nullum est enim genus rerum, quod aut avulsum a ceteris per se ipsum constare aut quo cetera si careant, vim suam atque aeternitatem conservare possint.* Sometimes the context, and particularly the meaning of the finite verb, is sufficient to suggest that the participle is conditional : e.g. invent. 1. 26 *commutabile, quod ab adversario* potest leviter mutatum *ex contraria parte dici* (the word *potest* suggests that *mutatum* represents 'si mutatum erit', rather than 'cum mutatum erit').

(c) Concessive

If a participle is to carry concessive force, there must be a clear and deliberate opposition in sense between it and the finite verb. Such deliberate opposition can always be achieved by adding the word *tamen* to the main clause, and this is done frequently by Cicero : e.g. invent. 1. 39 *et quae iam diu gesta et a memoria nostra remota tamen faciant fidem vere tradita esse* ; Caecin. 22 *quo loco depulsus*

Caecina tamen qua potuit ad eum fundum profectus est; Sest. 60 *quae* (sc. *virtus*) . . . *pulsa loco manet tamen atque haeret in patria* (cf. ibid. 58, 140, 142); Marcell. 31 *ingratus est iniustusque civis qui armorum periculis liberatus animum tamen retinet armatum*, &c. If the participle is qualified by a strong negative like *nullus* or *ne* . . . *quidem*, the concessive force of the participle is sufficiently established: Manil. 14 *si propter socios nulla ipsi iniuria lacessiti maiores nostri* . . . *bella gesserunt*; fin. 5. 48 *ut nemo dubitare possit quin ad eas res hominum natura nullo emolumento invitata rapiatur*; Phil. 2. 1 *tu ne verbo quidem violatus* . . . *ultro me maledictis lacessisti*.

Where the participle and the finite verb are expressed in directly antithetical terms, no further device is necessary: invent. 1. 94 *si plura pollicitus pauciora demonstrabit*; leg. 1. 14 *sed eos magna professos in parvis esse versatos*; Brut. 280 *atque hic parum a magistris institutus naturam habuit admirabilem ad dicendum* (where the antithesis is between *ars* and *ingenium*). Even where there was no direct verbal antithesis, it was often obviously more artistic and effective, from the orator's standpoint, to allow incongruity of ideas by itself to indicate the concessive colour of the participle. The following passage, for instance, would have been weakened, and its sarcasm blunted, if any less subtle means had been adopted: Flacc. 34 *est enim, credo, is vir iste ut civitatis nomen sua auctoritate sustineat, damnatus turpissimis iudiciis domi, notatus litteris publicis.*

(4) Equivalent to a predicative adjective

Though the predicative past participle in Cicero generally represents a clause, temporal or quasi-temporal, it is sometimes used rather as an emphatic predicative adjective (Type 1), more stress being laid on the result produced by the action of the participle than on the action itself. This is a primitive use, in keeping with the probable origin of the past participle, and there are many instances in early Latin: e.g. Plaut. Aul. 695 *ut istuc quod me oras impetratum ab eo auferam*; Trin. 817 *eumque huc ad adulescentem meditatum probe mittam*; Ter. Andr. 406 *venit meditatus alicunde ex solo loco*, &c. Ciceronian examples of this type of participle, in its simplest form, are: Flacc. 92 *qui tamen, ut opinor, iacent victi*; Att. 13. 48. 2 *laudationem Porciae tibi misi correctam*; fin. 4. 34 *non enim ipsa genuit hominem sed accepit a natura incohatum.* But, as we would expect, Cicero exploits this use with considerable sophistication and variety: Phil. 10. 6 *quod verbum tibi non excidit, ut saepe fit, fortuito: scriptum, meditatum, cogitatum attulisti*; Vatin. 1 *sic sum incitatus ut, cum te non minus contemnerem quam odissem, tamen vexatum potius quam despectum vellem dimittere* (where the participles are neatly made to correspond chiastically to *contemnerem* and *odissem*); Mur. 32 *quem L. Murena, pater huiusce, vehementissime vigilantissimeque vexatum repressum magna ex parte, non oppressum reliquit*; dom. 23 *homini taeterrimo . . . L. Pisoni nonne nominatim populos liberos, multis senatus consultis, etiam recenti lege generi ipsius liberatos, vinctos et constrictos tradidisti?* The last two passages are particularly interesting, for each shows Cicero using, side by side, two predicative past participles of different function, both agreeing with the same noun or pronoun. The first is a 'normal' temporal participle (*vexatum, liberatos*[1]); the second is a participle of the predicative adjective type (*repressum, vinctos*). The complex participial constructions, to which these two passages belong, will be fully discussed in a later chapter.

(5) Past participle used with present sense

It has been said that the past participle is sometimes used in Latin to supply the lack of a present participle passive.[2] So far as passive, as distinct from deponent, participles are concerned, this is not true of Cicero's practice, except in a limited sense. In so far as the perfect tense can imply the continuance in present time of a state produced by past action, the past participle may be said to partake of present sense. But it is misleading to equate *obsessi*, as K.–S. does, with πολιορκούμενοι. *obsidere* denotes the act of investing, and once that act is completed, those against whom it has been carried out are in a state of having been invested. *obsessi* is a proper past participle in every example of its use known to me. The same applies to the following Ciceronian passages, in which the participles, whilst they have come to

---

[1] *liberatos* might be taken as attributive, amplifying *liberos* (see pp. 57 f. below).
[2] e.g. by Kühner–Stegmann, 758.

denote primarily the state resulting from the action, are still strictly past: Manil. 9 *ut, cum duobus in locis disiunctissimis* . . . *a binis hostium copiis bellum terra marique gereretur, vos ancipiti contentione districti de imperio dimicaretis* (cf. de orat. 3. 131; Tusc. 4. 7 *adstricti*); off. 2. 39 *quod eam si non habebunt, nullis praesidiis saepti multis afficientur iniuriis* (cf. har. resp. 45 *circumsaepti*); de orat. 1. 124 *aut noluisse aut valetudine impediti non potuisse consequi id quod scirent putantur*; Sull. 51 *ego tectus praesidio firmo amicorum Catilinae tum et Autronii copias et conatum repressi.* In all these passages the participle describes not the process of being hindered, surrounded, protected, &c. (which would be the force of a true present participle passive), but a state resulting from such a process. The quasi-present sense is, in fact, produced by the inherent meaning of the verbs to which the participles belong. Verbs like 'besiege', 'hinder', 'surround', 'cover', imply, as the essential part of their meaning, a resultant state. Hence, the present participle *obsidentes* is regularly used not only of the act of laying siege, but, even more commonly, of remaining in position after doing so. In the case of a verb which does not carry this, as it were, 'built-in' implication (e.g. *oppugno* or *mitto*), the past participle is never found with quasi-present sense. Wackernagel (i. 288) is prepared to see a past participle with present sense in the Naevian line *laetus sum laudari me abs te, pater, a laudato viro*, which is quoted by Cicero in Tusc. 4. 67 and fam. 15. 6. 1, and paraphrased in fam. 5. 12. 7. But present sense is by no means compulsive here, and Schmalz–Hofmann 607 rightly draws attention to Cicero's explanatory sentence which follows the quotation in fam. 15. 6. 1: *ea est enim profecto iucunda laus, quae ab iis proficiscitur, qui ipsi* in laude vixerunt.

The following alleged Ciceronian examples are quoted by Kühner–Stegmann (loc. cit.). Not all the participles are predicative, but they may conveniently be considered together: Cato 61 *habet senectus, honorata praesertim, tantam auctoritatem.* Here *honorata* does not mean 'when it is held in honour', but 'when it has held public office'. Brut. 207 *his* (sc. *orationibus*) *scriptis ipse interfui. his scriptis* does not represent 'cum hae scribebantur', for which Cicero would have written 'his scribendis' (conjectured by

Lambinus). In this example of the *ab urbe condita* construction the use of the perfect participle implies the completion of the action in the past. Cicero is saying not that he saw the speeches being written, but that he was present at the time when, in fact, they were written—'cum scriptae sunt'.[1] Brut. 314 *quodvis potius periculum mihi adeundum, quam a sperata dicendi gloria discedendum putavi.* I cannot see why *sperata* should be supposed to mean 'quam sperabam', and not 'quam speraveram', which fits the context equally well, perhaps better.[2] Nor can I see any reason for not giving the participles their proper force in Tusc. 4. 58 *itaque bene adhibita ratio cernit, quid optimum sit; neglecta multis implicatur erroribus.* A more specious instance is Tusc. 5. 64 *cuius* (sc. *Archimedis) ego quaestor ignoratum ab Syracusanis, cum esse omnino negarent, saeptum undique et vestitum vepribus et dumetis indagavi sepulcrum.* Yet, here too, a careful reading of the passage shows that *ignoratum*, though it may include the actual moment when Cicero made the discovery, is intended primarily to convey the *past* ignorance of the Syracusans, which had lasted so long, that (*a*) they denied the existence of the tomb, and that (*b*) the tomb, when found, was overgrown with vegetation. Nägelsbach (p. 412) adduces two other instances, neither of which seems defensible. dom. 67 *ex quo iudicare potestis, quanta vis illa fuerit oriens et congregata, cum haec Cn. Pompeium terruerit iam distracta et exstincta.* Cicero is emphasizing the power of Clodius at its peak, when he (Cicero) was exiled, by showing that, even when that power had disintegrated and virtually vanished, it was still able to terrorize Pompey. R. G. Nisbet (edition, p. 133), apparently accepting Nägelsbach's view that the past participles have present sense, translates *distracta et exstincta* by 'in process of disintegration'. But it is rhetorically

---

[1] See pp. 94 f. below.

[2] Nägelsbach (p. 411) quotes other instances of *speratus*, in which present sense is less easy to deny: nat. deor. 1. 116 *qui quam ob rem colendi sint non intellego, nullo nec accepto ab iis nec sperato bono*; fam. 2. 9. 1 *primum tibi, ut debeo, gratulor laetorque cum praesenti, tum etiam sperata tua dignitate* (cf. fin. 1. 41 *nulla neque praesenti neque exspectata voluptate*); fin. 2. 63 *nulla nec adiuncta nec sperata voluptate.* It is worth observing (*a*) that *spero* often expresses a state of mind entered upon in the past and persisting in the present (cf. the similar deponent verbs discussed on p. 14); this applies especially to nat. deor. 1. 116; (*b*) that in the other examples the 'present' colour of the past participle is, in each case, helped by a word of unmistakably present sense (*praesenti, adiuncta*).

much more effective to give all four participles their proper force (*distracta* seems to be confirmed as past by the preceding phrase *cum iam a firmissimo robore copiarum suarum relictus esset*); they then describe Clodius' progressive rise and fall, and Cicero makes his point by a characteristic exaggeration. Phil. 2. 81 *et, si qui servavit* (sc. *de caelo*), *non comitiis habitis, sed prius quam habeantur, debet nuntiare. comitiis habitis* means not 'when the assembly is being held', but 'after the election has taken place'. That this interpretation is essential to Cicero's argument is seen from section 83: *confecto negotio* (i.e. after the votes had been declared) *bonus augur . . . 'alio die' inquit.*

The case for admitting the existence of deponent past participles with present sense seems, at first sight, stronger. A number of participles like *usus, veritus, oblitus, secutus, complexus,* appear, in many contexts, to have a force indistinguishable from that of a present participle active. Yet if we examine Cicero's usage carefully, we find that the number of deponent verbs whose participles have this property is limited, and that their 'present' character is more apparent than real. Many deponent participles in Cicero, including some of those which he uses most often, such as *nactus, adeptus, profectus, progressus, functus, lapsus, locutus,* and *expertus,* are never used except with their proper preterital force. The most valuable function of the deponent past participle was, in fact, that it provided an occasional substitute for the missing past participle active.

The deponent (or semi-deponent) verbs, whose participles often appear to have present sense, are, if my observation is correct, little more than a dozen in number, and they may be divided into two groups.

(i) Verbs in which (as in the case of *obsideo*) the essential meaning is the state resulting from the act, rather than the act itself. *amplecti* (*complecti*) describes the act of embracing (i.e. putting the arms round), *amplexus,* the embrace itself; *niti*—the act of leaning, *nixus*—the subsequent position; *confidere* (*diffidere*)—the act of putting (losing) trust in, *confisus* (*diffisus*)—the state of trust (distrust); *oblivisci*—the coming into a state of forgetfulness, *oblitus*—the state of forgetfulness. Sull. 59 *qui tanto amore suas possessiones amplexi tenebant* (its use with *tenebant* here illustrates the proper force of *amplexus*) ; Q. Rosc. 2 *sed ego copia et facultate causae confisus vide quo progrediar* (the meaning of *confisus* is strictly 'having put my trust in') ; Sull. 46 *coges me oblitum nostrae amicitiae habere rationem meae dignitatis* (we may translate *oblitum* by 'forgetting' or 'forgetful of', but its true force, freely rendered, is more like 'having banished from my mind').

(ii) Verbs expressing a state of mind which gives rise to an action, though it may still persist when the action takes place : *arbitror, adsentior, admiror, (aegre) patior, vereor*; similarly, certain verbs—notably *utor, sequor, imitor*—which essentially describe not a completed act, but a practice or process. This process may lead to a result, and in so far as it does so, though it may still continue side by side with that result, it is logically prior to it. Priority of this kind may be seen, to a greater or lesser degree, in the following typical Ciceronian instances, in each of which the participle would be idiomatically translated as if it were present: div. 1. 4 *furoris divinationem Sibyllinis maxime versibus contineri arbitrati eorum decem interpretes delectos e civitate esse voluerunt*; Phil. 6. 14 *huic enim adsensi septemvirum acta sustulimus*; off. 3. 45 *admiratus eorum fidem tyrannus petivit, ut se ad amicitiam tertium adscriberent*; Att. 1. 18. 3 *Menelaus aegre id passus divortium fecit*; fin. 1. 2 *plura suscepi veritus ne movere hominum studia viderer, retinere non posse*; off. 3. 38 *itaque hac opportunitate anuli usus reginae stuprum intulit*; Lig. 25 *cuius auctoritatem secuti in societatem belli veneratis*; leg. 2. 14 *quos imitatus Plato videlicet hoc quoque legis putavit esse.*

It is not to be supposed that Cicero and his contemporaries applied any conscious criterion in their use of these deponent participles, and indeed the corresponding present active forms (e.g. *verens, imitans*) are not infrequently found with no perceptible difference in sense. The development of the quasi-causal type of present participle (see below, pp. 28 ff.) would tend further to obscure any distinction which might have been felt. What we can say with certainty is that deponent past participles with virtually present sense are confined to a limited number of verbs, whose meanings have certain features in common.

(6) Some characteristic Ciceronian uses

Under this heading I propose to single out three characteristic ways in which Cicero uses the predicative past participle in his sentence structure: in antithetic phrases, in close juxtaposition with the finite verb, and appended to the finite verb.

(a) In antithetic phrases

Of all stylistic devices in the ancient world antithesis was probably the one most diligently cultivated and most effectively employed. The participle, by its versatility and conciseness, lent itself to antithetic expressions, and it is not surprising that we find Cicero using in this way participles of all types, past and present, predicative, attributive, and substantival. I quote here a selection of passages in which the predicative past participle is so used. The antithesis may be between participle and finite verb (or infinitive); to the examples already given on p. 7 above we may add the following: off. 3. 34 *hanc igitur partem relictam explebimus*; Planc. 11 *nostrum est autem . . . ferre modice populi voluntates, adlicere alienas, retinere partas, placare turbatas*; leg. 2. 31 *quid enim maius est . . . quam posse a summis imperiis et summis potestatibus comitiatus et concilia vel instituta dimittere vel habita rescindere?* It may be between two past participles: dom. 85 *et tu unus pestifer civis eum restitutum negas esse civem, quem eiectum universus senatus . . . egregium civem semper putavit* (cf. Tusc. 5. 13), or between a past and a present: dom. 27 *desinant homines isdem machinis sperare me restitutum posse labefactari, quibus antea stantem perculerunt* (cf. Phil. 5. 31).

(b) In juxtaposition with finite verb

When the action of a predicative past participle closely precedes, or virtually forms part of, the action of the finite verb of the clause or sentence in which it stands, Cicero habitually places participle and verb in close juxtaposition. This was, no doubt, a natural thing to do, but it occurs so often in Cicero as to be a noticeable and characteristic feature of his usage. The following examples are typical: S. Rosc. 15 *nam patrimonium domestici praedones vi ereptum possident* ('have seized and hold'); Manil. 11 *qui legatum populi Romani consularem vinculis ac verberibus atque omni supplicio excruciatum necavit* (death in the midst of, or soon after, torture; cf. Phil. 13. 37 *discruciatos necaret*); Cluent. 37 *in harenarias quasdam extra portam Esquilinam perductus occiditur*; fin. 2. 114 *cum omnes sensus dulcedine omni quasi perfusi moverentur*. Sometimes the force of the participle, when thus used, is almost that of a modal adverb: invent. 1. 102 *quintus locus est per quem ostendimus ceteras res perperam constitutas intellecta veritate commutatas corrigi posse*; Vatin. 2 *et loquacitatem paucis meis interrogationibus inretitam retardarem* (cf. har. resp. 55). Frequently it is tautological, and little more than a means of amplification: Verr. II. 5. 160 *cum ... ex illo metu mortis et tenebris quasi luce libertatis et odore aliquo legum recreatus revixisset*; Flacc. 25 *libertas in re publica constituta est, quae usque ad hoc tempus honoribus, imperiis, rerum gestarum gloria continuata permansit*; nat. deor. 2. 25 *omnes igitur partes mundi ... calore fultae sustinentur*.

(c) Appended

Cicero shows a marked tendency to place the predicative past participle after the finite verb to which it belongs. This device had an obvious advantage, in that it enabled the participial phrase to be expanded to considerable length without impairing the clarity of the main sentence. Many Ciceronian examples are evidently due primarily to this consideration: e.g. Mur. 54 *nunc mihi tertius ille locus est relictus orationis, de ambitus criminibus, perpurgatus ab iis qui ante me dixerunt, a me, quoniam ita Murena voluit, retractandus*; Manil. 16 *nisi eos qui vobis fructui sunt conservaveritis non solum, ut ante dixi, calamitate sed etiam calamitatis formidine liberatos*; de orat. 3. 43 *studiorum quibus vacant cives, peregrini fruuntur capti quodam modo nomine urbis et auctoritate* (the appended position is necessary to achieve the chiastic pattern *vacant cives, peregrini fruuntur*). An appended participle may, indeed, act as the pivot of a period, as in Catil. 2. 5 *itaque ego illum exercitum prae Gallicanis legionibus et hoc dilectu quem in agro Piceno et Gallico Q. Metellus habuit, et prae his copiis quae a nobis cotidie comparantur, magno opere contemno*, collectum *ex senibus desperatis, ex agresti luxuria, ex rusticis decoctoribus, ex iis qui vadimonia deserere quam illum exercitum maluerunt*.

The length of the participial clause is not, however, the only factor; in many examples it is relatively short. Sometimes

Cicero's intention seems to have been rather to give the participial clause more prominence than it would have had in a more normal subordinate position within the main sentence: Cluent. 10 *abs te peto, Oppianice, ut me invitum de patris tui causa dicere existimes adductum fide atque officio defensionis*; leg. 2. 49 *haec nos a Scaevola didicimus non ita descripta ab antiquis* (*descripta* is a generally accepted conjecture of Ascensius); Phil. 12. 6 *ex pacis patrocinio repentino, quod subito suscepit eodem captus errore quo nos.* Occasionally the participial clause acquires the force of an added statement, parallel in effect with the main sentence, rather than subordinate to it: Verr. II. 1. 61 *haec, inquam, duo* (*signa*) . . . *quae sectorem exspectant relicta ac destituta a ceteris signis*; de orat. 3. 197 *quorum illa summa vis carminibus est aptior et cantibus, non neglecta, ut mihi videtur, a Numa rege doctissimo maioribusque nostris.* In all these examples the prominence of the participial clause is rhythmically enhanced by the clausula immediately preceding it.

It is hard to resist the conviction that this practice of Cicero influenced Livy, in whose writing the appended past participle is very frequent. Livy, however, took a significant step beyond Cicero, in that he was prepared to use such a participle without reference to its proper anterior force, allowing it sometimes to express an action contemporaneous with that of the finite verb, or even subsequent to it: e.g. Livy 25. 11. 20 *hunc statum rerum Hannibal Tarenti relinquit regressus ipse in hiberna* ('and himself returned'); ibid. 25. 13 *post paucos dies rediit multis . . . donis ex Hieronis gaza ab Epicyde donatus* ('and was presented with many gifts', i.e. after his return). There is no trace of such a development in Cicero's usage.

(7) An ancient pattern in Cicero

One of the earliest uses of the predicative past participle is in phrases of the type: *accepi, acceptam servabo* (Ter. Andr. 298). The popularity in early Latin of figura etymologica, of which this phrase is an example, is attested by the most cursory reading of Plautus. This particular manifestation of the figure appears not only in Plautus and Terence, but in two fragments of prose of the second century B.C.: Plaut. Amph. 278 *optumo optume optumam operam das, datam pulchre locas*; Cato *ap.* Gell. 3. 7. 16 (= Peter, fr. 83) *Romani milites circumveniuntur, circumventi repugnant*; P. Scipio Africanus Minor, fr. 33 (Malcovati[2], p. 134) *vi atque ingratiis cum illo sponsionem feci, facta sponsione ad iudicem adduxi, adductum primo coetu damnavi, damnatum ex voluntate dimisi* (where the pattern is exploited for the purpose of climax). In the next century examples appear in Sisenna (Peter, fr. 27) *Romanos impetu suo protelant, protelatos persecuntur*, and in the *Rhetorica ad Herennium* 4. 66 *ego libertatem quae non erat peperi, vos partam servare non vultis*; ibid. 2. 27 *nam fere non difficile invenire, quid sit causae adiumento; difficillimum est inventum expolire et expedite pronuntiare*. In both of the last two examples the pattern is modified, in the first by the antithetic change of subject (*ego–vos*), in the second, by the separation of *invenire* and *inventum* to an extent which minimizes, if it does not remove, the obtrusiveness of figura etymologica.

In Cicero's early period the archaic pattern is twice found in its simple, primitive form: Caecin. 23 *improbus fuit quod homines coegit armavit, coactis armatisque[1] vim fecit*; Verr. II. 5. 61 *pretio certo missos facere nautas, missorum omne stipendium lucrari*. But figura etymologica had doubtless come to be regarded as naïve and old-fashioned, and we find the youthful Cicero already modifying the pattern, either by separating the participle from the cognate verb preceding it, invent. 1. 50 *atque inveniri quidem omnis ex his locis argumentatio poterit: inventam[2] exornari et certas in partes distingui et suavissimum est et summe necessarium* (cf. Rhet. Her. 2. 27 above), or by substituting a synonym, S. Rosc. 32 *patrem meum, cum proscriptus non esset*, iugulastis, *occisum in proscriptorum numerum rettulistis*. In his later work, whenever he makes use of the pattern, Cicero's treatment shows a sophisticated approach; direct juxtaposition of the related verb and participle is avoided, and the syntactical connexion between the participle and the preceding clause becomes more subtle: de orat. 2. 79 *deinde quinque faciunt quasi membra eloquentiae, invenire quid dicas, inventa disponere, deinde ornare verbis*, &c. (not *inventum*, cf. Rhet. Her. 2. 27 and invent. 1. 50,

---

[1] I have found no other Ciceronian instance of the ablative absolute in this kind of expression, but cf. the fragment of Scipio Africanus quoted above.

[2] H has *inventa*. The generally accepted reading *inventam* is supported by the fact that it is more in keeping with the development of the pattern here discussed.

above); prov. 7 *emisti a foedissimo tribuno plebis tum in illo naufragio huius urbis . . . tum, inquam, emisti grandi pecunia, ut tibi de pecuniis creditis ius in liberos populos . . . dicere liceret. id emptum ita vendidisti, ut aut ius non diceres aut bonis cives Romanos everteres* (the pattern is spread over two sentences); Lael. 44 *plurimum in amicitia amicorum bene suadentium valeat auctoritas, eaque et adhibeatur ad monendum . . . et adhibitae pareatur* (change from personal to impersonal construction); Mil. 104 *hunc sua quisquam sententia ex hac urbe expellet, quem omnes urbes expulsum a vobis ad se vocabunt?* (the cognate forms are separated not only by the intervening words, but by antithesis between the two clauses, which have different subjects); Manil. 58 *propterea quod alter uni illud bellum suscipiendum vestris suffragiis detulit, alter delatum susceptumque confecit.* In the last passage, drawn from a comparatively early work, not only are the members of the pattern held apart by concinnity, *alter . . . alter*, but they are duplicated, each double-member having reference to both of the persons about whom Cicero is speaking (Gabinius and Pompey). Their arrangement varies the traditional pattern in a way which it is much easier to admire than to analyse.[1]

B. PRESENT PARTICIPLE

Modern views about the Latin present participle are largely based on the valuable study published by J. Marouzeau in 1910, *L'emploi du participe présent latin à l'époque républicaine.*[2] Because of the very importance of this work, it is necessary, at the outset, to indicate the one fundamental part of Marouzeau's treatment with which I find myself in disagreement. Setting out from the affirmation that the Latin present participle is in itself devoid of temporal value, he goes on to attribute the element of concomitance or simultaneity, which is very often apparent in this participle,

---

[1] We find one of Cicero's contemporaries (Lentulus) using the pattern in a formal letter to the Senate in 43 B.C.: fam. 12. 15. 6 *facilius et reliqua exigere vectigalia et exacta servare poterimus.* The simplicity of this example makes the subtlety of Manil. 58 all the more apparent.

[2] Originally published in *Mémoires de la Société de Linguistique de Paris*, vol. 16. It has since been printed separately. When I cite this work, the number in square brackets refers to the page in *M.S.L.* 16.

to the 'aspect' of participle and finite verb; it is brought about by the juxtaposition of the imperfective aspect of the one and the perfective aspect of the other.[1] The same effect might be produced by the use of a purely adjectival form in place of a participle. To demonstrate this, Marouzeau quotes Juvenal 8. 243 f. :

> sed Roma parentem,
> Roma patrem patriae Ciceronem libera dixit.

But leaving aside the fact that *libera* here may be simply emphatic ('it was a free Rome which . . .'), as Marouzeau honestly admits, it is misleading to draw conclusions about the basic functions of the Latin adjective from a text belonging to the beginning of the second century A.D. This kind of predicative use, as has already been said, is comparatively infrequent with adjectives; with participles, on the other hand, it predominates overwhelmingly. If the participle borrowed some of its functions from the adjective, it may, in its turn, as the language developed, have influenced the adjective. Certain adjectives (e.g. *vivus, saucius*), as well as certain substantives (e.g. *puer, senex*), can assume a relation of concomitance to a finite verb. But the number of adjectives and nouns regularly so used seems to be limited, and it is possible to argue that analogy with the present participle has been a factor in enabling them to acquire this property.

(1) Concomitant and adverbial uses

In any case, the problem just raised belongs to the prehistory of the Latin language. All that need here be said is that from the first appearance of the present participle in our written records the character of concomitance is established as one of the two basic relationships which it can assume towards its finite verb.[2] In this relationship the participle expresses an activity or state existing at the time of the action of the finite verb, and, as it were, forming a background to it. It is thus roughly equivalent in sense to *dum*+present indicative. The participle and finite verb represent either the activities of different persons or distinct activities of the same person: Plaut. Aul. 303 *ne quid animae forte*

---

[1] Op. cit., pp. 6 [138] f.
[2] 'Finite verb' is to be understood to include here the infinitive in oratio obliqua.

amittat dormiens; Cas. 1003 *nulla causast quin pendentem me, uxor, virgis verberes.* The activities of participle and finite verb may be so distinct as to be opposed to one another (*vigilans somniat*), whence the participle may readily take on a concessive colour. In its second basic use the present participle takes the place of an adverb of manner; it describes an activity closely associated with that of the finite verb, with the subject of which it must, of course, agree. In early Latin this function appears, in its simplest form, in such participles as *flens, lacrimans, plorans, currens*. It is an easy step from the physical to the mental accompaniment of an action: Plaut. Mil. 201 *curans, cogitans*; ibid. 1386 *exspectans*. Hence verbs of thinking, fearing, hoping, &c., with their appropriate constructions, come to be used in the participle at an early period: Rud. 560 f. *signum flentes amplexae tenent* | nescioquem metuentes *miserae*; Amph. 1112 f. *ego cunas recessim rursum vorsum trahere et ducere* | metuens pueris mihi formidans; Bacch. 109 f. *iam dudum, Pistoclere, tacitus te sequor* | exspectans quas tu res hoc ornatu geras. Terence shows a greater freedom than Plautus in giving to adverbial participles their own verbal construction: Andr. 74 f. *primo haec pudice vitam parce ac duriter* | agebat, lana ac tela victum quaeritans; Eun. 583 f. *virgo in conclavi sedet* | suspectans tabulam quandam pictam; Hec. 162 f. *et illam et hanc quae domi erat cognovit satis,* | ad exemplum ambarum mores earum existimans; ibid. 365 f. *nam modo intro me ut corripui timidus,* alio suspicans | morbo me visurum adfectam ac sensi uxorem. Thinking, fearing, hoping, and the like, are often not merely the accompaniment of an action, but also its motive. Consequently participles of such verbs, when used adverbially, tend to have a quasi-causal sense. Another important development of the adverbial participle, which had begun at an early period, was its gerundial use: Plaut. Asin. 709 *postidea ad pistores dabo, ut ibi cruciere currens* (= *currendo*); Men. 922 *occidis fabulans*;[1] Ter. Haut. 138 f. *interea usque illi de me supplicium dabo* | laborans, parcens, quaerens, illi serviens; Phorm. 615 f. *nam hercle ego quoque id quidem agitans mecum sedulo* | inveni, opinor, remedium huic rei.

---

[1] *fabulans* is a certain conjecture of Acidalius; cf. Pseud. 931 *occidis me cum istuc rogitas*; Merc. 893 *enicas me miserum tua reticentia*.

In Cicero's writings the concomitant present participle preponderates over the adverbial at all periods and in all genres. In the earlier and middle periods the average preponderance is 2 : 1 ; in the treatises written after 49 B.C. the adverbial use becomes almost equally frequent. The ordinary concomitant participle scarcely needs illustration, but typical examples are : S. Rosc. 18 *occiditur ad balneas Pallacinas rediens a cena Sex. Roscius*; Manil. 42 *utrum hostes magis virtutem eius pugnantes timuerint an mansuetudinem victi dilexerint.* Contrast with the latter instance the adverbial use of the same participle in Sest. 45 *restitisses, repugnasses, mortem pugnans oppetisses.* In his use of this type of participle Cicero's practice shows little significant change between his earlier and his later writings; he is as ready to give such participles verbal construction in the Verrines as in the Philippics.

The adverbial use, however, with its various types, is progressively developed by Cicero. In the *Pro Roscio Amerino, Pro Roscio Comoedo, Pro Caecina,* and *Pro Lege Manilia* there are no examples. In the *Pro Quinctio* there are only two, one a simple *lacrimans* (97), the other (96) *obsecrans* with an *ut*-clause, of which examples are to be found in early Latin: Plaut. Cist. 567 f. *obsecrans ne deserat se* (cf. Ter. Haut. 725). Of the six instances in the *Pro Cluentio* five are simple adverbs: *flens* (22, 103), *lacrimans* (144), *lacrimantes* (197), *maerens* (178). The remaining instance (20), *nemo vestrum mirabitur illum diffidentem rebus suis ad Staienum atque ad pecuniam confugisse,* has precedents in a republican inscription of the early second century B.C., *quod re sua d⟨if⟩eidens asper afleicta parens timens heic vovit,*[1] and in Amph. 1113 *metuens pueris, mihi formidans.* Only fourteen adverbial instances are to be found in the whole of the Verrines. The majority are simple, but four passages prefigure the greater freedom which was to follow : Verr. II. 4. 67 *Rex . . . in foro, inquam, Syracusis* flens ac deos hominesque contestans *clamare coepit;* II. 5. 155 *qui eum non solum cognoscerent, sed etiam* lacrimantes ac te implorantes *defenderent* (it is noticeable that in these two examples the participle with verbal construction is, in each case, coupled with a simple adverbial participle of the most common type, an artistic touch which raises those trite words from the

[1] *Carm. Epigraph.* 4.

level of the commonplace, and gives them the required dignity and pathos); II. 5. 21 *totiens te senatum Panhormitanum adiisse* . . . orantem atque obsecrantem ut *aliquando ille miser atque innocens calamitate illa liberaretur*; ibid. 129 *et ita* me suam salutem appellans, te suum carnificem nominans, fili nomen implorans *mihi ad pedes misera iacuit* (the participle is exploited primarily as a means of introducing tricolon with homoeoteleuton). The four examples offered by the speeches against Catiline are all developed uses: Catil. 4. 6 (hoc malum) *manavit non solum per Italiam verum etiam transcendit Alpes et* obscure serpens *multas iam provincias occupavit*; 4. 3. *neque ille qui* exspectans *huius exitum diei stat in conspectu meo gener*; 1. 26 *iacere humi non solum* ad obsidendum stuprum *verum etiam* ad facinus obeundum, *vigilare non solum* insidiantem somno maritorum *verum etiam* bonis otiosorum (the participle provides variety of construction in two carefully balanced clauses); 2. 26 Q. *Metellus quem ego* hoc prospiciens *in agrum Gallicum Picenumque praemisi*. In the last example the participle expresses the mental background of the action of the main verb. This is the first appearance in Cicero of the quasi-causal type of adverbial present participle, which subsequently became common.

In the *Pro Sestio*, richest of all the speeches in the frequency and variety of its participles, we find the only two Ciceronian instances known to me of adverbial *flens* with verbal construction: Sest. 60 *et post meum discessum iis Pisonem verbis* flens *meum et rei publicae casum vexavit*; ibid. 120 flens *et recenti laetitia et mixto dolore ac desiderio mei egit apud populum Romanum multo gravioribus verbis meam causam quam egomet de me agere potuissem*. The use, with full verbal construction, of a participle which in Cicero's day had become stereotyped as a simple adverb-equivalent is significant evidence that the adverbial participle has now achieved complete emancipation as a subordinating element in the period.

In fact, during the last fifteen years of his literary activity Cicero uses the present participle in all genres with complete freedom of verbal construction, though it would perhaps be true to say that the developed use of the adverbial participle is less prominent in the speeches than in the letters and treatises.

(2) Adverbial uses

Since it is the adverbial participle which chiefly lends itself to subtle and varied uses in the period, it will be convenient to illustrate each of its developed types by a selection of representative examples.

(a) Modal

The simple adverbial participle of manner (*flens, lacrimans, properans*, &c.) has now acquired full verbal power to take a construction and to form a subordinate clause. This development had already begun in Plautus and Terence, in whom the number of instances is slightly less restricted than Marouzeau suggests,[1] and it was evidently well established in the Latin of the rhetorical schools, when Cicero was a student: Rhet. Her. 4. 51 *volitabit et vagabitur in foro, acuens dentes in unius cuiusque fortunas, in omnes amicos atque inimicos* . . . *incursitans, aliorum famam depeculans, aliorum caput oppugnans, aliorum domum et omnem familiam perfringens, rem publicam funditus labefactans* (cf. ibid. 68). Cicero's own use of this type of participle seems in his early works, as I have suggested, to be restrained, but in his middle and later periods he employs it freely: e.g. Planc. 99 *o reliquos omnes dies noctesque eas quibus iste* a me non recedens *Thessalonicam me in quaestoriumque perduxit!* (the participial clause describes the manner of *perduxit*); Att. 16. 4. 4 *deinde, quantum intellego, tarde est navigaturus*, consistens in locis pluribus (the participial clause stands in the same relation to the main verb as *tarde*, which it resumes and makes explicit); ad Q. fr. 2. 15. 2 *de quo petis ut ad te* nihil occultans, nihil dissimulans, nihil tibi indulgens *genuine*[2] *fraterneque rescribam*; fin. 5. 43 *e quibus accendi philosophi ratio debet, ut* eam quasi deum ducem subsequens *ad naturae perveniat extremum*; Brut. 281 *quae si ille audire voluisset, maxima cum gratia et gloria ad summam amplitudinem pervenisset*, ascendens gradibus magistratuum, *ut pater eius fecerat, ut reliqui clariores viri*. The last two passages are a reminder that the stock English translation of *pervenire* ('reach', 'arrive at') is often inadequate, since in this compound the simple verb *venire* retains its full

---

[1] Op. cit., pp. 13 [145] f. To the examples given by M. should be added Bacch. 277 and Rud. 561.

[2] Boot's conjecture *ingenue* is adopted by Watt in his O.C.T.

force, and can therefore properly be qualified by a modal participle. This fact throws light on a similar participial example in Horace (Sat. 1. 5. 94) which has exercised the grammarians:[1]

> inde Rubos fessi pervenimus utpote longum
> carpentes iter.

A special type of the modal participle is that which J. Lebreton calls a participle 'au sens d'équivalence'.[2] Here the force of the participle is not so much to express an activity accompanying the action of the main verb, as to describe or make explicit the action of the main verb itself, or vice versa. Its function is more easily illustrated than formulated in words: fin. 2. 39 *huius ego nunc auctoritatem sequens idem faciam*; ibid. 3. 35 *quas Graeci πάθη appellant, poteram ego verbum ipsum interpretans morbos appellare*; div. 2. 126 *praesertim cum Chrysippus Academicos refellens permulto clariora et certiora esse dicat quae vigilantibus videantur, quam quae somniantibus*; Tusc. 3. 69 *itaque Aristoteles veteres philosophos accusans, qui existimavissent philosophiam suis ingeniis esse perfectam, ait eos aut stultissimos aut gloriosissimos fuisse* (in this example, as in the one preceding it, the content of the participle is made explicit by the main clause). To this category we should probably assign off. 1. 14 *quam similitudinem natura ratioque ab oculis ad animum transferens multo etiam magis pulchritudinem . . . in consiliis factisque conservandam putat*, where the participial clause refers to the activity described in the main clause. Cf. Tusc. 1. 52; nat. deor. 2. 140; ac. 2. 106.

This 'descriptive' type of modal participle seems to be virtually confined to the treatises of Cicero's latest period. The only example which I have noticed elsewhere is Att. 7. 2. 6 *nostrum, inquam, te coniungens.*

(b) Gerundial

Between the modal and the instrumental or gerundial use of the present participle no sharp distinction can be drawn; one type merges into the other, and many examples stand on the border-line. The gerundial use, as we have seen, is present in

---

[1] Cf. A. Palmer ad loc.; Riemann–Ernout, *Syntaxe latine*[7], 277; A. Draeger, *Historische Syntax der lat. Sprache*, Leipzig, 1881, 773; S. Lyer, *R.É.L.*, 1929, 323 f.

[2] J. Lebreton, *Études sur la langue et la grammaire de Cicéron*, 401 f.

early Latin. To the examples already given (p. 21) may be added Plaut. Stich. 406 (*abiens*) and Ter. Phorm. 68 (*pollicens*). It is found in the *Rhetorica ad Herennium*: e.g. 1. 25 *conferens*; 3. 24 *amplificans* (cf. *amplificatione* in the next sentence). In Cicero's youthful *De Inventione* five of the dozen instances of the present participle are of this type: 1. 2 *inducens*; 1. 24 *faciens*; 2. 100 *redarguentem*; 2. 125 *admirantem . . . revertentem . . . quaerentem*; 2. 157 *captans*. 2. 125 is worth quoting: *quem locum multis modis variare oportebit, tum ipsum secum* admirantem, *quidnam contra dici possit, tum ad iudicis officium* revertentem *et ab eo* quaerentem *quid praeterea audire aut exspectare debeat; tum ipsum adversarium in testis loco* producendo, *hoc est* interrogando . . . &c. The participles and gerunds are evidently equivalent in function.

This preponderance in the *De Inventione* is abnormal. The work is not representative of Cicero's mature style, and in later years he was half inclined to disown it.[1] The construction in 2. 125 of an object-accusative with the gerund disappears from his later writing. If, as F. Marx believed,[2] the *De Inventione* was compiled from notes on the lectures of a Latin rhetorician who transmitted the precepts of some Greek textbook of rhetoric, the work no doubt preserves some of the lecturer's language, as well as his material. Certainly the gerundial present participle is not very frequent in the writing of Cicero's maturity, though Lebreton exaggerates when he remarks that the instrumental gerund and gerundive are very common in Cicero, the instrumental present participle very rare[3] (he quotes only nat. deor. 2. 126; off. 2. 67; Lael. 22). In fact, whilst the instrumental gerund is not uncommon, it is generally found in the form of the simple verbal noun; there appears to be a reluctance to use the instrumental gerundive, though the predicative use of the gerundive, especially after prepositions (*ad rem gerendam, in consiliis capiendis*, &c.) is very frequent. An experimental survey of the *Pro Sestio*, the Second Philippic, and *De Officiis I* revealed ten instances of the simple gerund used as a verbal noun (e.g. *discendo, negando, cogitando*),[4]

---

[1] de orat. 1. 5 *ex commentariolis nostris incohata ac rudia exciderunt, vix hac aetate digna et hoc usu.*   [2] Prolegomena to edition of Rhet. Her. (1894), 80 f.

[3] Op. cit., 400 f.

[4] Sest. 8, 25, 40, 47; Phil. 2. 52; off. 1. 22, 50, 59, 102, 105.

compared with only three instances of the instrumental gerundive: Sest. 58 *iniuriis in socios nostros inferendis*; Phil. 2. 110 *addendo die* (Mueller, *diem* codd.); off. 1. 2 *legendis nostris*. This result confirms the view that, outside the compact predicative use mentioned above (where the predominance of the prepositional type emphasizes the substantival character of the gerundive phrase), the *verbal* character of gerund and gerundive is little developed in Cicero.[1]

The following is a representative selection of the gerundial participles in Cicero: Att. 1. 16. 8 *idem, inquam, ego recreavi afflictos animos bonorum* unumquemque confirmans, excitans; insectandis vero exagitandisque nummariis iudicibus *omnem omnibus studiosis ac fautoribus illius victoriae* παρρησίαν *eripui* (in this elevated passage participles and gerundives are obviously equivalent in force, and their parallel use provides syntactical variety); nat. deor. 2. 132 *iam diei noctisque vicissitudo conservat animantes* tribuens *aliud agendi tempus aliud quiescendi* (the close proximity of *agendi* and *quiescendi* would be sufficient to recommend the use of the participle here); Tusc. 5. 51 *quid ergo aut hunc prohibet aut etiam Xenocratem illum gravissimum philosophorum* exaggerantem tantopere virtutem, extenuantem cetera et abicientem, *in virtute non beatam modo vitam sed etiam beatissimam ponere?* (cf. off. 1. 17; 2. 67); Lael. 22 *nam et secundas res splendidiores facit amicitia et adversas* partiens communicansque *leviores*; Cato 52 *quam serpentem multiplici lapsu et erratico* ferro amputans *coercet ars agricolarum*; Tusc. 3. 58 *hi enim omnes* diu cogitantes de rebus humanis *intellegebant eas nequaquam pro opinione volgi esse extimescendas*; Lig. 2 *cum* diu recusans *nihil profecisset*; div. 2. 59 *quasi vero quicquam intersit mures* diem noctem aliquid rodentes *scuta an cribra corroserint*.

In the last three examples it is clear that any idea of temporal concomitance is quite out of place. But it would be wrong to suppose that the participles are used loosely in an aoristic sense. Marouzeau regards the last passage as illustrating the juxtaposition of perfective main verb and imperfective participle,[2] but he

---

[1] Cf. S. Lyer, *R.É.L.*, 1932, 222–32 and 382–99; Schmalz–Hofmann, 596.

[2] Op. cit., 6 [138] f. S. Lyer, *R.É.L.*, 1929, 324, adopts a similar view. He explains the apparent anomaly as being due to an 'inexactitude dans l'interprétation de l'aspect' in the case of certain participles.

does not indicate how he would actually translate. In view of the other developed adverbial instances already quoted, it is far more natural to take these participles as gerundial.

nat. deor. 2. 126, which is one of the three examples given by Lebreton, can only be regarded as valid, if we accept the text of C. F. W. Mueller, who follows Madvig and Baiter: *vomitione canes, purgantes autem alvos ibes Aegyptiae curantur*. For *purgantes* the manuscripts vary between *purgante* and *purgare* (of which *purgatione* in two *deteriores* appears to be an attempted emendation); all manuscripts read *curant*. The solution of O. Plasberg in his editions of 1911 and 1917, now followed by A. S. Pease,[1] is: *vomitione canes, purgando autem alvo se ibes Aegyptiae curant*. Plasberg, in his *editio maior* (1911), points out in a note that copyists often confuse gerund and present participle. Notwithstanding the comparative rarity of instrumental gerundives in Cicero, Plasberg's conjecture is probably to be preferred; it certainly does less violence to the textual tradition than does the gratuitous alteration of *curant* to *curantur*.

It is not easy to say whether there is any essential difference in meaning between the participle and the gerund or gerundive, when used instrumentally. Many of the contexts in which it occurs suggest that, where the instrumental act was continued or repeated, the participle may have been felt to be more appropriate. Technically the participle had the advantage, over the gerund and gerundive, of greater lightness and greater ability to take verbal construction.

(c) Quasi-causal

In this use the present participle expresses a state of mind or emotion which not only accompanies the action of the finite verb, but is also its motive. Such states of mind are thinking, realizing, suspecting, believing, expecting, hoping, fearing, and the like. Examples of the use in Plautus and Terence have already been given (p. 21). To these may be added Bacch. 278 *cupientes*, Andr. 585 *metuens*, Eun. 133 *sperans*, Phorm. 45 *existumans*. An instance occurs in the *Rhetorica ad Herennium*, in an illustrative passage,

---

[1] A. S. Pease, *De Natura Deorum*, Cambridge, Mass., 1955–8.

possibly drawn from a *controversia* in which Scipio Nasica was accused of the death of Tiberius Gracchus (Marx, op. cit., p. 105), and therefore to be dated earlier than the treatise itself: 4. 68 *quod simul atque Gracchus prospexit, fluctuare populum verentem, ne ipse auctoritate senatus commotus sententia desisteret, iubet advocari contionem.* In Cicero the earliest example is Catil. 2. 26 (*prospiciens*), already quoted. In his maturity quasi-causal instances form, on the average, rather more than 1 per cent. of all participles. This in itself does not appear to be a striking proportion, but it is noteworthy that in the letters the percentage is greater, rising almost to 2 per cent. in his latest period. The passage from Rhet. Her., quoted above, shows that the usage was established before Cicero came on the scene, but he shows an increasing partiality for it in his later writing. The following illustrations will give some idea of its scope and frequency:

FEARING: leg. 2. 57 *quod haud scio an timens ne suo corpori posset accidere, primus ... igni voluit cremari*; fam. 13. 19. 2 *cuius dubia fortuna timidius tecum agebamus verentes, ne quid accideret eius modi* (cf. Att. 3. 18. 2 *metuens*; 10. 8. 5 *verens*; fam. 15. 17. 2 *verentem*; fin. 1. 7 *reformidans*; off. 1. 84 *timens*; 2. 25 *metuens*; nat. deor. 2. 59 *verens*).

THINKING, BELIEVING: nat. deor. 1. 7 *philosophiam nostris hominibus explicandam putavi magni existimans interesse . . . res tam graves tamque praeclaras Latinis etiam litteris contineri* (cf. fam. 15. 21. 4 *existimans*; ad Brut. 17. 2 *aestimans*; Att. 7. 1. 6 *putans*; 10. 7. 3 *putans*; fam. 1. 9. 6 *reputans*; Att. 11. 1. 2 *credens*; Tusc. 1. 111 *existimans* (cf. Cato 84); Tusc. 3. 63 *opinantes*; ibid. 3. 64 *putantes*).

SUSPECTING: Phil. 3. 26 *modo enim ex Africa decesserat et quasi divinans se rediturum duos legatos Uticae reliquerat* (cf. Att. 1. 19. 4 *suspicans*; fam. 9. 2. 3 *suspicans*; ibid. 9. 24. 1 *non suspicans*).

REALIZING, ETC.: nat. deor. 1. 33 *tum caeli ardorem deum dicit esse, non intellegens caelum mundi esse pariem*; Phil. 13. 19 *quem tum ille demens laedere se putabat edictis ignorans, quaecunque falso diceret in sanctissimum adulescentem, ea vere recidere in memoriam pueritiae suae* (cf. Att. 1. 16. 2 *perspiciens*; nat. deor. 1. 123 *videns*; fin. 2. 17 *providens*; fam. 4. 1. 1 *providentem*).

HOPING, ETC.: fam. 7. 3. 2 *quae cum vidissem, desperans victoriam primum coepi suadere pacem* (cf. fam. 6. 6. 1 *exspectans*; Phil. 3. 33 *exspectans*).

The following may also be noted: Att. 4. 19. 1 *recordans*; 5. 6. 2 *dubitans*; Lig. 3 *cupiens*.

As a development of the adverbial usage, this type of participle always agrees with the subject of the clause in which it stands. An apparent exception to this rule is fam. 9. 16. 1 *delectarunt me tuae litterae, in quibus primum amavi amorem tuum, qui te ad scribendum incitavit* verentem *ne Silius suo nuntio aliquid mihi sollicitudinis attulisset.* The pronoun *te*, with which *verentem* agrees, whilst it is grammatically the object of *incitavit*, contains the logical subject of the final gerund *scribendum.* The relative clause is logically equivalent to 'quo incitatus es ut scriberes verens &c.'. A similar example is to be found in de orat. 3. 33.

Quasi-causal participles occur six times in Cicero's correspondents: fam. 5. 10b. 1 (Vatinius) *existimans*; 8. 8. 3 (Caelius) *ignorans*; 10. 17. 2 (Plancus) *existimans*; 10. 18. 2 (Plancus) *extimescens*; 10. 21. 2 (Plancus) *existimans*; 11. 4. 1 (D. Brutus) *captans, cupiens*.

This usage, which Cicero undoubtedly established more firmly in the literary language, has a special significance in the development of the Latin present participle as a subordinating element. From 'propter hoc' to 'post hoc' is no great step, and there is justification for assuming that this quasi-causal type helped to prepare the way for the aoristic present participle which became common in later Latin.

(d) In place of a final clause

An idiomatic use of the quasi-causal participle, frequent enough in Cicero to deserve special mention, is his habit of using the present participle of verbs of seeking and avoiding as equivalent to a clause of purpose. Such participles are noteworthy not for their syntax, which is quite normal, but as a feature of style which appears to be virtually confined to Cicero's latest period: Phil. 5. 19 *ipse interea septemdecim dies de me in Tiburtino Scipionis declamitavit sitim quaerens* (cf. Brut. 251 *quaerens*; fin. 5. 74 *quaerentes*; Tusc. 1. 115 *quaerentem*); off. 1. 69 *qui eam, quam dico, tranquillitatem expetentes a negotiis publicis se removerint ad otiumque perfugerint* (cf. fin. 2. 86

expetentes; nat. deor. 2. 125 *petentes*); orat. 226 *quam* (sc. *numerosam comprehensionem*) *perverse fugiens Hegesias* . . . *saltat incidens particulas* (cf. fin. 4. 79; Att. 8. 12. 2 *fugiens*; off. 3. 3 *fugientes*). Under the same heading we may include de orat. 2. 59 *non ego utilitatem aliquam ad dicendum aucupans horum libros et nonnullos alios, sed delectationis causa, cum est otium, legere soleo.*

The adverbial participle, by its nature, is closely attached to the subject of the finite verb, and therefore regularly appears in the nominative or, if the verb of its clause is an infinitive in oratio obliqua, in the accusative. Attention has already been drawn to two instances in which a quasi-causal participle qualifies the logical subject of a sentence. The same is true of the following passages: de orat. 2. 257 *saepe etiam versus facete interponitur* . . . *aut aliqua pars versus, ut Stati* a Scauro stomachante (Scaurus is the logical subject. Cf. Sull. 86 *a me sciente*); Marcell. 33 *sed quia non est omnibus* stantibus *necesse dicere* (cf. orat. 171 *contemnenti*; fat. 14 *dissentienti*); Planc. 47 *itaque* haesitantem te *in hoc sodaliciorum tribuario crimine ad communem ambitus causam* contulisti; Phil. 14. 12 *quanto enim honore, laetitia, gratulatione in hoc templum ingredi debent illi ipsi huius urbis liberatores, cum hesterno die propter eorum res gestas* me ovantem et prope triumphantem *populus Romanus in Capitolium domo tulerit, domum inde reduxerit* (*me* contains the logical subject of the *cum*-clause, corresponding to *liberatores*, which is both logical and grammatical subject of the main clause). For a probable genitive example, see p. 62 below.

(3) Concomitant uses

The concomitant is the most frequent and familiar type of present participle. Its ordinary use needs no further illustration. Before we consider some of its modifications, this may be a suitable point to bring forward a few statistics. Marouzeau argues that in early Latin the nominative present participle shows an overwhelming preponderance over the oblique cases, and only rarely has verbal construction,[1] and that Cicero is the first fully to exploit the verbal potentialities of the participle, and to use it

---

[1] Op. cit., pp. 13 [145] ff., followed and summarized by F. Horn, *Zur Geschichte der absoluten Partizipialkonstruktionen im Lateinischen*, Lund–Leipzig, 1918, 4 ff.

freely in all the cases.[1] With this statement we may, in general, agree, but it is based on a limited selection of Cicero's writings, and needs some modification in the light of a comprehensive survey. The concomitant participle, which, unlike the adverbial, is not tied to the subject of the clause or sentence in which it appears, will provide a good test of any trend which is to be observed in Cicero. In the following tables 'nominative' includes subject-accusative in oratio obliqua; 'verbal construction' includes direct or indirect object, dependent clauses, prepositional phrases,[2] and the accusative or ablative with verbs of motion. For convenience the writings are divided into three periods, separated by Cicero's exile and by the Civil War.

		NOMINATIVE		OBLIQUE	
		With verb. constr.	*Without verb. constr.*	*With verb. constr.*	*Without verb. constr.*
I. Before 60 B.C.	Speeches	15	21	32	31
	Letters	..	..	..	..
	Treatises³	..	..	..	..
	TOTAL	15	21	32	31
II. 57–50	Speeches	21	7	42	42
	Letters	24	9	33	27
	Treatises	17	12	25	26
	TOTAL	62	28	100	95
III. 47–43	Speeches	15	13	29	13
	Letters	30	14	23	24
	Treatises	138	62	85	65
	TOTAL	183	89	137	102

Reduced to percentages, the totals appear as follows:

	NOMINATIVE		OBLIQUE	
	With verb. constr.	*Without verb. constr.*	*With verb. constr.*	*Without verb. constr.*
I	15	21	32	31
II	21	10	35	34
III	36	17	27	20

[1] Marouzeau, op. cit., p. 18 [150]; Horn, op. cit., p. 6.

[2] Marouzeau apparently does not admit the prepositional phrase as a criterion; but can it be maintained that in the phrase *de his rebus disputans* the participle is any less verbal than in *haec disputans*?

[3] Examples in the *De Inventione* are too few to be statistically useful.

From these two tables some interesting facts emerge. In the first place, the percentage of present participles, both nominative and oblique, taking verbal construction rises steadily: Period I— 47 per cent., II—56 per cent., III—63 per cent. Yet we do not find, what we might expect, a corresponding increase in the frequency of oblique participles. On the contrary, whilst in periods I and II oblique participles predominate in all genres in the average ratio of 2 : 1, in period III the balance is in favour of the nominative (53% against 47%). This result is largely brought about by the treatises, which form the overwhelming bulk of Cicero's output during his last years. But the same trend is to be observed in the other two genres also.

	Period I		Period II		Period III	
	Nom. %	Obl. %	Nom. %	Obl. %	Nom. %	Obl. %
Speeches	36	63	25	75	40	60
Letters	..	..	35·5	65·5	48·4	51·6

If adverbial participles were taken into account, the prepon- derance of the nominative in period III would be much more striking. It is tempting to conclude that, after experimenting in his early and middle periods with a wider and freer use of oblique participles as subordinating elements, Cicero, in the writings of his last years, began to revert to a more conservative practice, in which, while he continued to exploit the subordinating powers of the present participle, he tended to keep it more often in agree- ment with the subject of the sentence. We cannot, for instance, in the latest speeches find a sentence such as the following, in which two oblique present participles in different cases are used with verbal construction, and two participles in the same case are used in complex construction:[1] Sest. 118 *sed quid ego populi Romani animum virtutemque commemoro, libertatem iam ex diuturna servitute dispicientis, in eo homine cui tum petenti iam aedilitatem ne histriones quidem coram sedenti pepercerunt?*

It might be expected that among the oblique uses the accusa- tive case would predominate, and this is true of the speeches,

[1] See p. 128 below.

although the margin by which it surpasses the dative is only slight. In the treatises, on the other hand, the dative is roughly twice as common as the accusative.[1] The genitive is rare at first, but its use shows an increasing freedom. In the ablative the predicative present participle is seldom found.

GENITIVE: The present participle in the genitive is very rare in early Latin; there are only two instances in Plautus, and none in Terence. There is none in the *Rhetorica ad Herennium*. The Plautine instances are: Aul. 811 *certo enim ego vocem hic loquentis modo mi audire visus sum*; Rud. 260 *nam vox me precantum huc foras excitavit*. The participle has no noun or pronoun in agreement, but is given substantival force to enable it to depend on the noun (*vox* in each case). The meaning is approximately 'someone speaking', 'people entreating'. Perhaps the use of a genitive present participle with *vox* was a colloquial idiom, for the first example in Cicero is of a very similar type: Cluent. 30 *et ad hanc mortem repentinam* vocemque morientis *omnia praeterea quae solent esse indicia . . . veneni in illius mortuae corpore fuerunt*. Two instances in the speeches against Catiline show development: Catil. 1. 20 *quid exspectas auctoritatem loquentium, quorum voluntatem tacitorum perspicis?*; 4. 11 *versatur mihi ante oculos aspectus Cethegi et furor in vestra caede bacchantis*. In both these participles, the one without, the other with verbal construction, some concomitant force is to be discerned, though it is naturally less obvious, when the noun with which the participle agrees depends on another noun, instead of being immediately associated, as direct or indirect object, with the finite verb. Later we find a number of examples where the concomitance is clearer: dom. 101 *Sp. Maeli regnum adpetentis domus est complanata*; Att. 8. 14. 2 *cuius fugientis comes, rem publicam recuperantis socius videor esse debere*; ibid. 10. 9. 2 *lacrimae meorum me interdum molliunt precantium . . .*; off. 2. 51 *ut nos et saepe alias et adulescentes contra L. Sullae dominantis opes pro Sex. Roscio Amerino fecimus*; Deiot. 20 *vultus hominum te intuentium atque admirantium recordare* (here the concomitance is not with the main

---

[1] Naturally, I do not include subject-accusative in oratio obliqua. Cicero's predilection for using the present participle in dative constructions is remarked on by Seyffert–Mueller, *Laelius*, 184.

verb, but with the time in the past implied in the phrase *vultus* . . .
recordare = 'quales vultus fuerint').

The substantival bias in the genitive present participle, already noted in the two instances from Plautus, and inherent in
the fact that it depends upon a noun, appears in Cicero's developed
usage in two ways. Occasionally the participle is used as a quasi-
substantive, though with clear reference to a particular person
named. In Cluent. 30, quoted above, the phrase *vocem morientis*,
whilst it closely resembles *vocem* . . . *loquentis* and *vox* . . . *precantum*,
has a particular reference (Cluentia) such as is absent from the
Plautine passages. Similarly, in Att. 7. 7. 6 *quid ergo?* exercitum
retinentis, *cum legis dies transierit, rationem haberi placet*, the reference to Caesar, whose name is prominent in the immediate
context, is even more unmistakable. A more elaborate example is
found in Phil. 11. 4 *in Galliam invasit Antonius, in Asiam Dolabella, in
alienam uterque provinciam. alteri se Brutus obiecit impetumque* furentis
atque omnia divexare cupientis *vitae suae periculo conligavit*. To
explain the participles here as being in agreement with a pronoun
(*eius*) understood, would be wide of the mark. The participle is
allowed to assume the substantival force natural to the construction, while the reference to a particular person is left quite clear.
This use may well be an innovation on the part of Cicero. It is
perhaps worth noting that in phrases of this kind, where the
noun or pronoun is expressed, e.g. in Vatin. 15 *et* Vatini *latronis
ac sacrilegi vox audietur hoc* postulantis, noun and participle, whilst
their separate force is discernible, come near to forming a single
idea.

In fact, this is the second way in which the substantival bias
manifests itself: the tendency—exhibited by a number of passages in the later writings—of the participle and its noun to
coalesce into a single concept, which thus becomes invested with
the grammatical functions of a substantive. English has the same
idiom; it is equally possible to say 'the thought of him-returning'
('him-returning' being a single, quasi-substantival concept) or
'the thought of his return'. fam. 4. 4. 3 *ut speciem aliquam viderer
videre quasi* reviviscentis rei publicae ('the revival of the republic');
fin. 5. 3 *me quidem ad altiorem memoriam* Oedipodis huc venientis et

illo mollissimo carmine quaenam essent ipsa haec loca requirentis *species quaedam commovit* ('the arrival of Oedipus and his inquiry') ; Phil. 9. 15 *notetur etiam* M. Antoni nefarium bellum gerentis *scelerata audacia. his enim honoribus habitis Ser. Sulpicio repudiatae reiectaeque legationis ab Antonio manebit testificatio sempiterna* (not Antony's effrontery, but rather the effrontery of his conducting a *nefarium bellum.* This interpretation is confirmed by *repudiatae . . . legationis ab Antonio . . . testificatio* in the next sentence, where the past participle is used in the same way).

The last three examples properly belong to the discussion of the *ab urbe condita* construction. They are treated here because they are part of a development of the genitive present participle which is almost certainly an innovation on the part of Cicero himself.

DATIVE: Of the ordinary concomitant use of the predicative present participle in the dative nothing need be said. But there is one idiomatic type, the frequency of which in Cicero's writings goes far to explain the marked preponderance, in the latest period, of the dative over the accusative. An example of the basic pattern is found in Plaut. Merc. 515: LY *rogare hoc unum te volo.* PA *roganti respondebo.* It is a pattern of what might be termed 'reciprocity', in which participle and finite verb are complementary to one another in meaning. Such complementary pairs are: ask—answer, request—give (grant, refuse), seek—find, say (deny, swear, promise)—believe (disbelieve, agree, disagree). The dative is not essential in pairs of this kind. *roganti respondebo* does not appear elsewhere in Plautus or in Terence, but *iacentem tollere* is already a stereotyped expression with Plautus (Cist. 659, Most. 330, Pseud. 1247), and it appears several times, with characteristic variations, in Cicero (e.g. Marcell. 8 *extollere iacentem,* dom. 96 *iacentem—excitari,* Brut. 13 *iacentem excitavit*). Similarly, as against numerous examples of *petenti concedere, dare,* &c., we find *petentem repudiare* (Arch. 25) and *rogantem impetrare* (fam. 5. 12. 8). But because verbs of answering, giving, denying, allowing, believing, take a dative of the indirect object, the 'reciprocal' type of participle is found almost invariably in the dative. A small selection from a multitude of instances will illustrate its use: Q. Rosc. 50 *aut Cluvius Roscio petenti concessisset, si universae praedae particeps esset;*

Verr. II. 1. 128 *nolite Cn. Fannio dicenti credere*; Flacc. 47 *in Asiam venit Hermippoque percontanti de nomine Fufiano respondit se omnem pecuniam Fufiis persolvisse*; Cael. 5 *quem et absentem in amplissimum ordinem cooptarunt et ea non petenti detulerunt quae multis petentibus denegarunt* (contrast with this the normal concomitant participle in Mur. 7 *nihil tibi* consulatum petenti *a me defuit*—'when you were a candidate for').

Examples of this type are not very frequent in the earlier writings, but the variety of vocabulary which Cicero employs from the outset suggests that he was working on a familiar pattern, which was well established when his literary career began. Some idea of this variety is given by the following random selection: Att. 1. 16. 10 *iuranti—non crediderunt*; ibid. 4. 1. 7 *postulanti—negarunt*; dom. 40 *quaerenti—respondit*; Pis. 45 *nuntiantibus—non crederet, postulantibus—denegaret*; de orat. 2. 128 *postulanti—recusabo*; ibid. 130 *monenti—adsentiemur*; fam. 13. 24. 2 *adfirmanti—credas*; ad Q. fr. 3. 1. 11 *petenti—veniam non dedit.*

There is one form of the reciprocal pattern which Cicero made peculiarly his own. Here the complementary concepts are those of thinking, on the one hand, and getting an idea, on the other. Since the notion of thinking is intrinsically more durative than those of asking, promising, &c., the concomitant value never disappears in this formula, and in the earliest example of its use the participle is predominantly concomitant: har. resp. 55 *nisi forte existimatis hanc tantam conluvionem illi tantamque eversionem civitatis in mentem subito* in rostris cogitanti *venire potuisse* ('while he was pondering on the rostra'). In the *De Oratore* Cicero has begun to use the pattern freely. It is noteworthy that the first six sections of the first book contain four reciprocal datives (1 *cogitanti*, 2 *cupientibus*, 4 *hortanti*, 6 *intuenti*), two of which are of the new type. The first is worth quoting, since it illustrates a characteristic way in which Cicero was to exploit the pattern: de orat. 1. 1 *cogitanti mihi saepenumero et memoria vetera repetenti perbeati fuisse, Quinte frater, illi videri solent, qui in optima re publica, cum et honoribus et rerum gestarum gloria florerent, eum vitae cursum tenere potuerunt, ut vel in negotio sine periculo vel in otio cum dignitate esse possent.* Apart from the general structural value of a participle in a long period (ability to form a clause, and syntactical economy), there is here the added advantage that the link of reciprocity between *cogitanti* and *videri* helps to hold together the first part of the period. The second book of the *De Divinatione* opens with a period in which the same pattern appears, and where its linking force is even better demonstrated: div. 2. 1 quaerenti mihi multumque et diu cogitanti, *quanam re possem prodesse quam plurimis, ne quando intermitterem consulere rei publicae, nulla maior* occurrebat, *quam si optimarum artium vias traderem meis civibus.* One further example may be given. It occurs, like the previous two, in an opening period, this time of a carefully composed letter: fam. 4. 13. 1 (to Figulus) quaerenti mihi iam diu, *quid ad te potissimum scriberem, non modo certa res nulla sed ne genus quidem litterarum usitatum* veniebat in mentem.

It seems almost certain that Cicero introduced the pattern into Latin. The nearest approach to it in early Latin is to be seen perhaps in Most. 84 ff. and Trin. 223 ff., but apart from the presence of the same complementary concepts, the formal resemblance is insignificant. The fact that two of Cicero's most striking examples come from dedicatory opening paragraphs suggests the possibility that he may have derived this particular formula from Greek models. I have not found any strong confirmation of this, but the following opening sentences may be worth noting: Isocrates, *Evagoras* ὁρῶν, ὦ Νικόκλεις, τιμῶντά σε τὸν τάφον τοῦ πατρὸς ... ἡγησάμην ... κ.τ.λ.: [Longinus] *De Sublimitate* τὸ μὲν τοῦ Κεκιλίου συγγραμμάτιον, ὃ περὶ ὕψους συνετάξατο, ἀνασκοπουμένοις ἡμῖν ὡς οἶσθα κοινῇ, Ποστούμιε Τερεντιανὲ φίλτατε, ταπεινότερον ἐφάνη τῆς ὅλης ὑποθέσεως ... κ.τ.λ.[1] Of this pattern Cicero's correspondents offer no example, though the *roganti–respondere* type occurs several times (e.g. fam. 10. 21. 1; 10. 32. 3; 11. 28. 6).

(4) Apparent breaches of concomitance

In certain contexts the concomitant present participle appears to express action not simultaneous with that of the main verb, but either immediately preceding or immediately following. This is most evident with verbs of arrival and departure, and is fairly

[1] I assume that there is no question of a Latin idiom being transferred to Greek, even in the first century A.D.

common in Plautus and Terence, in whom, because of the many comings and goings of New Comedy, such verbs abound: e.g. Amph. 665 *quia domi daturus nemo est prandium advenientibus*; Capt. 914 *adveniens deturbavit totum cum carne carnarium*; Persa 731 *transcidi loris omnis adveniens domi*; Poen. 652 *adiit ad nos extemplo exiens*. Marouzeau (op. cit., pp. 6 [138] ff.), followed by Lyer (*R.É.L.*, 1929, 322 ff.) and Schmalz–Hofmann 604, maintains that the appearance of simultaneity, which is usually found with the present participle, results from the juxtaposition of the imperfective aspect of the participle and the perfective aspect of the finite verb. Given this imperfective or durative character, he argues, the action of the present participle may, and normally does, overlap the action of the finite verb, and thus, in certain cases, gives an appearance of anteriority. This theory seems attractive in the abstract, but I find it difficult to apply to the interpretation of particular passages. Marouzeau goes on to say (p. 10 [142]) that since the present participle is, in his view, incapable of expressing relative time, it is necessary, in order to give it temporal value, to attach to the participle an adverb of time. To illustrate this principle as applied to cases where the participle is intended to express immediate anteriority, he quotes six instances in which such an adverb (*extemplo, continuo, ilico*) is found: Amph. 714, 799 f., Epid. 361, Most. 570, Poen. 652, Haut. 182. But as many instances can be quoted where there is no adverb; to Amph. 665, Capt. 914, and Persa 731 (see above) one may add Bacch. 361, Curc. 660, and Truc. 382. The conclusion must be that, whilst an adverb may be used to emphasize the immediacy of the action of the main verb, it is not a necessary adjunct to the participle in expressions of this kind. This participial usage seems to be a colloquial idiom, confined to a limited number of verbs, among which *advenio* overwhelmingly predominates. S. Lyer (loc. cit.) adduces Capt. 8 f. *alterum quadrimum puerum servos surpuit | eumque hinc profugiens vendidit in Alide*. But *hinc profugiens* is not aoristic, as Lyer supposes; it means 'while he was a fugitive from here'.[1]

---

[1] So Tammelin, 18 f. When the statement is repeated, Capt. 17 f. *fugitivos ille, ut dixeram ante, huius patri | domo quem profugiens dominum apstulerat vendidit*, the participle is concomitant.

The same idiomatic use appears in a number of Ciceronian passages: e.g. Att. 7. 12. 5 *si ita factum esset, ut ille Romam veniens magistratus et senatum Romae offenderet*; dom. 4 *quo restituto senatus auctoritatem restitutam putabamus quam primum adveniens prodidisti.* More common in Cicero is a corresponding use of the present participle of verbs of departure, in which the participle appears to be not simultaneous with the finite verb, but rather prospective. Here, too, there are early Latin precedents: Plaut. Epid. 90 *fidicinam emit, quam ipse amat, quam abiens mandavit mihi*; Ter. Phorm. 288 *quoi commendavi filium hinc abiens meum.* Most frequent in Cicero is *proficiscens*, e.g. Mur. 42 *habuit proficiscens dilectum in Umbria*, but we also find *discedens* (Verr. II. 4. 85 *discedens mandat proagoro Sopatro . . . ut demoliatur . . . et statim ex illo oppido proficiscitur*), *decedens* (fam. 2. 15. 4 *ego de provincia decedens quaestorem Coelium praeposui provinciae*), and *egrediens* (Att. 12. 1. 1 *hoc litterularum exaravi egrediens e villa ante lucem*). Cf. fam. 9. 3. 1 *eunti.* Among Cicero's correspondents, such participles occur four times in letters of Caelius: fam. 8. 1. 1; 8. 3. 1; 8. 6. 2; 8. 10. 5.

What should be said about these uses is that they indicate not any irregularity in the present participle, but an inherent character of certain verbs, which happens in these instances to be exhibited by the present participle. Thus, verbs of departure were evidently capable of including a period of preparation before the physical act of setting out: e.g. Att. 7. 19 *Capuam tamen proficiscebar haec scribens.* Similarly, in Catullus 101 *advenio has miseras, frater, ad inferias*, the present tense is equivalent to 'adveni et adsum' (see Kroll ad loc.), and covers some time after Catullus' actual arrival.

Here, too, we can find the true explanation of the so-called 'conative' present participle, for which two Ciceronian passages have been adduced: Lael. 75 *si Lycomedem, apud quem erat educatus, multis cum lacrimis* iter suum impedientem *audire voluisset*; Cato 11 *C. Flaminio tribuno plebis, quoad potuit,* restitit agrum Picentem et Gallicum viritim contra senatus auctoritatem dividenti. On *Laelius* 75 Seyffert, in his edition of 1844, quoting Cato 11 in support, maintained that the present participle, in so far as it corresponded to an imperfect tense, could be used *de conatu.* This view was

vigorously rejected, in his revision of Seyffert's commentary, by
C. F. W. Mueller,[1] who declared that the theory of a conative
participle had only gained currency through misleading translation; Lycomedes was not merely 'trying to' hinder, but was in the
act of hindering. Mueller is surely right. While the act is in
process, whether it is destined to be successful or not, there is no
difference between hindering and trying to hinder. The same
character belongs to *dare* and its compounds. The activity of
giving is not completed until the gift is accepted. In the present
and imperfect tenses the activity is incomplete, and therefore, in
some contexts, the English translation 'offer' is appropriate. But
before an offer has been accepted (*dedit*—the completed act—
implies acceptance), the activity of giving and of offering is one
and the same. This character belongs to a large number of Latin
verbs which in their present systems denote an action still incomplete (it does not apply, for instance, to such verbs as *tango* or
cado). Hence, in Cato 11 *dividenti* is used with normal concomitant
force—'in the act of dividing'—and is not to be regarded, with
Schmalz–Hofmann 605, as having any future or prospective
sense.[2]

(5) Some passages of special interest

I propose to discuss a number of passages which do not fall
readily or obviously into any of the categories treated in the
previous pages. Marouzeau (op. cit., p. 11 [143]), when putting
forward his theory that an adverb is attached to the present
participle to give it temporal force—a theory which we have seen
reason to doubt—quotes, as an illustration of repeated action,
div. 2. 121 *nemo est quin* saepe iactans *Venerium iaciat aliquando*. Immediately after, to illustrate 'la durée de l'action', he quotes,
from the same context, *quis est enim, qui* totum diem *iaculans non
aliquando conliniet?* It is clear from the actual context (in which the
second passage precedes), as well as from the close similarity of
the language, that Cicero, by two different pictures, is illustrating
an identical thought: if one goes on throwing dice long enough,

[1] Seyffert–Mueller, *Laelius* (1876), 458.
[2] See Kühner–Stegmann, 120 ff.; Wackernagel, i. 165.

one is sure to throw a 'Venus', just as, if one goes on throwing a dart long enough, one is bound to hit the target. In both cases the participle is concomitant; *saepe-iactans* ('in the course of frequent throwing') forms, as it were, a single verbal idea, and expresses a continued activity. A similar explanation will apply to ac. 2. 148 *tum Lucullus, non moleste, inquit, fero nos haec contulisse.* saepius enim congredientes *nos, et maxime in Tusculanis nostris, si quae videbuntur requiremus (saepius-congredientes*—'in the course of frequent meetings').

There are, however, some clear instances of frequentative use of the present participle without an adverb's help: Phil. 2. 58 *lictores laureati antecedebant, inter quos aperta lectica mima portabatur, quam* ex oppidis *municipales homines honesti ob viam necessario* prodeuntes *non noto illo et mimico nomine, sed Volumniam consalutabant* (the participle is concomitant with *consalutabant*; the frequentative force is given mainly by the plural *ex oppidis*); ad Q. fr. 2. 6. 2 *M. Furium Flaccum, equitem Romanum, hominem nequam, Capitolini et Mercuriales de collegio eiecerunt praesentem* ad pedes unius cuiusque iacentem (here it is the words *unius cuiusque* which give to the participle the character of repeated action; we might translate 'while he was going through the performance of prostrating himself before each member in turn').

Marouzeau (p. 8 [140]) quotes two passages from the *De Divinatione*, in which the present participle is used of future facts or events: div. 1. 111 *orientem tyrannidem multo ante prospiciunt*; 2. 16 *medicus morbum ingravescentem ratione providet.* He rightly translates 'la naissance de la tyrannie . . . l'aggravation d'une maladie', and observes that, in each case, the futurity lies in the main verb. In fact, these are examples of the same sort of coalescence between participle and noun as has already been noticed among genitive uses (pp. 35 f.), and they properly belong to the *ab urbe condita* construction, which is discussed in a later chapter.

Finally, a passage in which, at first sight, the participles seem hard to explain: nat. deor. 1. 54 *confugitis ad deum; cuius operam profecto non desideraretis, si immensam et interminatam in omnis partes magnitudinem regionum videretis,* in quam se iniciens *animus* et intendens *ita late longeque peregrinatur, ut nullam tamen oram ultimi videat, in qua possit insistere.* It would appear that, if the participles *se iniciens* . . . *et intendens* express an act, they cannot be concomitant with *peregrinatur*, which is a continued activity. They cannot be frequentative, for the idea of repetition would make no sense here. If Cicero is using the present participle with aoristic force, it is an isolated instance, for which I have found no parallel, even remote, in the whole of his writing. The difficulty, however, disappears, when one realizes that the participles do not describe a completed act. The mind launching itself into infinity is an act which can have no end; the phrase *se iniciens* . . . *et intendens* describes the manner of *peregrinatur*. These are, in fact, modal participles, and nothing could more vividly suggest the *immensam et interminatam in omnis partes magnitudinem regionum.*

(6) Graecisms

The tendency, once prevalent, to find syntactical Graecisms in Latin writers provoked a strong reaction, the influence of which still remains. But it is possible, as E. Löfstedt has remarked, that scepticism has gone too far.[1] This is specially true of Cicero, who, despite his conscious endeavour to mould the Latin language into a literary instrument as artistic and flexible as Greek, was himself a great philhellene, and the close friend of another, and during the last few years of his literary activity was mainly occupied in reading and reproducing Greek philosophical treatises. It would not be surprising, in such circumstances, if borrowed Greek constructions should occasionally have found their way into his writing, particularly into his letters and treatises.[2]

There is a familiar Greek idiom, very common in Plato, but by no means confined to him, in which a participle bears the main weight of a clause or sentence; and when, as often, the clause is interrogative or relative, it is to the participle, not to the finite verb, that the relative or interrogative pronoun or adverb is attached:[3] e.g. Plato, Rep. 1. 332 d 1 ἦ οὖν δὴ τίσιν τί ἀποδιδοῦσα

[1] *Syntactica*, ii. 408 f.

[2] W. Kroll recognizes their presence, especially in the letters: *Studien zum Verständniss d. römischen Literatur*, 251 n.

[3] Cf. J. N. Madvig, *Syntax of the Greek Language* (Eng. edn., 1873), sect. 176, pp. 157 f.; Kühner–Gerth, *Ausführliche Grammatik der griechischen Sprache* (4th edn.), vol. ii, 100 f.; J. M. Stahl, *Kritisch-historische Syntax des griech. Verbums* (1907), 698 f.

τέχνη δικαιοσύνη ἂν καλοῖτο; ; Theaet. 184 a φοβοῦμαι οὖν μὴ οὔτε τὰ λεγόμενα συνιῶμεν, τί τε διανοούμενος εἶπε πολὺ πλέον λειπώμεθα. In pre-Ciceronian Latin I have found no traces of such a use, but Cicero offers no fewer than eight examples from his later writings: fin. 3. 37 quam vero utilitatem aut quem fructum petentes *scire cupimus illa, quae occulta nobis sunt* . . .? ibid. 5. 87 *patrimonium neglexit, agros deseruit incultos*, quid quaerens aliud nisi vitam beatam? Phil. 2. 86 *supplex te ad pedes abiciebas* quid petens? Tusc. 1. 31 *ut ait Statius in Synephebis*, quid spectans *nisi etiam postera saecula ad se pertinere?* fat. 33 quid enim spectans *deus ipse diceret Marcellum eum, qui ter consul fuit, in mari esse periturum?* ad Q. fr. 2. 13. 1 *sin minus, in illud ipsum mare deiciemus*, quod spectantes *scribimus*;[1] Att. 8. 9. 2 *si quidem etiam vos duo tales ad quintum miliarium* (sc. obviam ituri estis), *quo nunc ipsum unde se re-cipienti*, quid agenti, *quid acturo?* ibid. 16. 6. 2 *sed id satis superque tecum me non esse* quid fugientem?

With the exception of ad Q. fr. 2. 13. 1, none of these instances is earlier than 49 B.C. Their number suggests that Cicero was deliberately trying to make a syntactical innovation, borrowed from Greek.[2] In any case the idiom did not take root in Latin. One suspects that it would be difficult to assemble an equal num-ber of examples from the whole of post-Ciceronian Latin prose.

Apart from this idiom, which finds no mention in Schmalz–Hofmann,[3] possible Graecisms among Cicero's present participles are few and disputable. ad Brut. 23. 2 *quem cum a me dimittens graviter ferrem*—to which presumably one might add Att. 5. 1. 4 *dissimulavi dolens*—is unhesitatingly described by Schmalz–Hofmann (589, 605) as a normal predicative participle, but after long and careful observation of Cicero's participial usage in general, I cannot help feeling that, when he wrote these phrases, Cicero, perhaps without being conscious of it, had Greek idiom in mind.[4] The same applies to Tusc. 2. 19 *aspice Philoctetam, cui*

---

[1] The editions of Ascensius (2nd, 1522) and of Cratander (1528) printed *scriben-tes spectabamus*, thus showing, as Professor Fraenkel has pointed out to me, the early editors' instinct for the normal idiom.

[2] For similar Ciceronian instances with the ablative absolute, see pp. 111 f. below.

[3] But see Kühner–Stegmann, 785.

[4] Kühner–Gerth, op. cit. ii. 53 f.

concedendum est gementi (cf., for example, Plat. Rep. iii. 391 e πᾶς γὰρ ἑαυτῷ συγγνώμην ἕξει κακῷ ὄντι),[1] and perhaps also to off. 1. 71 *et iis forsitan concedendum sit* rem publicam non capessentibus, *qui . . . doctrinae sese dediderunt.*

The present participle, in the uses which have been described, steadily increases in frequency throughout Cicero's career. A table showing the percentage, in his total participial usage, represented by the predicative present participle speaks for itself:

	Speeches	Letters	Treatises
Period I (before 60)	11	11	..
Period II (58–50)	16	23	14
Period III (after 49)	22	26	26

Cicero's exploitation of the participle's aptitude for verbal construction also increases steadily. In the last period there is a notable development in the use of various adverbial types, particularly the quasi-causal participle, a development with which is associated a preponderance of nominative over oblique participles. The free use of oblique present participles reaches its peak in the middle period, after which it becomes less prominent in comparison with the nominative, though dative uses fully maintain their frequency. It is in the final period that we find the great majority of instances of the most subtle uses.

None of the inherent potentialities of the present participle was left undeveloped by Cicero.[2] The only step remaining for later writers—a step which went beyond the legitimate scope of the participle—was to give it full aoristic value. Even for this Cicero had prepared the way by his unmistakable development of the quasi-causal type.

[1] Ibid. 55.
[2] I have not thought it necessary to illustrate Cicero's use of the present participle with conditional or concessive force, since his corresponding treatment of the past participle has been fully discussed.

NOTE 1

ON THE POSITION OF THE PREDICATIVE PARTICIPLE IN RELATION TO ITS NOUN

It is hazardous to make pronouncements about word-order in a language so flexible in this respect as is Latin. This is well illustrated by the fact that the two most authoritative Latin grammars of modern times express almost diametrically opposite views about the position of the attributive adjective.[1] When we are dealing not merely with the natural flexibility of the language, but also with an individual and subtle stylist like Cicero, dogmatic generalization is even more liable to be mistaken. Nevertheless, with due allowance for this, it does seem possible to discern the influence of certain broad principles on the position of the predicative participle in relation to the noun which it qualifies.

In the great majority of instances the predicative participle follows its noun. Most deviations from this normal position seem to fall under two main heads: either the participle is intended to carry more emphasis than its noun (or pronoun), or it stands in a clause introduced by a connecting relative or demonstrative pronoun, with which its juxtaposition is syntactically natural, if not necessary.

(1) Emphasis

When the participle (i) qualifies an unemphatic proper name or pronoun, or (ii) itself carries a special emphasis, it may be put first.

(i) Att. 9. 10. 2 *et me una haec res torquet quod non omnibus in rebus labentem vel potius ruentem Pompeium tamquam unus manipularis secutus sim*; Verr. II. 4. 76 *itaque aliquando multis malis magnoque metu victi Segestani praetoris imperio parendum esse decreverunt*; Cluent. 175 *cum vagus et exul erraret atque undique exclusus Oppianicus in Falernum se ad L. Quinctium contulisset* (it is clear from the context that Cicero is talking about Oppianicus, and this sentence would be just as intelligible without the name; but since it has not occurred for twenty lines, and Cicero is beginning a new paragraph, he inserts it here merely for the sake of complete clarity); Planc. 13 *deinde sitientem me virtutis tuae deseruisti ac reliquisti*; fam. 14. 5. 1 *de nave exeuntibus nobis Acastus cum litteris praesto fuit.*

(ii) The clearest instances where a participle carries more emphasis than its noun are those in which it is enhanced by antithesis or parallelism: e.g. Balb. 16 *cuius igitur* audita *virtus dubitationi locum non daret,* huius visa atque perspecta *obtrectatorum voce laedetur* (*visa* is a conjecture of Halm); p. red. in sen. 36 *ne* a me defensa *res publica* per eundem me extremum in discrimen vocaretur; Tusc. 4. 58 *itaque* bene adhibita *ratio cernit, quid optimum sit,* neglecta *multis implicatur erroribus*; ad Q. fr. 2. 14. 5 *erat aliqua suspicio dictaturae,* . . . *summum otium forense, sed* senescentis magis *civitatis* quam adquiescentis;

---

[1] Compare Schmalz–Hofmann 616 with Kühner–Stegmann 605 f. According to S.–H., the adjective, when emphatic, is placed before the noun; according to K.–S., it is placed after.

leg. 3. 44 discriptus *enim populus censu, ordinibus, aetatibus* plus *adhibet ad suffragium consilii* quam fuse in tribus convocatus; Cato 2 *hoc enim onere* . . . aut iam urgentis aut certe adventantis *senectutis et te et me ipsum levari volo* (cf. div. 1. 128; 2. 100).

Sometimes the emphasis is sufficiently obvious from the context: Cato 56 *in agris erant tum senatores* . . . *si quidem aranti L. Quinctio Cincinnato nuntiatum est eum dictatorem esse factum*; Att. 11. 17. 1 *properantibus tabellariis alienis hanc epistulam dedi; eo brevior est et quod eram missurus nostros* (the reason why Cicero has written a shorter letter is not that he is sending it by someone else's couriers, but that they are in a hurry, and, because they are not his own, he can hardly keep them waiting); Cluent. 164 *habetis, iudices, quae in totam causam de moribus A. Cluenti, quem illi invidiosum esse reum volunt, annos octo meditati accusatores collegerunt* (the nature of the emphasis is to be seen from *totam* and from the relative clause *quem* . . . *volunt*; Cluentius is alleged to have a bad reputation, yet, for the whole case against his character, this is all that the prosecution has been able to collect, in spite of eight years of preparation); Sest. 76 *venientem in forum virum optimum et constantissimum M. Cispium, tribunum plebis, vi depellunt* (that the phrase *venientem in forum* is emphatic becomes clear when we notice the prominence of the word *forum* in the remainder of the sentence: *caedem* in foro *maximam faciunt, universique destrictis gladiis et cruentis* in omnibus fori partibus *fratrem meum* . . . oculis *quaerebant, voce poscebant*); Mil. 38 *cuius vis omnis haec semper fuit ne P. Clodius, cum in iudicio detrahi non posset, vi oppressam civitatem teneret* (the emphasis in *vi oppressam* is made plain by the preceding *vis*); prov. 32 *ipse ille C. Marius* . . . *influentis in Italiam Gallorum maximas copias repressit, non ipse ad eorum urbis sedisque penetravit* (Cicero's argument is summed up by the sentence with which this section begins: *bellum Gallicum* . . . *C. Caesare imperatore gestum est, antea tantum modo repulsum*; the sense is evidently: 'Marius checked large forces of Gauls, (but only) when they were pouring into Italy'); Phil. 14. 24 *quam ob rem aut supplicatio re publica pulcherrime gesta postulantibus nostris imperatoribus deneganda est, quod praeter A. Gabinium contigit nemini, aut supplicatione decernenda hostis eos, de quibus decernitis, iudicetis necesse est* (the granting of a *supplicatio* involved regarding the defeated as *hostis*; unless the Senate was prepared to accept this logical corollary in the case of the defeated Antony, they must refuse a *supplicatio*, even in circumstances in which the granting of it was virtually inevitable); Tusc. 3. 31 *quare accipio equidem a Cyrenaicis haec arma contra casus et eventus, quibus eorum advenientis impetus diuturna praemeditatione frangantur* (*advenientis*—'as soon as they arrive'; this interpretation is supported by the word **prae**meditatione, which otherwise would be rather pointless); leg. agr. 2. 13 *concurrunt iussu meo plures uno tempore librarii, descriptam legem ad me adferunt* (*lex* occurs in the previous sentence, and *legem* here is as unemphatic as the pronoun *eam* would have been; the important fact is that the law was copied); Tusc. 1. 73 *quod iis saepe usu venit, qui acriter oculis deficientem solem intuerentur, ut aspectum omnino amitterent* ('the sun in eclipse'). Prominence is similarly to be given to the participial phrase in the following examples: Verr. II. 1. 7 *quod iste inventus est qui e complexu parentum abreptos filios ad necem duceret*; orat. 42 *sed quod educata huius nutrimentis eloquentia ipsa se postea colorat et roborat* (cf. ibid. 68 *seiunctus*).

It is instructive to compare the following three passages: Phil. 3. 32 *magna vis est, magnum numen* unum et idem sentientis *senatus*; ibid. 5. 32 *experietur consentientis senatus nervos atque vires*; Deiot. 11 *cum audiret* senatus consentientis *auctoritate arma sumpta.* In both of the extracts from the Philippics Cicero is addressing the Senate; what he wishes to impress on its members is the importance of unity. In the *Pro Deiotaro* he is seeking to justify to Caesar Deiotarus' behaviour at the time of the Civil War. For this purpose, the fact that the Senate had initiated the hostilities was just as important as its unanimity. Perhaps a shift of emphasis is similarly to be seen in Sest. 145: *quia me lugenti patriae, flagitanti senatui, poscenti Italiae, vobis omnibus orantibus reddiderunt.* The participles are parallel in function. The first three bear the main weight of their clauses, and are naturally placed first. To have put the less colourful and forceful *orantibus* in the same position would have satisfied formal concinnity, but at the expense of anticlimax. Cicero avoids this by changing the position of the participle and, by the addition of *omnibus*, transferring the main weight of the clause to *vobis.*

Occasionally one cannot readily decide whether a participle in prior position is to be regarded as predicative with emphasis or as attributive, since, as will later be shown, the attributive participle, when its character is not otherwise indicated (and sometimes when it is), tends to be put before its noun. In the following examples the participle might be taken as attributive, without materially affecting the sense: Quint. 10 *orat atque obsecrat ut multis iniuriis iactatam atque agitatam aequitatem in hoc tandem loco consistere . . . patiamini*; ibid. 74 *unus fuit . . . qui . . . cupidissime contenderet ut per se adflictum atque eversum propinquum suum . . . communi luce privaret*;[1] de orat. 1. 202 *idemque* (possit) *languentem labentemque populum aut ad decus excitare aut ab errore deducere.*

(2) Syntactical necessity

Sometimes the syntax of a participial clause is such, that the only natural position for the participle is before the noun. This situation occurs most frequently with the past participle passive, in clauses where the ablative of agent or instrument belonging to the participle is, or includes, a relative or demonstrative pronoun introducing the clause: Att. 6. 1. 6 *et quidem habuerat turmas equitum, quibus inclusum in curia senatum Salamine obsederat*; rep. 2. 46 *quo auctore et principe concitata civitas . . . exulem et regem ipsum et liberos eius et gentem Tarquiniorum esse iussit*; nat. deor. 2. 118 *quibus* (sc. *vaporibus*) *altae renovataeque stellae atque omnis aether refundunt eadem et rursum trahunt indidem* (cf. rep. 6. 29; dom. 42; orat. 187; off. 2. 15; div. 1. 115; Phil. 12. 15); rep. 6. 19 *hoc sonitu oppletae aures hominum obsurduerunt*; Cluent. 192 *atque his rebus cum instructum accusatorem filio suo Romam misisset*; Lig. 7 *a quo hoc ipso C. Pansa mihi nuntium perferente concessos fasces laureatos tenui quoad tenendos putavi.* Essentially similar to the above are Tusc. 4. 6 *cuius libris editis commota multitudo contulit se ad eam potissimum disciplinam* and invent. 1. 103 *quibus ex omnibus acriter excitata indignatio summum in eum qui violarit horum aliquid odium commovere poterit.* Clauses thus introduced in which the noun precedes the

---

[1] It is more likely that the participles here are predicative, and that their position is due to the emphasis attached to *per se* (see p. 6 above).

participle are quite exceptional, e.g. leg. agr. 1. 2 *videte* . . . *ut a maioribus nostris possessiones relictas disperdat ac dissipet*, where Cicero may have wished to enhance by juxtaposition the contrast of ideas between *relictas* and *disperdat*. The same principle operates with other constructions which link the introductory pronoun closely with the participle: nat. deor. 2. 137 *per quas lapsus cibus* . . . *in eam venam, quae cava appellatur, confunditur* (compare the phrase, a few lines earlier, in which the participle is not in direct syntactical connexion with the relative pronoun: *per quas cadit cibus a iecore dilapsus*); orat. 183 *neque enim ipse versus ratione est cognitus, sed natura atque sensu, quem dimensa ratio docuit quid accideret*; off. 2. 9 *in quo verbo lapsa consuetudo deflexit de via*; Phil. 2. 64 *una in illa re servitutis oblita civitas ingemuit*.

We may include under the same heading of syntactical necessity the following examples: nat. deor. 2. 135 *atque is agitatione et motibus linguae cum depulsum et quasi detrusum cibum accepit, depellit* (the prominence given to *agitatione et motibus linguae*, at the head of the sentence, has entailed the position of *depulsum et quasi detrusum*); Pis. 74 *nam cum tu timidus ac tremens tuis ipse furacissimis manibus detractam e cruentis fascibus lauream ad portam Esquilinam abiecisti* (an example very similar to the previous one; the position of *detractam* is entailed by the emphatic prominence given to *tuis . . . furacissimis manibus*); div. 1. 79 *noctu lumine apposito experrecta nutrix animadvertit puerum dormientem circumplicatum serpentis amplexu* (*lumine apposito* gives the reason for *experrecta*). Syntactical effectiveness, if not necessity, is to be seen in Phil. 10. 9 *esset vel receptaculum pulso Antonio vel agger oppugnandae Italiae Graecia*, where there is a complementary affinity between *receptaculum* and *pulso* similar to that present in the corresponding *agger oppugnandae*. Concinnity, in fact, has doubtless played its part in this instance.

Most departures from the normal position of the predicative participle fall into one or other of these two categories. But there remains a number of examples in which the governing factor has evidently been Cicero's own artistic sense, and in these, so far as the particular reason for his choice is concerned, we can only make tentative conjectures: Tusc. 1. 96 *cum iam praecordiis conceptam mortem contineret* (perhaps to avoid the harsh juxtaposition of *conceptam contineret*); Verr. II. 4. 107 *qua Ditem patrem ferunt repente cum curru exstitisse, abreptamque ex eo loco virginem secum asportasse*; div. 1. 73 *qui cum per agrum Leontinum iter faciens equum ipse demisisset in flumen, submersus equus voraginibus non exstitit* (in both these narrative passages the position of the participle, at the beginning of the second clause, seems to give an added impression of vividness and rapidity); rep. 2. 7 *nec vero ulla res magis labefacta- tam diu et Carthaginem et Corinthum pervertit aliquando quam hic error ac dissipatio civium* (it is not easy to suggest a reason here, unless the connexion of the participial phrase *labefactatam diu* with both the nouns is felt to be clearer than if it had followed *Corinthum*).

Finally, it may be worth while to examine in some detail a case of emphasis which editors seem not to have noticed, but which is of importance in its context: orat. 200 *ante enim circumscribitur mente sententia, confestimque verba concurrunt, quae mens eadem, qua nihil est celerius, statim dimittit, ut suo quodque loco respondeat; quorum* discriptus *ordo alias alia terminatione concluditur. atque omnia illa et prima et media verba spectare debent ad ultimum.* Cicero is answering the question whether rhythm is to be observed throughout a period, or only at the beginning and the end. His reply (199) is that, whilst the final cadence must be rhythmical, its rhythm must be such, that it appears to be the natural and inevitable conclusion of what has gone before. To achieve this the orator must first formulate in his mind the whole idea which he wishes to express, and, like a commander disposing his troops, arrange the words each in its proper place. Only when the word-order has been thus 'marshalled' (*discriptus*—the quasi-military metaphor is sustained), is the appropriate clausula to be chosen. Kroll's note here (edition, p. 172) is surely wrong. His interpretation is that, because the clausulae must be varied, for the reason given in section 197 (i.e. to avoid an impression of conscious artificiality), the preceding rhythms must be varied accordingly. In fact, as the whole context shows, and as the emphatic *discriptus* puts beyond doubt, Cicero is here mentioning another factor in the variation of the clausula: it must be a natural close to the preceding rhythms.

NOTE 2

THE COMPLETIVE PARTICIPLE

The predicative participle is used in Latin to complete the verbal statement in certain cases where, without the participle, the verb would be either imprecise or meaningless. A use, confined to early Latin, of *do* and *reddo* with the past participle has already been mentioned (p. 3). A similar use of the present participle is found in Plautus, where it has the force of a simple predicative adjective: e.g. Stich. 407 *eos nunc laetantis faciam* (*laetantis = laetos*). Cicero provides more elaborate examples of the same type: e.g. de orat. 3. 172 *quae vinctam orationem efficit, quae cohaerentem, quae levem, quae aequabiliter fluentem*; fin. 2. 45 *eademque ratio fecit hominem hominum appetentem* cumque iis natura et sermone et usu congruentem. Another type of completive participle, well established in early Latin, is the present participle with various verbs of perception: e.g. Plaut. Asin. 878 *si forte accubantem tuom virum conspexeris*; Most. 934 *neque tibicinam cantantem neque alium quemquam audio*; Ter. Haut. 285 *texentem telam studiose ipsam offendimus*. This participial use was continued throughout the classical period, side by side with the infinitive construction, and in a general way may be said to express actual, as opposed to intellectual, perception. This distinction, however, cannot be strictly maintained, because of the defectiveness of the Latin participial system, which makes the use of the infinitive obligatory in the passive.[1] Cicero does not seem to have made any striking innovation in this type. The range of verbs with which such a participle is used—*video, audio, aspicio, offendo, animadverto* (Tusc. 3. 48), *reperio* (fin. 2. 99)—is somewhat wider than that which appears in Plautus and Terence, but this is no more than we would expect. More interesting is the fact that Cicero has several examples in which the participle is not present, but past: invent. 2. 162 *aut si quid*

---

[1] E. C. Woodcock, *A New Latin Syntax*, pp. 74 f.

eorum, quae ante diximus, a natura profectum maius factum propter consuetudinem videmus; div. 1. 91 *licet autem videre et genera quaedam et nationes huic sententiae deditas*; fin. 3. 7 *M. Catonem* . . . *vidi in bibliotheca sedentem, multis circumfusum Stoicorum libris* (*circumfusum* stands in the same relationship to *vidi* as does *sedentem*; cf. div. 1. 79 *animadvertit puerum dormientem circumplicatum serpentis amplexu*). Here, too, the lack of examples in early Latin may be fortuitous.[1]

A development which, if not due to Cicero himself, seems to belong to his age or to the immediately preceding generation, since there is no trace of it in early Latin, is the use of a completive participle after verbs of representing.[2] Verbs used in this way by Cicero are *facio, trado, induco,* and *fingo*: Cato 54 *at Homerus* . . . *Laertem lenientem desiderium, quod capiebat e filio,* colentem agrum et eum stercorantem facit (cf. Tusc. 5. 115; nat. deor. 1. 31); Brut. 50 *Menelaum ipsum dulcem illum quidem tradit Homerus, sed pauca dicentem*; Tusc. 2. 27 *lamentantis inducunt fortissimos viros* (cf. div. 2. 40; orat. 138); Att. 9. 5. 2 *finge me quamvis* εὐστομάχως *haec ferentem*. Particularly interesting examples of this type are passages in which *est* is used as a verb of representing: div. 1. 52 *est apud Platonem Socrates, cum esset in custodia publica,* dicens *Critoni, suo familiari, sibi post tertium diem moriendum* (cf. orat. 41). Perhaps we should also add *profero* in de orat. 1. 38 *plura proferre possim detrimenta publicis rebus quam adiumenta per homines eloquentissimos importata*. It will be noticed that in the last passage the participle is past; two further instances can be quoted: nat. deor. 2. 64 *ex se enim natos comesse fingitur solitus*; Tusc. 1. 97 *quae est igitur eius oratio, qua facit eum Plato usum apud iudices, iam morte multatum*.

With the exception of Att. 9. 5. 2 and de orat. 1. 38, all the examples of this type quoted above come from treatises of Cicero's latest period, and whilst the significance of this ought not to be exaggerated, since they are utterances which find their most natural expression in reflective writing, it is tempting to see here a Ciceronian innovation.

---

[1] Cf. Tammelin, 114 ff. Tammelin believes that in all the apparent examples the past participle should be regarded as a shortened form of the perfect infinitive.

[2] Tammelin, 67. In Ter. Eun. pr. 36, which he tentatively adduces in a footnote (cf. p. 70), *currentem* is attributive.

II

THE ATTRIBUTIVE PARTICIPLE

W HEN a participle is used attributively it performs the regular function of a true adjective, that of attaching to a noun a permanent or quasi-permanent characteristic, irrespective of the action of the main verb. From a very early time some participles (like *rectus* and *sapiens*) were used exclusively, and many more (like *doctus* and *diligens*) frequently, as simple attributive adjectives, admitting degrees of comparison. In two places Cicero goes so far as to allow a participle in the superlative—and therefore in a characteristically adjectival form—to retain verbal function: dom. 23 *homini taeterrimo, crudelissimo, fallacissimo, omnium scelerum libidinumque maculis notatissimo*; de orat. 3. 31 *ut unus ad dicendum instructissimus a natura esse videatur.*

The two passages just quoted illustrate the special advantages which the attributive participle offered, as sentence-structure became more complex. Its verbal function enabled it to be attached, with the force of a relative clause, to any noun in the sentence, whilst its adjectival termination ensured that, however extended its own construction, the framework of the main sentence, of which it formed a part, remained clear and closely knit. Good examples of this are seen in Cael. 12 *neque ego umquam fuisse tale monstrum in terris ullum puto, tam ex contrariis diversisque et inter se pugnantibus naturae studiis cupiditatibusque conflatum* and in nat. deor. 1. 114 *comprehende igitur animo et propone ante oculos deum nihil aliud in omni aeternitate nisi 'mihi pulcre est' et 'ego beatus sum' cogitantem.*

At the same time, it became increasingly necessary to distinguish the attributive use from other subordinating uses of the participle, and to make its particular function recognizable. In observing Cicero's use of the attributive participle, the chief interest lies in noticing the various ways in which this distinction is made. Occasionally the participle is found in syntactical correspondence to a relative clause, so that its force is obvious: e.g. ad Q. fr. 1. 1. 11 *quaestorem habes* non tuo iudicio delectum, sed eum quem sors dedit; rep. 1. 5 *et Themistoclem patria, quam liberavisset, pulsum atque proterritum non in Graeciae* portus per se servatos, *sed in* barbariae *sinus confugisse*, quam adflixerat. But in this juxtaposition Cicero's primary object was no doubt to avoid monotony, rather than to establish the character of the participle. It is instructive to observe, in the following passage, the taste which leads Cicero to substitute a participle in the last clause, thus avoiding the frigid and mechanical concinnity which a third relative clause would have produced: div. in Caec. 72 *habet honorem, quem petimus, habet spem, quam propositam nobis habemus, habet existimationem multo sudore labore vigiliisque collectam.* The ways by which an attributive participle was distinguished as such were for Cicero inherited or instinctive, rather than deliberate devices consciously adopted on each occasion. It is when we find rhythm and sentence-balance playing their part in determining the use of the participle and in keeping its function clear, that we can recognize the authentic hand of Cicero.

(1) In definitions

We may conveniently begin with the use of the participle in definitions, since here its attributive character is explicit and prominent. The definition is a sophisticated form of expression, and presupposes some familiarity with philosophical modes of thought. We may, therefore, assume with some confidence that Latin borrowed this convenient use from Greek; and this assumption is confirmed by the fact that a relatively large number of such participles occur not only in Cicero's late philosophical works, but also in the *De Inventione*, which is believed to be founded on the same Greek original as the *Rhetorica ad Herennium*, a work similarly characterized by a frequent use of defining participles. A few examples drawn from an anonymous Greek rhetorical τέχνη (*Rhet. Gr.*, Spengel–Hammer, i, pp. 352 ff.) will serve to illustrate the type upon which the Latin definition-formula was modelled:

6 ἔστι δὲ πάθος πρόσκαιρος κατάστασις ψυχῆς, σφοδροτέραν ὁρμὴν

54 THE ATTRIBUTIVE PARTICIPLE

ἢ ἀφορμὴν κινοῦσα; 48 Ζήνων δὲ οὕτω φησί· διήγησίς ἐστι τῶν ἐν
τῇ ὑποθέσει πραγμάτων ἔκθεσις εἰς τὸ ὑπὲρ τοῦ λέγοντος πρόσωπον
ῥέουσα; 159 ὡς δὲ Ἁρποκρατίων, ἐνθύμημά ἐστι λόγος πρὸς ἀπό-
δειξιν λαμβανόμενος τῶν ὑποκειμένων; 198–9 ἐπίλογός ἐστιν, ὡς
μὲν Νεοκλῆς, λόγος ἐπὶ προειρημέναις ἀποδείξεσιν ἐπιλεγόμενος,
πραγμάτων ἀθροισμὸν καὶ ἠθῶν καὶ παθῶν περιέχων. ὡς δέ τινες,
μέρος λόγου ὕστατον ἑπόμενον ἀποδείξεσιν. This is the same pattern of formula which we find Aristotle using in, for instance, his
famous definition of tragedy (*Poetics* 1449ᵇ24: ἔστιν οὖν τραγῳδία
μίμησις . . . δι᾽ ἐλέου καὶ φόβου περαίνουσα τὴν τῶν τοιούτων
παθημάτων κάθαρσιν). We encounter this pattern frequently in the
Rhetorica ad Herennium and in the parts of Cicero's writings most
subject to Greek influence: Rhet. Her. 3. 3 *iustitia est aequitas ius
uni cuique re tribuens pro dignitate cuiusque*; 4. 43 *circumitio est oratio
rem simplicem adsumpta circumscribens elocutione* (cf. ibid. 46); invent.
1. 10 *constitutio est prima conflictio causarum ex depulsione intentionis
profecta*; ibid. 20 *exordium est oratio animum auditoris idonee comparans
ad reliquam dictionem* (cf. invent. 1. 40, 44, 49, 57, 106; 2. 160);
Tusc. 3. 24 *altera* (sc. *perturbatio*), *quae est immoderata appetitio opinati
magni boni rationi non obtemperans*; nat. deor. 3. 64 *Neptunum esse
dicis animum cum intelligentia per mare pertinentem.*

In his later works Cicero allows himself to vary the stereotyped
definition-formula: off. 3. 118 *prudentiam introducunt scientiam sup-
peditantem voluptates, depellentem dolores*; fin. 5. 65 *quae animi affectio
suum cuique tribuens atque hanc, quam dico, societatem coniunctionis
humanae munifice et aeque tuens iustitia dicitur*; part. 79 *custos vero
virtutum omnium dedecus fugiens laudemque maxime consequens vere-
cundia est*; nat. deor. 1. 36 *Zeno autem . . . naturalem legem
divinam esse censet, eamque vim obtinere recta imperantem prohibentemque
contraria.*

(2) Completing *res, homo* &c.

Some nouns tend to attract adjectival description, because by
their nature they are generic, and need specification before they
can be used in a particular context. The two words of this kind
which are most frequently met in Latin are *res* and *homo*, and
when a participle is found in agreement with either of these

nouns, the presumption is that it has the function of an attributive adjective, specifying the noun and completing the sense: e.g.
invent. 1. 98 *enumeratio est per quam* res disperse et diffuse dictae
unum in locum coguntur; fin. 4. 50 *placet igitur tibi, Cato, cum* res
sumpseris non concessas, *ex illis efficere quod velis*; Verr. II. 5. 49
habemus hominem in fetialium manibus educatum; de orat. 2. 136
atque haec forsitan homini non omnia, quae sunt in natura rerum,
celeriter animo comprehendenti *permulta videantur.* Further illustration is unnecessary, since examples of participles completing
res and *homo* are frequent in Cicero's writing at all periods, and
obviously reflect regular usage. More interesting is Cicero's
readiness to extend the same principle to other nouns, where they
carry a generic significance: dom. 123 *si postem tenuerit pontifex et*
verba ad religionem deorum immortalium composita *ad perniciem
civium transtulerit*; orat. 163 verba . . . *legenda sunt potissimum* bene
sonantia; fin. 1. 6 *cum tractat* locos ab Aristotele ante tractatos;
Att. 1. 19. 1 *et primum tibi, ut aequum est* civi amanti patriam, *quae
sint in re publica exponam*; Catil. 4. 18 *habetis* consulem ex plurimis
periculis et insidiis atque ex media morte non ad vitam suam, sed
ad salutem vestram reservatum (the phrase *habetis consulem* (cf.
Verr. II. 5. 49, above) establishes the generic force of the noun
and enables the adjectival character of *reservatum* to be clearly felt,
despite the length and comparative complexity of its intervening
construction); Mur. 78 *audite, audite* consulem, *iudices, nihil dicam
adrogantius, tantum dicam* totos dies atque noctes de re publica
cogitantem (the generic force of *consulem* is less certain here, but
may be regarded as probable—'a consul who . . .'); Phil. 2. 45
nemo umquam puer emptus libidinis causa *tam fuit in domini potestate
quam tu in Curionis* (the generalizing effect of *nemo* helps to establish the attributive character of *emptus*). To this category belong
nat. deor. 1. 114 *comprehende igitur animo et propone ante oculos* deum
nihil aliud in omni aeternitate nisi 'mihi pulcre est' et 'ego beatus
sum' cogitantem and Tusc. 1. 37 animos enim per se ipsos
viventes *non poterant mente complecti.* In each of these two passages
the main sentence implies that the noun is incomplete without an
adjectival description. (Other examples with *animus* in off. 1. 13
and Tusc. 2. 15.)

(3) Completing certain pronouns and pronominal adjectives

Certain demonstrative and indefinite pronouns and pronominal adjectives, notably *hic, ille, iste, aliquis, quidam, quisquam*, have a natural tendency to be accompanied by further specification, so that a participle in agreement with one of them is likely to be attributive: Brut. 124 *atqui* haec, *inquam, de incestu* laudata *oratio puerilis est locis multis*; Mur. 72 hae *conquestiones* in senatu habitae; Manil. 7 *delenda est vobis* illa *macula* Mithridatico bello superiore concepta; Sest. 72 illa ex vepreculis extracta *nitedula*; fin. 3. 76 illum a Cyro exstructum *rogum*; Verr. II. 3. 187 iste *anulus aureus* abs te datus; invent. 1. 36 *corporis* aliquam *commoditatem* non natura datam, sed studio et industria partam (cf. Mur. 12); invent. 1. 97 *ille putat oportere* quandam *inferri orationem* a causa atque a iudicatione ipsa remotam; de orat. 3. 199 *his tribus figuris insidere* quidam *venustatis* non fuco illitus sed sanguine diffusus *debet color* (cf. Verr. II. 4. 38; Brut. 263). *ille* and *quidam* are the pronouns most frequently associated with participles in this way by Cicero.

Though in the great majority of instances the pronoun is adjectival, a specifying participle is sometimes found with substantival uses of *aliquis* and *quidam*: Manil. 41 *itaque omnes nunc in iis locis Cn. Pompeium sicut* aliquem non ex hac urbe missum, sed de caelo delapsum *intuentur*; fin. 1. 41 *statue contra* aliquem confectum tantis animi corporisque doloribus, *quanti in hominem maximi cadere possunt*; Catil. 4. 16 *quam* quidam hic nati, et summo nati loco, *non patriam suam, sed urbem hostium esse iudicaverunt*; fin. 3. 18 *quod . . . contineant* quiddam *in se* ratione constitutum et via. To these we may add an example with *quisquam*: fam. 10. 2. 1 *sed nec sine periculo* quisquam libere de re publica sentiens *versari potest in summa impunitate gladiorum*.

The same tendency is to be seen with some other pronominal adjectives which, by their indefinite nature, frequently entail the addition of a more specific attribute; chief among these are *omnis, multi, nullus, alius*: orat. 198 *sed omnis nec claudicans nec quasi fluctuans et aequaliter constanterque ingrediens numerosa habetur oratio*; Verr. II. 5. 48 *multas pecunias isti erogatas* ('quae isti erogatae essent') *in operum locationes falsas atque inanes esse perscriptas*; nat. deor. 1. 111

nullam enim novistis nisi profectam a corpore et redeuntem ad corpus animi voluptatem. These pronominal adjectives may themselves be used as substantives, and when no other noun is present, it is impossible to decide whether the participle is to be regarded as attributive or substantival. Some examples of this kind will be given in the next chapter.

(4) Amplifying a true adjective

When a participle is used, with or without a conjunction, to amplify and reinforce a true attributive adjective, its own attributive function is quite clear. Plautus offers two examples: Mil. 649 f. *o lepidum senem . . . atque equidem plane educatum in nutricatu Venerio*; Pseud. 28 *lepidis tabellis lepida conscriptis manu.* These passages doubtless reflect artistic elaboration, rather than popular usage, but they show that from an early period such arrangement was natural to a Roman ear. Cicero's taste for fullness of expression predisposed him to use participles in this way, and there are numerous instances of amplifying participles, both with and without a conjunction, in all periods of his writing. They are least in evidence, as one would expect, in the generally less formal and elaborate language of his letters. The following are a representative selection.

(a) Without conjunction

Verr. II. 3. 43 *ut tuis* praeclaris abs te principe inventis et excogitatis *edictis atque institutis uteretur*; ibid. II. 4. 17 publicis *operis* publice coactis (cf. Plaut. Pseud. 28, above); ibid. II. 5. 60 *cognoscite nunc* novam *praedandi rationem* ab hoc primum excogitatam; Catil. 4. 9 *animum vere* popularem saluti populi consulentem; dom. 29 veteres multo ante suscepti et provisi *labores*; off. 1. 136 *ut perturbationes fugiamus, id est motus animi* nimios rationi non obtemperantes.

In his later works Cicero sometimes exploits the possibilities of this usage at considerable length: div. 1. 1 vetus *opinio est* iam usque ab heroicis ducta temporibus, eaque et populi Romani et omnium gentium firmata consensu, *versari quandam inter homines divinationem*; nat deor. 1. 67 *sed ubi est veritas?* in mundis, credo, innumerabilibus omnibus minimis temporum punctis aliis

nascentibus, aliis cadentibus; *an in* individuis *corpusculis* tam praeclara opera nulla moderante natura, nulla ratione fingentibus?

(b) With conjunction

Verr. II. 2. 82 *accipite nunc aliud eius facinus* nobile et multis locis
saepe commemoratum; leg. agr. 2. 5 exigua *laus* et ab invitis
expressa *proponitur*; Mur. 59 sapientes ac multum in posterum
prospicientes *iudices*; orat. 106 *huius* multiplicis et aequabiliter in
omnia genera fusae *orationis*.
The conjunction may be adversative: Pis. 4 *adulescentes* bonos et
fortes, sed usos ea condicione fortunae, *ut* . . .; Phil. 5. 35 *quae
sunt* maxima *illa quidem*, sed adhuc hominum magis iudiciis quam
publice laudata; Sest. 12 *homini* studioso fortasse victoriae, sed
tamen nimium communem Martem belli casumque metuenti.

This method of attaching to an adjective a longer participial
clause lent itself to the principle of expansion, which was fundamental to Cicero's sentence-structure, and it is obviously for this
reason that, especially in his later work, we find examples in
which a participle follows two or more adjectives: off. 1. 61
*splendidissimum videri quod animo magno elatoque humanasque res despi-
ciente factum sit*; fin. 2. 15 *nec de re obscura . . . sed de illustri et facili et
iam in vulgus pervagata loquitur*; ibid. 2. 45 *mentemque acrem et vigentem
celerrimeque multa simul agitantem*.

(5) Corresponding to a true adjective

If a participle is related to an adjective or adjective-equivalent
(e.g. possessive genitive) by explicit parallelism or antithesis, its
own attributive character is unmistakable: Verr. II. 2. 13 *non solum
istum bona* sua, *verum etiam sacra deosque penates* a maioribus traditos
ex aedibus suis eripuisse; ibid. 2. 121 *non modo* Siculorum *nihil in hac
re valuisse leges*, sed ne ab senatu quidem populoque Romano
datas; div. 1. 11 *nam* cum antiquissimam *sententiam*, tum omnium
populorum et gentium consensu comprobatam *sequor*; rep. 1. 36
quam ob rem peto a vobis ut me sic audiatis, neque ut omnino expertem
Graecarum rerum, neque ut eas nostris in hoc praesertim genere
anteponentem; Cluent. 2 *quae contionibus* seditiose concitatis *ac-
commodatior est*, quam tranquillis moderatisque iudiciis.

As the last example shows, where the parallelism or antithesis is explicit, it is not necessary that the true adjective should precede the participle, in order to give it attributive character. But, in fact, the possibilities of expansion offered by the participial phrase made it specially suitable for second place in a pair of terms, or for final place in a series: Cluent. 134 *quodsi hoc Habito facere licuisset, facile illis ipsis iudicibus et falsae suspicioni et invidiae populariter excitatae restitisset*; Tusc. 5. 3 *vereor enim, ne natura, cum corpora nobis infirma dedisset, iisque et morbos insanabilis et dolores intolerabilis adiunxisset, animos quoque dederit et corporum doloribus congruentes et separatim suis angoribus et molestiis implicatos.* The rhythmical convenience of the participial phrase is most clearly seen in those passages where Cicero uses a series of parallel clauses, often with anaphora: Verr. II. 2. 104 *ut in re tam clara, tam testata, tam abs te ipso pervulgata tabulas publicas corrumpere auderes*; de orat. 1. 226 *quis hoc philosophus tam mollis, tam languidus, tam enervatus, tam omnia ad voluptatem corporis doloremque referens, probare posset?*; Marcell. 22 *nam quis est omnium tam ignarus rerum, tam rudis in re publica, tam nihil unquam nec de sua nec de communi salute cogitans?*

(6) Corresponding to a substantive

When a noun with participle in agreement stands in apposition to another noun, or in syntactical correspondence to it, the participle is clearly attributive: Verr. II. 5. 73 *exsiluit conscientia sceleris et furore ex maleficiis concepto excitatus*; Phil. 5. 27 *quid interest, per deos immortales, utrum hanc urbem oppugnet an huius urbis propugnaculum, coloniam populi Romani praesidi causa conlocatam?*; dom. 89 *o speciem dignitatemque populi Romani, quam reges, quam nationes exterae, quam gentes ultimae pertimescant, multitudinem hominum ex servis, ex conductis . . . congregatam* (in apposition to *speciem dignitatemque*) ; p. red. in sen. 16 *non te illius unguentorum odor, non vini anhelitus, non frons calamistri notata vestigiis in eam cogitationem adducebat*; Deiot. 9 *nunquam tu illum accusavisti ut hostem, sed ut amicum officio parum functum* (cf. Pis. 28; ad Q. fr. 1. 2. 4).

(7) In prepositional phrases and with nouns in genitive

A participle agreeing with a noun in the genitive, or with a noun governed by a preposition, has a *prima facie* likelihood of being attributive, in the sense that, when used predicatively, the participle is generally associated with the subject or object (direct or indirect) of a finite verb. Predicative participles are, however, sometimes found in prepositional phrases: Lig. 22 *itaque in Africam venit* iam occupatam ('when it had already been seized'); Mil. 40 *in Cn. Pompeium pro Milone* dicentem *impetus factus est* ('while he was speaking'); dom. 134 *quos memoriae proditum est ab ipso Hercule* perfuncto iam laboribus *sacra didicisse* ('when he had completed'); Sest. 57 *de hoc* nihil cogitante, nihil suspicante, *eisdem operis suffragium ferentibus est rogatum, ut sedens cum purpura . . . praeconi publico subiceretur*; fin. 1. 39 *ut e patre audiebam facete et urbane* Stoicos irridente; rep. 1. 44 *atque hoc loquor de tribus his generibus rerum publicarum* non turbatis atque permixtis, sed suum statum tenentibus. (Cf. *ab* de orat. 2. 257; Lael. 42; Phil. 14. 30; orat. 190; nat. deor. 3. 84. *ex* nat. deor. 2. 93. *contra* rep. 1. 68.) Clearly, in an appropriate context there was nothing to prevent a participle in a prepositional phrase from functioning predicatively, and the same is true of participles agreeing with genitive nouns, though to a more limited extent. I have only found three examples in Cicero of the past participle thus used: Verr. II. 5. 61 *pretio certo missos facere nautas, missorum omne stipendium lucrari*; Att. 14. 9. 2 *eius interfecti morte laetamur cuius facta defendimus*; Mur. 34 *cuius expulsi et eiecti vita tanti aestimata est ut morte eius nuntiata denique bellum confectum arbitrarentur*. With the present participle the use is somewhat more frequent, but instances are still relatively few. To the examples quoted on p. 34 above I can add de orat. 2. 35 *et languentis populi incitatio et effrenati moderatio* and Phil. 3. 4 *quorum ante pedes eius morientium sanguine os uxoris respersum esse constabat*.

If there is nothing to prevent a participle in the genitive or following a preposition from being used predicatively, there is nevertheless a tendency for such participles to coalesce with the nouns with which they agree, either in an attributive sense or in the *ab urbe condita* construction, to be discussed later. Indeed, it is not always easy, even with the help of the context, to distinguish the one type from the other. In the following passages, for instance, the participle is to be regarded as attributive: Verr. II. 2. 184 *sic contendo, ex his libellis parvis* apud unum magistrum societatis repertis *vos iam coniectura adsequi posse cuiusmodi praedo iste in illa provincia fuerit* (apart from the sense—it was the *libelli*, not the finding of them, which provided the information—the use of *his* and *parvis* suggests that *repertis* has an amplifying force) ; dom. 11 *res erat non in opinione dubia, sed in praesenti* atque ante oculos proposito *periculo* (amplifying *praesenti*) ; nat. deor. 2. 137 *a corde autem in totum corpus distribuitur per venas admodum multas* in omnes partes corporis pertinentes (the preceding adjective *multas* helps to determine the attributive character of *pertinentes*). It is less easy to feel certain about passages such as these : fin. 4. 73 *omninoque de istis omnibus verbis a Zenone mutatis ita disputabat* (the context— a particular example of Piso's discussion of Zeno's terms has just been given—and the fact that *omnis* is often completed by an attributive participle favour the sense 'all those words which were changed by Zeno', rather than 'the changing of all those words') ; de orat. 2. 338 *habet enim multitudo vim quandam talem ut, quem ad modum tibicen sine tibiis canere, sic orator sine* multitudine audiente *eloquens esse non possit* (it is not clear—though the sense here is virtually unaffected—whether we are to understand *multitudine audiente* as 'multitudine quae audiat' or as 'audientia multitudinis'; certainly examples of *sine* with the *ab urbe condita* construction are very rare and doubtful) ; nat. deor. 2. 115 *haec omnis descriptio siderum atque hic tantus caeli ornatus ex* corporibus huc et illuc casu et temere cursantibus *potuisse effici cuiquam sano videri potest?* (here the sense is against taking *cursantibus* as attributive ; it is not the bodies, but their random movement, which could not have produced an ordered pattern) ; Brut. 164 *plura etiam dicta* (sc. *sunt*) *quam scripta, quod ex* quibusdam capitibus expositis nec explicatis *intellegi potest* (the tendency for an attributive participle to follow and complete *quidam* favours that interpretation of *expositis nec explicatis*, but it is more likely that the sense which Cicero intended is 'from the fact that certain headings are set forth but not developed').

Of participles agreeing with genitive nouns the following are examples of attributive use : Mil. 64 *plena omnia malleolorum ad urbis incendia comparatorum*; Phil. 1. 31 *oblitus auspiciorum a te ipso augure populi Romani nuntiatorum*; Brut. 201 *oratorum bonorum* . . .

duo genera sunt, unum attenuate presseque, alterum sublate ampleque dicentium; off. 1. 62 *id virtutis non est, sed est potius immanitatis omnem humanitatem repellentis*; div. 2. 105 *hic vero quanta pugna est doctissimorum hominum negantium esse haec a dis immortalibus constituta* (this is not a clear instance, for, though *negantium* might be regarded as amplifying *doctissimorum*, it seems preferable to regard it as an adverbial predicative participle agreeing with the logical subject,[1] the sense being 'quantum pugnant doctissimi homines negantes . . . &c.'). The following belong to the *ab urbe condita* type : Sull. 83 *totiens renovetur memoria per me inventae salutis*; de orat. 3. 206 *et adiunctio et progressio et eiusdem verbi crebrius positi quaedam distinctio*.

(8) Participles in common attributive use

In certain phrases concerned with common private or public activities some participles were used with attributive force so frequently, that in the absence of any indication to the contrary (such as might be given, for example, by word-order or concinnity) the reader would assume them to be so used. Such activities are the writing, sending, or receiving of a letter, the owing, depositing, or paying of money, the writing or delivery of a speech, the passing of a law. Typical examples are : fam. 10. 20. 2 *sed accepi litteras a collega tuo datas Idibus Maiis*; Att. 2. 13. 1 *facinus indignum! epistulam* αὐθωρεὶ *tibi a Tribus Tabernis rescriptam ad tuas suavissimas epistulas neminem reddidisse*; Phil. 2. 7 *quis enim umquam . . . litteras ad se ab amico missas . . . in medium protulit*; Flacc. 54 *invita solverat Castricio pecuniam iam diu debitam*; off. 2. 78 *aut pecunias creditas debitoribus condonandas putant*; Sest. 37 *cum unus in legem per vim latam iurare noluerat* (the participle is also in a prepositional phrase) ; Att. 15. 1a. 2 *Brutus noster misit ad me orationem suam habitam in contione Capitolina* (the attributive character is reinforced by *suam*) ; Tusc. 2. 9 *in qua* (sc. *Academia*) *disputationem habitam non quasi narrantes exponimus*. Cicero extends the scope of these regularly attributive participles, especially *scriptus* and *datus*; Verr. II. 3. 147 *cum lege aequissime scripta venderent*; Brut. 106 *isque et orationes reliquit . . . et annalis sane exiliter scriptos* (cf. ibid. 101) ; leg.

---

[1] See p. 31 above.

1. 33 *tantam autem esse corruptelam malae consuetudinis, ut ab ea tamquam igniculi exstinguantur a natura dati*; fin. 2. 34 *id est virtute adhibita frui primis a natura datis* (cf. ibid. 45). To the above participles we may add *factus* in such examples as Verr. II. 3. 144 *attuli sponsiones ipso praesente factas de decumarum societate, ab ipso prohibitas iudicari* (where *prohibitas* acquires its attributive character from its parallelism with *factas*), and ibid. II. 4. 32 *cum iste ab sese hydriam Boethi manu factam praeclaro opere et grandi pondere per potestatem abstulisset* (cf. ibid. II. 4. 64 *candelabrum e gemmis clarissimis opere mirabili perfectum*).

In the philosophical works Cicero regularly uses certain participles attributively, as part of his technical terminology. *Efficiens*, for example, is sometimes thus attached to *causa*, and perhaps represents Cicero's translation of ποιητικός : fat. 33 *erat hoc quidem verum ex aeternitate, sed causas id efficientes non habebat*; ibid. *causis enim efficientibus quamque rem cognitis posse denique sciri quid futurum esset* (cf. div. 1. 125; top. 58. 60).

(9) Participle preceding noun

The normal position for a predicative participle is after its noun, and the reasons for departing from this position have been discussed earlier (pp. 46 ff.). When a participle in this position is intended to be attributive, its character, unless it belongs to the limited number of participles in common attributive use, is regularly made clear in one or other of the ways already described in this chapter. Naturally, it could not be claimed that Cicero never uses a participle attributively after its noun, without such 'reinforcement'; but there are few such instances which could not equally well be taken as predicative, their sense remaining materially unchanged. Examples of this 'indifferent' kind are: Verr. II. 2. 158 *apud omnes Graecos hic mos est, ut honorem hominibus habitum in monumentis eiusmodi non nulla religione deorum consecrari arbitrentur*; Phil. 3. 15 *primum in Caesarem maledicta congessit depromta ex recordatione impudicitiae et stuprorum suorum*; ibid. 13. 38 *quo facilius reviviscat Pompeianorum causa totiens iugulata*; de orat. 2. 7 *ut laudem eorum iam prope senescentem . . . ab oblivione hominum atque a silentio vindicarem*.

On the other hand, there is considerable evidence to suggest that, when a participle precedes its noun, though it is not necessarily attributive, there is a *prima facie* likelihood that it may be. In many of the passages already quoted in this chapter attributive participles are found in prior position. I add a further selection of such instances, which could be multiplied : Verr. II. 3. 74 *verum non una te, sed universae similibus afflictae iniuriis et incommodis civitates* . . . *persequuntur* (the participle completes *universae*) ; Tusc. 1. 74 *vetat enim dominans ille in nobis deus iniussu hinc nos suo demigrare* (completes *ille*) ; de orat. 1. 92 *artem vero negabat esse ullam, nisi quae cognitis penitusque perspectis et in unum exitum spectantibus et nunquam fallentibus rebus contineretur* (completes *rebus*) ; div. 1. 125 *ea est ex omni aeternitate fluens veritas sempiterna* (amplifies a true adjective) ; de orat. 2. 39 *tibi enim adsentior vestrum esse hoc totum diserte dicere, idque si quis in alia arte faciat, eum adsumpto aliunde uti bono, non proprio nec suo* (corresponds to a true adjective) ; part. 77 *nam quae* (sc. *virtus*) *venientibus malis obstat, fortitudo, quae quod iam adest tolerat et perfert, patientia nominatur* (corresponds to adjectival relative clause) ; leg. agr. 1. 21 *nos caput patrimoni publici* . . . *subsidium annonae, horreum belli, sub signo claustrisque rei publicae positum vectigal servare non potuisse* (corresponds to a substantive) ; de orat. 2. 130 *nec quotiens causa dicenda est, totiens ad eius causae seposita argumenta revolvi nos oportet* (in prepositional phrase).

Even without any explicit reinforcement, the participle in this position is often unmistakably attributive, as in an apostrophe such as Verr. II. 5. 163 *o graviter desiderata et aliquando reddita plebi Romanae tribunicia potestas*, or in a descriptive ablative phrase such as Att. 4. 18. 2 *nemo enim in terris est mihi tam consentientibus sensibus*. In a large number of passages the context shows that the noun is being used in an indefinite or generic sense, and that the participle is a descriptive specification : e.g. Phil. 10. 5 *cupio sine offensione nostrae amicitiae sic tecum ut* a te dissentiens senator *queri* ('a senator who disagrees with you') ; Pis. 10 *an potest ulla esse excusatio non dicam* male sentienti, sed sedenti, cunctanti, dormienti in maximo rei publicae motu *consuli* ('a consul who . . .') ; leg. 3. 24 *quid enim illum aliud perculit, nisi quod potestatem* intercedenti collegae *abrogavit* ('a colleague who . . .') ; Lig. 2 *habes, igitur,*

Tubero, quod est accusatori maxime optandum, confitentem reum, *sed tamen hoc confitentem se in ea parte fuisse qua te* (the attributive character of the participle in *confitentem reum* is confirmed by the equivalent substantival clause *quod . . . optandum*) ; Pis. 4 *ego in C. Rabirio perduellionis reo* XL annis ante me consulem interpositam senatus auctoritatem *sustinui contra invidiam atque defendi* ('*a* decree which . . .' ;[1] cf. Cael. 55 *ex qua domo recitatur vobis iure iurando devincta auctoritas*) ; leg. 2. 8 *ita principem legem illam et ultimam mentem esse dicebant* omnia ratione aut cogentis aut vetantis dei ('*a* god who . . .' ; this interpretation is confirmed, a few lines later (ibid. 9), by the phrase *illius caelum atque terras tuentis et regentis dei*, where the participles complete *illius*, and are clearly attributive) ; Cato 22 *quem ad modum nostro more* male rem gerentibus patribus *bonis interdici solet.* Cf. Sest. 52 ; fam. 5. 8. 1 ; ad Q. fr. 1. 1. 5.

This long, but by no means exhaustive, list of clear examples justifies an attributive interpretation of many other passages in which the participle precedes the noun: e.g. Sest. 41 *neque se privatum publice susceptae causae defuturum esse dicebat* (cf. Quinct. 76 ; Att. 4. 16. 7 ; contrast fam. 1. 9. 20 *quam ob rem eius causam . . . susceptam defendi in senatu*) ; Caecin. 94 *qui colonus habuit conductum de Caesennia fundum* ; Verr. II. 2. 186 *inspiciebamus Syracusis a Carpinatio confectas tabulas societatis* ; Mur. 42 *ipse autem in Gallia ut nostri homines desperatas iam pecunias exigerent aequitate diligentiaque perfecit* ; Lael. 65 *deinde non solum ab aliquo allatas criminationes repellere, sed ne ipsum quidem esse suspiciosum* ; div. 1. 69 *ex horreis direptum effusumque frumentum vias omnes angiportusque constraverat* ; off. 2. 30 *familiaritates habere fidas amantium nos amicorum.* Cf. off. 3. 107 ; fam. 7. 26. 1.

Perhaps sufficient instances have now been quoted to support the claim that prior position tends to give a participle attributive force. There are passages where, as we have already noticed (p. 48), it is not possible to distinguish with certainty between an emphatic predicative and an attributive use. In Cluent. 28 *Larinum confestim exanimata venit et ibi de integro funus* iam sepulto *filio fecit* the participial phrase could equally well mean 'who had already been buried' or 'after he had already been buried'. Similarly, Mil. 32 *fortasse vix possent frangere hominis sceleratissimi*

---

[1] I take *auctoritas* in this passage to be equivalent to *consultum.*

corroboratam iam vetustate *audaciam* ('which was now toughened' or 'toughened as it now was'); de orat. 2. 21 *in media oratione* de maximis rebus et gravissime disputantem *philosophum omnes unctionis causa relinquunt* ('who is discussing' or 'even when he is discussing'). Cf. orat. 225 incisim autem et membratim tractata *oratio in veris causis plurimum valet*; leg. 1. 37 *quocirca vereor committere ut* non bene provisa et diligenter explorata *principia ponantur*; div. 1. 87 *quis est autem quem non moveat* clarissimis monumentis testata consignataque *antiquitas?* But most, if not all, of such instances are 'indifferent', in the sense that either interpretation will adequately convey Cicero's meaning.

(10) Examples of special interest

In the final section of this chapter I wish to consider some passages which are of special interest, either because they do not fall obviously under any of the preceding categories, or because they are particularly good illustrations of Cicero's handling of the attributive participle. I deal first with some apparent exceptions to the habit whereby an attributive participle following its noun is usually 'reinforced'.

That a participle or participial phrase immediately following a proper name could carry attributive force, without the normal appositional *homo*, seems to appear from the following three passages: Mur. 3 *et primum M. Catoni* vitam ad certam rationis normam derigenti et diligentissime perpendenti momenta officiorum omnium *de officio meo respondebo*; Phil. 3. 23 *quid enim attinuerat L. Cassio, tribuno plebis fortissimo et constantissimo civi, mortem denuntiare, si in senatum venisset; D. Carfulenum, bene de re publica sentientem, senatu vi et minis mortis expellere; Ti. Canutium, a quo erat honestissimis contentionibus et saepe et iure vexatus, non templo solum, verum etiam aditu prohibere Capitolii?*; ibid. 25 *familiarissimus eius, mihi homo coniunctus, L. Lentulus et P. Naso* omni carens cupiditate *nullam se habere provinciam . . . iudicaverunt.* It might, however, be argued that in the first example the participle represents not a relative, but a causal clause—'inasmuch as he . . .', and that in the other two the nature of the participial phrases is sufficiently established by the adjacent and corresponding clauses.

In the following examples *eiusmodi* and *horum* might be regarded as adjective-equivalents, which the participles amplify: de orat. 1. 208 *ipsaque illa quae in commentarium meum rettuli sunt* eiusmodi, *non aliqua mihi doctrina tradita, sed in rerum usu causisque tractata*; Lig. 34 *quis est qui* horum *consensum* conspirantem et paene conflatum in hac prope aequalitate fraterna *noverit, qui hoc non sentiat?* We could suggest that, in the same way, attributive colour is given to the participles by the genitives in Att. 13. 4. 1 *habeo munus a te elaboratum decem legatorum* and ibid. 47a. 3 *fratris epistulam ad te misi, non satis humane illam quidem respondentem meis litteris*, but we need not expect to find attributive reinforcement in every case, least of all in the language of informal letters. There is none, for instance, in Att. 4. 17. 4 *Scaurus . . . obnuntiationibus* per Scaevolam interpositis *singulis diebus usque ad pr. Kal. Octobr., quo ego haec die scripsi, sublatis populo tributim domi suae satis fecerat.* Nevertheless, it is noticeable how frequently Cicero, whether consciously or not, does indicate the character of his attributive participles, even if it is by no more than a hint contained in the language of the surrounding context. In fin. 5. 35, for example, *est etiam actio quaedam corporis, quae* motus et status naturae congruentes *tenet*, the participial phrase is foreshadowed, a couple of lines earlier, by the words *naturales motus ususque habere*. An excellent illustration of attributive reinforcement is to be seen in Catil. 4. 2 *ego sum ille consul, patres conscripti, cui non forum in quo omnis aequitas continetur, non campus* consularibus auspiciis consecratus, *non curia, summum auxilium omnium gentium, non domus, commune perfugium, non lectus* ad quietem datus, *non denique haec sedes honoris, sella curulis, unquam vacua mortis periculo atque insidiis fuit.* We see here more than a skilful exploitation of variety in concinnity; the relative clause *in quo . . . continetur* firmly establishes the character of the participles which follow, and this reinforcement the substantival phrases *summum auxilium* and *commune perfugium* strengthen. Kühner–Stegmann 770, quoting this passage as one of its few illustrations of attributive participles in Cicero, omits the clauses which make the instance particularly informative.

There remain a few passages where the interpretation presents difficulty. Verr. II. 5. 94 *tum imperator ab isto praepositus Cleomenes flagitabatur*. It is not easy to decide whether the participial phrase qualifies *imperator* (to which *Cleomenes* will then stand in apposition) or *Cleomenes* (with *imperator* as predicate of *praepositus*). If we are influenced by the attributive tendency of a participle in prior position, we shall choose the second alternative, and translate (probably rightly) : 'Cleomenes who had been put in command by him'. off. 3. 116 *atqui ab Aristippo Cyrenaici atque Annicerii philosophi nominati omne bonum in voluptate posuerunt*. The most likely interpretation of the words *ab Aristippo* . . . *nominati* seems to be 'the philosophers who are called, after Aristippus, Cyrenaics, and those who are called Annicerians'. But if *nominati* is thus attributive, its noun *philosophi* is in a very unusual position, separating, as it does, the participle from its predicate. Holden (edition, p. 401) takes *philosophi nominati* as an appositional phrase 'the Annicerians, philosophers in name only', which certainly gives a contemptuous flavour appropriate to the context. But his support for this use of *nominati* is not strong, and it is impossible to believe that the word is not being employed here in its normal sense. Perhaps *nominati* follows *philosophi*, instead of preceding it, because its characteristic clausula-rhythm (– ◡ – –) enhances a colon which helps to hold together the long attributive phrase and to keep its function clear. Alternatively, *nominati* might be substantival, with *philosophi* as part of its predicate, to be taken ἀπὸ κοινοῦ both with *Cyrenaici* and with *Annicerii*: 'those who are called . . . Cyrenaic philosophers and (those who are called) Annicerian philosophers'.

de orat. 3. 137 *qui* (sc. *Pisistratus*) *primus Homeri libros confusos antea sic disposuisse dicitur, ut nunc habemus*. It is unfortunate that, with hundreds of clear Ciceronian instances from which to choose, Kühner–Stegmann (770) should have quoted, as a representative example of the attributive participle, this passage, which, to say the least, is by no means characteristic. The fact that the participle follows its noun, without any attributive reinforcement, is a *prima facie* reason for assuming it to be predicative, and this is confirmed by the required sense. The participle is surely to be associated closely with *disposuisse*; its main point is to provide the reason for Pisistratus' action. The words *confusos antea* represent not 'qui antea confusi erant', but rather 'cum antea confusi essent'.

To end this chapter I cannot do better than present a few passages which show how effectively Cicero can, in the same sentence, attach an attributive and a predicative participle to the same noun, and even place them side by side, while yet keeping the function of each perfectly clear. dom. 25 *sed excitatus aliquando Cn. Pompei . . . excitatus, inquam, aliquando Cn. Pompei nimium diu reconditus et penitus abstrusus animi dolor subvenit subito rei publicae.* The different types of participle are here not juxtaposed; indeed, it is the emphatic position of *excitatus* at the head of the sentence, and widely separated from *dolor*, which chiefly establishes it as predicative. The other two participles are recognized as attributive mainly by their position immediately preceding the noun. fam. 1. 7. 3 *virum enim excellentem et tibi tua praestanti in eum liberalitate devinctum non nihil suspicantem propter aliquorum opinionem suae cupiditatis te ab se abalienatum illa epistula retinuisti. devinctum,* doubly reinforced by *virum* and by *excellentem,* is unmistakably attributive, and its close attachment to *virum* creates in the sentence a break, which makes it easier to recognize the different (predicative) function of *suspicantem.* Exactly the same kind of structure can be seen in Tusc. 5. 15 *quia motus turbulenti iactationesque animorum incitatae et impetu inconsiderato elatae rationem omnem repellentes vitae beatae nullam partem relinquunt. incitatae* corresponds to the true adjective *turbulenti,* and both reinforce *elatae,* after which a break is clearly felt.[1]

---

[1] See p. 126 below.

III

THE PARTICIPLE AS A SUBSTANTIVE

ANY Latin adjective can be used in the plural (masculine or neuter) as a noun, and some adjectives are regularly so used in the singular (e.g. *amicus, familiaris, iuvenis, dives*). That their substantival use is more restricted in the singular than in the plural is due to the fact that, when used as a noun, an adjective must necessarily describe a person or thing not as an individual, but as belonging to a certain class or type; and therefore, in most contexts, the plural number is more natural than the singular. This is true also of participles, which are as amenable as adjectives to substantival use, and have the additional advantage that they can be qualified by adverbs or prepositional phrases, or can govern a case. If Cicero does not exploit the substantival participle so extensively as the attributive, the reason lies in the inherent limitations of the device: in the main it can only be used of persons or things with typical or generic reference; in the masculine the participle is as indefinite as *homo*, in the neuter, as *res*.

(1) Singular

Except in the masculine present, singular participles are only rarely used by Cicero with substantival force, though perhaps not quite so rarely as the standard Latin grammars would lead one to suppose. Some participles, especially past participles, were already established in regular substantival use in the time of Cicero, so that their appearance in the singular would be felt as quite natural, e.g. Cluent. 170 *quid metuebat? ne oppugnaretur a perdito an ne accusaretur a damnato?*, where the correspondence of the two participles helps to reinforce the substantival character of each. So *debitum*, 'a debt': orat. 178 *mutila sentit quaedam et quasi decurtata, quibus tamquam debito fraudetur offenditur. praeteritum*, 'the past': off. 1. 11 *ad id solum quod adest quodque praesens est se accommodat, paulum admodum sentiens praeteritum aut futurum*, where the substantival force of *praeteritum* is anticipated by the corresponding *id . . . quod adest*. The singular use of *auditum*, in the sense of 'something heard', is to be found in Plautus, as well as the more common use of the plural: Merc. 903 *vidistin an de audito nuntias?* The single instance in Cicero is therefore no innovation: off. 1. 33 *nihil enim habeo praeter auditum*. Here, too, the substantival force of *auditum* is helped by the preceding *nihil*; cf. de orat. 3. 131 *non modo nihil acquisierint, sed ne relictum quidem et traditum et suum conservarint*. In fact, apart from stereotyped uses, substantival participles in the neuter singular are not easily found in Cicero, and Schmalz–Hofmann's statement (p. 458) 'häufig wird das Neutr. Sing. substantiviert' ought, to that extent, to be modified. Except for the passages given above, the only clear examples which I have noticed are invent. 2. 9 *non enim parum cognosse, sed in parum cognito stulte et diu perseverasse turpe est* and Att. 13. 22. 3 *tantum nolebam aut obsoletum Bruto aut Balbo incohatum dari* (*tantum* here is adverbial = 'only'). A doubtful instance is invent. 1. 26 *vitia vero haec sunt certissima exordiorum quae summo opere vitare oportebit: vulgare, commune, commutabile, longum, separatum, translatum*. The adjectives and participles here could be regarded as substantives— 'id quod vulgare sit', &c., but it is more likely that they remain adjectival, qualifying *exordium* (to be understood from the preceding *exordiorum*).

Kühner–Stegmann (p. 128) cites two Ciceronian examples of substantival participles in the nominative masculine singular: Pis. 53 *non ut redire ex Macedonia nobilis imperator sed ut mortuus infamis efferri videretur*; fin. 4. 51 *et beatus esse poterit virtute una praeditus, carens ceteris, nec tamen illud tibi concedet, praeter virtutem nihil in bonis esse ducendum.*[1] In fact, Cicero provides two other instances more striking than either of these: fam. 2. 15. 4 *neque erat superiore honore usus quem praeficerem* (it might be argued that *usus* is attributive, and qualifies the suppressed antecedent of *quem*, but its substantival character is confirmed by the similar plural

---

[1] Madvig (edition, p. 557) takes the subject of *poterit* and *concedet* to be not *virtute una praeditus*, but Polemo, who is mentioned at the beginning of this section. According to this interpretation, therefore, *praeditus* and *carens* are both predicative, qualifying the unexpressed subject.

instance in Phil. 8. 28 *huic se etiam summis honoribus usi contra suam dignitatem venditabant*) ; rep. 1. 51 *tam cito evertetur quam navis, si e vectoribus sorte ductus ad gubernacula accesserit.*

The examples which I have noticed of the masculine singular past participle in oblique cases are : Att. 6. 6. 4 *ego sorte datum offenderem, ut etiam inquireret in eum quem reliquissem?*; Mur. 4 *is potissimum summo honore adfecto defensor daretur qui eodem honore praeditus non minus adferret ad dicendum auctoritatis quam facultatis*; Tusc. 4. 74 *sic igitur adfecto haec adhibenda curatio est*;[1] Sest. 83 *qui cum causam civis calamitosi, causam amici, causam bene de re publica meriti . . . suscepisset.* From this handful of examples we can at least conclude that, in his restricted use of the masculine singular past participle as a substantive, Cicero made no special effort to avoid either the nominative or the oblique cases.

With present participles the situation is different. Whilst the neuter singular is very rare indeed, Cicero uses the masculine singular freely in all cases except the nominative. The fact that the two neuter examples known to me happen to be in the nominative is probably fortuitous. The first of these, which Kühner–Stegmann (p. 288) quotes as an isolated instance of the neuter singular present in Cicero, is not very significant : fin. 4. 68 *teneamus enim illud necesse est, cum consequens aliquod falsum sit, illud, cuius id consequens sit, non posse esse verum.* In his philosophical treatises Cicero uses the plural *consequentia* so frequently as a technical term that he may be said to establish it as a full noun, so that in an appropriate context the singular presents no difficulty. More noteworthy is ac. 2. 37 *deinde cum inter inanimum et animal hoc maxime intersit, quod animal agit aliquid* (nihil enim agens *ne cogitari quidem possit quale sit*), where, in spite of the fact that the neuter form is indistinguishable from the masculine, and the case is the avoided nominative, the sense is made perfectly clear by the surrounding context. I regard this passage as a much firmer instance of a substantival nominative singular present participle than that quoted by K.–S. 224 from Cato 74 *mortem igitur omnibus*

[1] Nägelsbach is wrong in maintaining (p. 143) that *adfecto* is not to be counted as substantival, because it refers to a person mentioned in the preceding context. That person has served merely as an illustration ; here Cicero is clearly speaking of the type.

horis impendentem timens qui poterit animo consistere? The validity of this example depends upon our interpretation of *qui*. If it is equivalent to *quomodo*—and there is some support for this assumption in the fact that, when Cicero uses *qui* = *quomodo*, it is generally with the verb *posse*[1]—*timens* must indeed be substantival = 'is qui timet'. On the other hand, one cannot ignore the possibility that *qui* is an interrogative pronoun in the nominative. It is recognized that in early and colloquial Latin—and in Cicero too—there was a good deal of fluctuation between interrogative *quis* and *qui*, both in adjectival and in substantival uses.[2] Even if we cannot believe that in Cato 74 Cicero used *qui* in the sense of *quis*, it could easily, in view of the fluctuation, have entered the tradition of the text at an early stage, and there is a considerable amount of manuscript authority for *quis*, which is the reading of V and of the second hands of P, L, and A; it was also (according to Orelli) adopted by Victorius in his edition. Considering that at S. Rosc. 96 *quis primus Ameriam nuntiat* and leg. 3. 34 *quis autem non sentit* all the manuscripts have *qui*, and the now universally accepted *quis* goes back to Halm, in the first case, and to Turnebus, in the second, there seem to be reasonably strong grounds for reading *quis* in Cato 74. If we were to do so, *timens* would become a normal predicative participle of the concomitant type.

The contrast in Cicero between the rarity of the singular substantival present participle in the nominative and its comparative frequency in other cases seems to reflect inherited usage. Plautus provides half a dozen examples in oblique cases, but, apart from *amans*, which was evidently already stereotyped as a full noun, no instance in the nominative. In Terence I can cite (hesitantly) only Phorm. 243 *peregre rediens semper cogitet*.[3]

Cicero uses substantival present participles both as simple *nomina agentis* (*audiens*, *somnians*, *consolans*, &c.) and with verbal construction. In their simple use substantival present participles

---

[1] G. Landgraf, *Pro Rosc. Amer.*, p. 341.

[2] Neue–Wagener, *Formenlehre*, ii. 430 ff.; Schmalz–Hofmann, 695; E. Löfstedt, *Syntactica*, ii. 79 ff., esp. 92.

[3] I cannot find justification for the reference in Schmalz–Hofmann (p. 457) to 'die bereits bei Plt. und Ter. nicht seltene Substantivierung des Part. Praes. im Nom. Sing.'

differ from nouns formed with the suffix *-tor* and *-sor* in that the latter are used, as a rule, without reference to a particular occasion, and sometimes imply a permanent or habitual quality or function, whilst the participle is used of a quality shown, or a function exercised, in particular circumstances. (When the participle has verbal construction, this particularization generally becomes explicit.) A pair of comparisons will serve to illustrate the distinction: Tusc. 3. 73 *quod aiunt plerosque consolationibus nihil levari adiunguntque consolatores ipsos confiteri se miseros, cum ad eos impetum suum fortuna converterit.* Compare with this ibid. 3. 75 *haec igitur officia sunt consolantium, tollere aegritudinem funditus aut sedare aut detrahere quam plurimum . . .* &c., where the participle 'those who are giving consolation' implies a function temporarily assumed to meet particular circumstances. The essential difference is even clearer, when we compare de orat. 2. 54 *ceteri non exornatores rerum, sed tantum modo narratores fuerunt* with part. 32 *probabilis autem erit* (sc. *narratio*) *. . . si probitas narrantis significabitur* (*narrantis*—'the person who is setting forth the facts' on a particular occasion).

Of the masculine singular substantival participles used by Cicero about 50 per cent. are in the genitive. This predominance is not surprising, for since it is the primary function of the genitive case to assert a relationship between nouns, the substantival character of a participle was doubtless more readily felt in the genitive than in the other cases. The following typical examples need no comment: orat. 132 *nullo enim modo animus audientis aut incitari aut leniri potest, qui modus a me non temptatus sit*; div. 1. 63 *iacet enim corpus dormientis, ut mortui*; ibid. 1. 121 *sic castus animus purusque vigilantis . . . est paratior*; Tusc. 3. 26 *est autem impudens luctus* maerore se conficientis, *quod imperare non liceat liberis*; off. 2. 48 *magna est enim admiratio* copiose sapienterque dicentis.

Cicero shows a special readiness to exploit the substantival present participle as a characterizing genitive: e.g. Att. 14. 16. 3 *non est* fidentis *hoc testimonium, sed potius* timentis; Planc. 75 inridentis *magis est quam* reprendentis; div. 2. 112 *hoc scriptoris est,* non furentis, adhibentis diligentiam, *non insani*; Tusc. 1. 80 *haec refelli possunt. sunt enim* ignorantis, cum de aeternitate animorum dicatur, de mente dici; fin. 5. 22 *ad eas enim res referre, quae agas . . .*

obscurantis est omnem splendorem honestatis, ne dicam inquinantis. Cf. Tusc. 5. 28; fin. 5. 72.

In the foregoing examples there is present, to a greater or less degree, a vague kind of personification; the participle expresses a human being behaving in a certain way. This personal image is comparatively strong in, for instance, div. 1. 63 *iacet enim corpus dormientis, ut mortui*; it is much weaker in some of the characterizing genitive examples, such as fin. 5. 22, where *obscurantis est* does no more than provide an elegant stylistic variation for *obscurare est*. Similarly, in div. 2. 69 *at paulo post audita vox est* monentis ut providerent (cf. Plaut. Aul. 811 *vocem hic loquentis modo mi audire visus sum*, quoted on p. 34, above) the reader receives no such impression of personality as, for instance, in off. 2. 48 *admiratio copiose sapienterque dicentis*. If we translate *vox monentis* as 'a voice warning (them)', we are probably not far from the effect which the phrase had on the Roman reader's mind. Another example in which the grammatically substantival participle carries with it no personal image occurs in a list of recommended figures of speech and thought in de orat. 3. 203 *tum illa, quae maxime quasi inrepit in hominum mentes*, alia dicentis ac significantis *dissimulatio* ('the dissembling which consists in saying one thing and meaning another'). What is said here applies also to some genitive plural instances, such as Brut. 216 *in utroque* cachinnos inridentium commovebat ('scornful laughter').

Of the other cases the dative is the most frequently used, and is almost always unqualified. Typical examples are: orat. 76 *nam orationis subtilitas imitabilis illa quidem videtur esse existimanti sed nihil est experienti minus*; Tusc. 4. 59 *alia est enim lugenti, alia miseranti aut invidenti adhibenda medicina*. Qualification or verbal construction, in the few examples in which it appears, is of the simplest kind: Phil. 11. 20 *etsi quis potest refragari* non modo non petenti verum etiam recusanti?; Tusc. 1. 57 bene interroganti *respondentem*; Mur. 68 consulatum petenti *solet fieri*.

In fact, the general tendency for verbal construction, if any, to be short and simple, is in keeping with the essential character of the substantival participle. Its chief virtue was its conciseness; it lent itself to the economical and pithy type of utterance such as is represented by the popular proverb. We find traces of such proverbial use in Cicero: fin. 4. 80 scrupulum, *inquam* abeunti; de orat. 2. 186 *facilius est enim* currentem, *ut aiunt,* incitare,[1] *quam commovere languentem* (it is interesting to note how Cicero develops the proverbial phrase, and in the next section goes on to use a number of singular substantival participles in similar concise, antithetic phrases: 187 *ut* (sc. *oratio*) *non modo inclinantem excipere aut stantem inclinare sed etiam adversantem ac repugnantem, ut imperator fortis ac bonus, capere possit*). Similarly, Ennius' phrase *qui erranti comiter monstrat viam,* quoted in Balb. 36 and off. 1. 51, has an echo in off. 3. 54 *quid est enim aliud erranti viam non monstrare.* A good illustration of Cicero's effective juxtaposition of the conciseness of a substantival participle with the diffuseness of an equivalent relative clause is Lig. 10 *arguis fatentem. non est satis: accusas eum, qui causam habet aut, ut ego dico, meliorem quam tu aut, ut tu vis, parem.*

When a general statement in the accusative and infinitive, such as is often introduced by an impersonal expression like *honestum est* or *licet,* contains a masculine singular participle with no noun or pronoun in agreement, one may be tempted to understand the participle as substantival. Thus, in orat. 4 *prima enim sequentem honestum est in secundis tertiisque consistere* it seems appropriate to take *prima sequentem* as = 'eum qui prima sequatur'. But in all such passages we should probably regard the participle as predicative, qualifying the unspecified subject of the infinitive (*aliquem* or *hominem*); so that *sequentem* means 'when one is aiming at'. The same applies to *licet* in, e.g., off. 1. 92 *haec praescripta servantem licet magnifice, graviter, animoseque vivere* (cf. Tusc. 1. 91; 5. 44; off. 2. 67; fat. 35). de orat. 1. 184 *haec igitur et horum similia iura suae civitatis ignorantem erectum et celsum, alacri et prompto ore atque vultu, huc atque illuc intuentem vagari cum magna caterva toto foro, praesidium clientibus atque opem amicis et prope cunctis civibus lucem ingeni et consili sui porrigentem atque tendentem, nonne in primis flagitiosum putandum est?* It would be wrong to take *ignorantem* as substantival. All the participles in this elaborate passage are predicative, and all qualify *vagari, ignorantem* (concomitant) in a general way, *intuentem, porrigentem,* and *tendentem* more closely (adverbial).

---

[1] A. Otto, *Sprichwörter der Römer,* 102 f.

It is an example of complex participial construction of a type which is fairly common in Cicero, and which will be fully discussed in a later chapter.

(2) Plural

Neuter participles are used substantivally with much greater freedom in the plural than in the singular. The accusative case shows a marked predominance, partly no doubt because its form clearly distinguishes it from the masculine. The nominative, equally distinguishable, is comparatively infrequent. The reason for this cannot lie merely in the fact that things are more likely to be found in the position of grammatical object than in that of subject, since the same infrequency, though less pronounced, is to be seen in Cicero's use of the nominative plural masculine. Perhaps in this he was following an inherited tendency. He certainly seems to avoid the oblique cases of the neuter plural which are identical in form with the masculine. I have found only one instance of the dative (Cluent. 84 *proxime accedere illum qui alterius bene inventis obtemperet*) and only four of the ablative. Of these four two hardly count (invent. 2. 32 *ex ante factis*; ibid. 2. 37 *ante factis omissis*), since the participle involved had become stereotyped as a noun before the time of Cicero. In Quinct. 90 *ex quo et ex ceteris dictis, factis,* cogitatisque *Sex. Naevi* the nature of *cogitatis* is established by the recognizably substantival *dictis* and *factis*; one might add that *cogitata* had already been used substantivally by Terence (Phorm. 283); it is used elsewhere by Cicero in leg. agr. 1. 1 and Deiot. 21. The fourth example is Cael. 48 *sed abhorret non modo ab huius saeculi licentia, verum etiam a maiorum consuetudine atque concessis.* The reading *concessis* has been suspected, but it is questionable whether Ernesti's alternative suggestion *concessu* is admissible in a construction such as this, and C. F. W. Mueller's *consensu* seems too remote from the required sense. On the other hand, substantival *concessa* is not found elsewhere, and one would hardly expect a participle not established as a substantive to be used in dependence on a genitive.[1] The instance should perhaps

---

[1] Orelli's attempt to mitigate this difficulty by putting a comma after *consuetudine* is ruled out by the requirements of concinnity; the balance intended with *huius saeculi licentia* must be the whole phrase *maiorum . . . concessis.*

be considered doubtful; but, assuming that the reading is genuine, the parallel *consuetudine* makes it sufficiently clear that *concessis* cannot be anything but neuter. Similarly, of the five genitive examples noted three involve a stereotyped participial substantive: Att. 15. 4a *actorum*; fin. 1. 63 and part. 41 *consequentium*. In the other two the fact that the participle is neuter is made explicit: orat. 200 *qui et multa scripserint et quaecumque etiam sine scripto dicent similia scriptorum effecerint* (*scriptum* was established as a substantive; in this case, however, the existence of the identical genitive plural form of *scriptor* created a potential ambiguity); ibid. 227 *non quin idem sint numeri non modo oratorum et poetarum, verum omnino loquentium, denique etiam* sonantium omnium quae metiri auribus possumus.

Only a small proportion of neuter plural substantival participles are found with verbal construction, and these are all past participles, with the exception of one present example, in which the qualification is of the simplest kind: fin. 5. 85 *alterum non dubitabunt quin et Stoici* convenientia sibi *dicant et vos repugnantia*. With the past participle, the two most elaborate examples of qualification are: orat. 89 *vitabit etiam quaesita*, nec ex tempore ficta sed domo adlata; ac. 1. 14 *quid est enim quod malim quam* ex Antiocho iam pridem audita *recordari?*

The concise antithetic phrase, which we have already observed to be characteristic of Cicero in his use of predicative past participles (p. 15), appears also in his handling of substantival past participles in the neuter plural: leg. 1. 9 *neque tam facile* interrupta contexo *quam* absolvo instituta; orat. 235 *facilius est enim* apta dissolvere *quam* dissipata conectere; Mur. 50 *qui* consumpta replere, erepta recuperare *vellent*; fin. 5. 51 *praetermissa repetimus, incohata persequimur*.

The neuter plural of the present participle is used substantivally by Cicero only in the rhetorical and philosophical treatises, where it provides abstract concepts with a suitably generalized form of expression, and, in particular, furnishes a comparatively small number of convenient quasi-technical terms which are often used, especially *consequentia* (*sequentia*) 'consequences' and *repugnantia* (*pugnantia*) 'contradictions'. Tusc. 4. 64 *quibus igitur rationibus* instantia *feruntur, eisdem contemnuntur* sequentia; orat. 168 *meae quidem (aures)* . . . *et curta sentiunt nec amant* redundantia; de orat. 2. 166 *nam et coniuncta quaeremus* . . . *et similitudines et dissimilitudines et contraria et consequentia et consentanea et quasi praecurrentia et repugnantia*; ibid. 2. 281 *ridentur etiam discrepantia*; div. 2. 150 *nec ii quidem contemptissimi* (sc. *philosophi*) *sed in primis acuti et* consequentia et repugnantia *videntes*.

Of substantival participles in the masculine plural it is worth while to observe that, if we leave out of account the *De Inventione*, on the ground that its language is likely to be exceptionally influenced by Greek syntax, apart from a single instance of a neuter plural *(cogitatis)* in Quinct. 90 and a masculine singular in Caecin. 39 *ut ille cogatur restituere qui ingressum expulerit, ille qui ingredientem reppulerit non cogatur*, all the substantival participles which occur in Cicero's writing before 60 B.C. are masculine plural. Nor are they negligible in number; I have noticed eight examples in the *Pro Roscio Amerino*, the Verrines and the Catilinarians. This seems to suggest, as indeed we might expect, that it was in the masculine plural that the substantival use of the participle first became current in literary prose at Rome. At least, this was the use which first came readily to Cicero's pen.

The two examples from the *Pro Roscio Amerino* appear in a passage celebrated for its concinnity, and recalled by Cicero, in later years, with a certain amount of amused pride:[1] S. Rosc. 72 *etenim quid tam est commune quam spiritus vivis, terra mortuis, mare* fluctuantibus, *litus* eiectis? It is to be observed that in this passage the substantival force of *fluctuantibus* and *eiectis* is anticipated and made easier, because, preceding these participles and corresponding to them are two words more fully established in substantival use, and we have already noticed that attributive participles are often 'supported' in this way. Nägelsbach (p. 138) suggests that this type of reinforcement is characteristic of participles used substantivally. It is true that similar examples occur in Cicero's writing: e.g. fam. 2. 13. 1 *tamen confirmantur nostra consilia, cum sentimus* prudentibus fideliterque suadentibus *idem videri*; off. 2. 77 *nullum igitur vitium taetrius est* . . . *quam avaritia, praesertim in*

---

[1] orat. 107.

principibus et rem publicam gubernantibus; Att. 7. 13. 2 *nam dilectus adhuc quidem invitorum est* et a pugnando abhorrentium. But the number of such examples is small, compared with the many passages where there is no such reinforcement, even when the participle has verbal construction, and might be considered, for that reason, less easily recognizable as substantival: e.g. Verr. II. 5. 151 ex Hispania fugientes *se excepisse et supplicio adfecisse dicit*; Phil. 1. 21 *altera promulgata lex est, ut* de vi et maiestatis damnati *ad populum provocent*; ibid. 8. 28 *huic se etiam* summis honoribus usi *contra suam dignitatem venditabant* (cf. ibid. 32 *hoc honore usi*); off. 1. 83 *consuetudo imitanda medicorum est, qui* leviter aegrotantes *leniter curant*; leg. 1. 39 sibi autem indulgentis et corpori deservientis atque omnia, quae sequantur in vita quaeque fugiant, voluptatibus et doloribus ponderantis . . . *in hortulis suis iubeamus dicere.* (Cf. Tusc. 5. 28; ac. 2. 20.)

It seems reasonable to conclude that in the use of substantival participles, at any rate in the masculine plural, Cicero felt no need of any reinforcing element. When he chose to use such a participle in a pair or series with proper substantives or substantival adjectives, it was doubtless natural to proceed from the more familiar to the less. But we may be sure that his chief consideration—probably his only conscious consideration—was stylistic effectiveness. What must generally have determined the position of a participle or participial phrase at the end of such a series was its greater weight or compass. This factor is evident, for instance, in Mil. 92 *si in gladiatoriis pugnis . . . timidos atque supplices et* ut vivere liceat obsecrantes *etiam odisse solemus*, and there is a good example in Catil. 1. 25 *nactus es ex perditis atque* ab omni non modo fortuna verum etiam spe derelictis *conflatam improborum manum.* On the other hand, in the following passage—drawn, it will be observed, from Cicero's early period—the substantival participles precede the substantives proper: Verr. II. 5. 12 *ut damnati in integrum restituantur, vincti solvantur, exules reducantur, res iudicatae rescindantur.*

The 47 instances which I have observed of substantival past participles in the masculine plural comprised 28 with verbal construction and 19 without. The case distribution was: nominative 11 (24%), accusative 19 (40%), genitive 5 (11%), dative 9

(19%), ablative 3 (6%). With present participles the situation was very different. Of 86 observed instances 25 had verbal construction, 61 were unqualified. The cases were distributed thus: nominative 5 (6%), accusative 9 (10%), genitive 35 (41%), dative 30 (35%), ablative 7 (8%). The striking feature about these figures is the spectacular rise, in the present participle, of the proportion of genitive and dative instances, at the expense of the nominative and accusative. Cicero's apparent reluctance to admit substantival present participles in the nominative is in contrast to his tendency, already observed (p. 33), towards an increasingly frequent use of predicative present participles in this case. Of the 65 genitive and dative instances three-quarters were unqualified. It was, in fact, in phrases such as *discentium studia*, *animos audientium*, *dolorem maerentium*, *officia consolantium*, *percontantibus* (*quaerentibus*, *consulentibus*) *respondere*, *laborantibus succurrere*, and the like, that Cicero found the substantival participle most convenient.

The low percentage of past participles in the genitive plural is probably to be explained by the fact that there was often the possibility of confusion with the identical form of a noun ending in -*sor* or -*tor*, which would, of course, have conveyed a meaning directly opposite to that intended. We may detect Cicero's care to avoid such confusion in off. 2. 66 *quid enim eloquentia praestabilius vel admiratione audientium vel spe indigentium vel* eorum qui defensi sunt *gratia?* (not *defensorum*, since *defensor* is a word used frequently by Cicero). On the other hand, in off. 2. 43 *at eius filii nec vivi probabantur bonis et mortui numerum obtinent* iure caesorum, there was no danger of misunderstanding, since, apart from the fact that *caesor* was not in use, the Roman reader would recognize an allusion to a phrase in the XII Tables—'iure caesus esto'.[1]

Schmalz–Hofmann (p. 458) explains the relative clause in off. 2. 66 as an illustration of an alleged principle whereby Cicero only admits the substantival past participle in the masculine plural 'um eine Klasse von Menschen zu bezeichnen'.[2] The

---

[1] *Fontes iuris Romani*, I Leges, ed. Riccobono, p. 57.
[2] Nägelsbach (p. 140) formulates the principle as 'eine geschlossene, bestimmt bezeichnete Klasse von Individuen'.

validity of such a principle is open to question. It is true that the substantival participle is commonly used, both in the singular and in the plural, to describe things or persons as belonging to a type or class, without reference to a particular time or context. But sometimes Cicero does use the participle, both present and past, masculine and neuter, with just such particular reference: Verr. II. 5. 151 ex Hispania fugientes *se excepisse . . . dicit*; Pis. 89 *cum concursum* plorantium *. . . ferre non posses, in oppidum devium Beroeam profugisti*; Phil. 8. 28 *huic se etiam* summis honoribus usi *contra suam dignitatem venditabant*; fam. 13. 36. 1 *tabulam in qua nomina* civitate donatorum *incisa essent*; off. 2. 24 *sed iis, qui* vi oppressos *imperio coercent, sit sane adhibenda saevitia*. The last passage is a striking example of particularization; *vi oppressos* is closely attached to *imperio coercent*, and is virtually equivalent to 'eos quos vi oppresserunt'.

One particularized instance of the present participle is worth quoting, as the only occurrence in Cicero of a feminine substantival participle. Describing the migration of cranes Cicero says: nat. deor. 2. 125 *eaeque* (sc. *grues*) *in terga* praevolantium *colla et capita reponunt*. It would be pedantic, as well as unnecessary, to attempt to defend strict usage by arguing that *praevolantium* should be regarded as attributive, with *gruum* understood; it is a perfectly natural and intelligible extension of the substantival use to non-human beings which, considered grammatically, happen to be regularly feminine.

Finally, I would draw attention to a type of participial expression in which it is usually impossible to decide whether the participle is to be regarded as attributive or substantival. These are expressions introduced by certain adjectives or pronouns which themselves are often used substantivally. In the following passages the participle is substantival, if the introductory adjective or pronoun is taken adjectivally: invent. 1. 61 (partitio) *quam* omnes ab Aristotele et Theophrasto profecti *maxime secuti sunt*; off. 3. 60 *ergo et Pythius et* omnes aliud agentes aliud simulantes *perfidi, improbi, malitiosi*; de orat. 2. 355 *eidemque* multa ex aliis causis aliquando a se acta, multa ab aliis audita *meminerunt* (*multa* is probably the substantive here); Brut. 258 *confluxerunt enim et Athenas et in hanc urbem* multi inquinate loquentes *ex diversis locis*; Tusc. 1. 98 *quanta delectatione autem adficerer, cum Palamedem, cum Aiacem, cum* alios iudicio iniquo circumventos *convenirem*; leg. 1. 61 ipsumque ea moderantem et regentem *paene prenderit* (Ziegler proposed the insertion of *deum* after *regentem*).

Having noted the ambivalence of this type of phrase, one should add that it matters not at all which way the participle is understood, since in either case the sense is exactly the same; and it would no more occur to the Roman to analyse the nature of the participle in such a phrase than it would occur to the modern Englishman to ask himself, whether a notice saying 'all persons trespassing will be prosecuted' meant 'all persons who trespass' or 'all trespassers'.[1]

[1] The few instances of future participles used substantivally will be separately considered in a later chapter.

IV

THE *AB URBE CONDITA* CONSTRUCTION

A WELL-KNOWN participial usage in Latin is that whereby a predicative participle, usually past, coalesces with its noun in such a way that the two together form a complex of substantival character, capable of standing as subject or object of a verb, or of being governed by a preposition. This complex, in which the meaning of the participle predominates, is in many modern languages often best translated by a verbal noun with dependent genitive ('the foundation of the city'), though, as will be suggested later, such a translation does not do justice to the precision of the Latin idiom. Because of the difficulty of finding a clear and concise definition in grammatical terms, Livy's familiar title will serve as a convenient description,[1] though I know of only one instance of the construction with *ab* in Cicero (Phil. 3. 9), and none before him, apart from a Republican inscription of 105 B.C.[2]

The construction is regarded as being specially characteristic of Latin,[3] though a considerable number of examples can be found in Greek, especially in Thucydides: e.g. 3. 20. 1 τῷ σίτῳ ἐπιλιπόντι ἐπιέζοντο; 4. 26. 5 αἴτιον δὲ ἦν οἱ Λακεδαιμόνιοι προειπόντες; 4. 29. 3 καὶ αὐτῷ ἔτι ῥώμην καὶ ἡ νῆσος ἐμπρησθεῖσα παρέσχε; 6. 3. 3 μετὰ Συρακούσας οἰκισθείσας. An attempt has been made by F. P. Jones ('The *ab urbe condita* construction in Greek', University of Wisconsin Dissertation, 1939) to show that there is a much greater number of instances in Greek than had hitherto been supposed, but he does so at the expense of blurring

---

[1] It is used in this way, though not apparently for the first time (see his opening para.), by O. W. Heick, 'The *ab urbe condita* construction in Latin', University of Nebraska, 1936. Apart from its title and collection of examples, I have not derived great benefit from this work.

[2] Dessau, *I.L.S.* 5317 *ab colonia deducta anno xc.*

[3] e.g. Schmalz–Hofmann, 608 'eine Eigenheit des Lateinischen'.

the distinction between this construction and similar uses of the predicative participle. For example, ἅμα τῇ ἐσόδῳ γιγνομένῃ (Thuc. 2. 6. 3), where the participle is merely supplementary, and could be omitted without essentially changing the meaning of the prepositional phrase, cannot be put in the same category as μετὰ Συρακούσας οἰκισθείσας, in which the participle is needed to make the phrase intelligible.

Even if the *ab urbe condita* construction is more common in Greek than has hitherto been assumed, it remains true that it is less characteristic than in Latin. Not only has Greek richer resources in the way of alternative modes of expression—notably the articular infinitive—but in Latin the cognate gerundival construction, to which there is nothing corresponding in Greek, helps to give prominence to the participial usage. Kühner–Gerth compares the Greek use to the Latin in a way which seems implicitly to recognize that in Latin the construction has a more fundamental role.[1]

The suggestion that the Latin use was derived from the Greek has recently been adopted by E. Schwyzer, who, in his *Griechische Grammatik*, Band II, p. 404, describes the Latin construction as 'Nachahmung'. Schwyzer refers to a footnote in Jones's monograph which he has apparently misunderstood. In that note,[2] after quoting a passing remark of Gildersleeve in *A.J.P.* 13. 258 ('It would be too horrible if *post conditam urbem* were a Graecism, as Milton's "since created man" is a Latinism'), Jones concludes: 'the number alone of the Greek examples which I have collected makes the suggestion of Gildersleeve seem less absurd than he apparently thought it'. It is unfortunate that, through a misunderstanding of this note, the most recent and influential work on Greek syntax should have lent its authority to an idea which has never been seriously put forward, and which is manifestly untenable. A construction which is not only used by Plautus and Cato but appears in the fragments of the XII Tables cannot be regarded as anything but indigenous. The appearance of the usage in both languages, before they came

[1] *Ausführliche Grammatik der griechischen Sprache*, ii. 78, Anm. 1.
[2] Op. cit., p. 6, note 3.

into close literary contact, is surely to be explained by the assumption that they independently inherited it from a common parent.

A. EARLY LATIN

In Plautus and Terence the construction, in the form in which it later becomes common, appears rarely. We have a handful of instances with prepositions and one doubtful case of nominative use (Cist. 686), which will be examined later. Four Plautine examples involve what were obviously established phrases for sunrise and sunset: Bacch. 424 *ante solem exorientem*; Epid. 144 *ante solem occasum* (cf. Men. 437, 1022). The latter is the phrase which appears in the XII Tables (Table I): *sol occasus suprema tempestas esto*.[1] Apart from these, we find, with *post*, Cas. 84 *post transactam fabulam* and Ter. Hec. 742 *post factam iniuriam*; with *super*, Bacch. 367 *super auro amicaque eius inventa Bacchide* (Heick[2] wrongly adduces Trin. 305 (cf. 301) *ab ineunte aetate*, where the participle is used as an attributive adjective (= *prima*), and Ter. Ad. 199 *ob male facta haec*, where *male facta* is substantival). From Cato can be quoted fr. 84 (Peter) *post dimissum bellum* and mil. fr. 2 Jordan (p. 80) *ob rem bene gestam*.

The form in which this usage is most prominent in early Latin is in phrases with *opus* (or *usus*) *est*, in which either the past participle of an intransitive verb is used impersonally, *obvigilatost opus* (Bacch. 398), *cauto opust* (Merc. 466), or, when the participle is transitive, it is accompanied by a noun in agreement. Characteristic Plautine examples of the latter type are: Curc. 302 *mihi homine convento est opus* (cf. 322); Mil. 914 *quid istis nunc*

---

[1] In Bruns, *Fontes iuris Romani*[7], p. 19, followed by Riccobono, op. cit., p. 28, the reading accepted, on Mommsen's authority, is *solis occasus*. Mommsen's judgement was governed by the fact that the phrase appears in this form in all ancient authorities who refer to it from Varro onwards, with the exception of Gellius 17. 2. 10, where, however, one manuscript (the best) has *solis*. But the fact that Gellius is using the phrase to illustrate the 'non insuavis vetustas' of the words *sole occaso*, together with the three Plautine examples, convinces me that the original phrase was *sol occasus*. It was obviously particularly liable to later 'normalization', and it is significant that at Men. 437 the manuscript reading, clearly wrong, is *solis*.

[2] Op. cit., pp. 13 f.

memoratis opust?; Pseud. *732 sed quinque inventis opus est argenti minis*; Asin. *312 nunc audacia usust nobis inventa et dolis.*[1]

Moreover, we should not ignore the fact that the gerundive, which is undeniably peculiar to Latin, and which, in some of its most characteristic uses, shows a striking similarity to the *ab urbe condita* construction, is already in Plautus a comparatively common mode of expression. Without attempting to go into the vexed question of the nature of the gerundive, it is sufficient to note that, in a phrase like *ad aquam praebendam* (Amph. 669), the noun and gerundive coalesce to form a single idea, and that the gerundive is the predominant component, and cannot be removed without destroying the intelligibility of the phrase. The effective difference between the gerundive and the past participle, when used in this way, is that the participle expresses an action as complete, the gerundive as incomplete or prospective. I hope that the validity of this distinction between the participial and gerundival uses, as well as their kinship with one another, will be confirmed by some Ciceronian passages which I shall quote presently in the course of a survey of the construction in Cicero.

B. THE CONSTRUCTION IN CICERO

(1) With prepositions

Among the prepositions with which the construction is used, it is perhaps not surprising that *post*, which figures comparatively prominently in the early Latin examples, also predominates in Cicero. I have counted well over fifty instances, of which about a quarter consist of the phrase *post urbem* (or *Romam*) *conditam*. The majority of Cicero's examples are phrases of similar conciseness, e.g. *post homines natos*, *post sacra instituta*, &c. But Cicero is prepared, even in his earlier writing, to allow the construction to occupy quite extensive clauses: Verr. II. 3. 74 *testari ac dicere numquam* post populi Romani nomen ab Siculis auditum et cognitum *Agyrenses . . . dixisse aut fecisse quippiam*; Sull. 81 *cui cum adfuit* post delatam ad eum primam illam coniurationem, *indicavit se audisse*

---

[1] Tammelin (pp. 104–14) has a full discussion of the usage in Plautus and Terence.

aliquid; Cluent. 200 *qui nunc primum* post illam flammam aliorum facto et cupiditate excitatam . . . *paulum respirare a metu coepit.* Cicero shows a special predilection for associating the construction with a superlative, a negative (or equivalent interrogative), *primus, unus,* or *solus.* About one-third of his examples with *post* are of this type. In addition to Verr. II. 3. 74 and Cluent. 200, above, the following may be quoted as characteristic: Catil. 4. 14 *causa est enim post urbem conditam haec inventa sola, in qua omnes sentirent unum atque idem*; leg. agr. 2. 36 *sunt sacella quae post restitutam tribuniciam potestatem nemo attigit*; dom. 95 *at id quod mihi crimini dabatur . . . erat res post natos homines pulcherrima*; har. resp. 16 *de mea domo, quam senatus unam post hanc urbem constitutam ex aerario aedificandam . . . putarit*; Vatin. 34 *quaero ex te, Vatini, num quis in hac civitate post urbem conditam tribunos plebis appellarit ne causam diceret.*

The examples already quoted illustrate the fact that in the *ab urbe condita* construction—and this applies to its use in general—the position of the participle in relation to its noun is syntactically indifferent. No principle of varying emphasis can be detected, and the position seems to have been governed by purely subjective considerations of rhythm or euphony.

The preposition *de* is also used by Cicero with relative frequency (about 25 instances). It provided a neat and concise way of referring to a past event: e.g. Verr. II. 2. 111 *quare de hospitio violato et de tuo isto scelere nefario nihil queror*; Rab. perd. 8 *an de peculatu facto aut de tabulario incenso longa oratio est expromenda?*; opt. gen. 21 *non enim tam multa dixit de rationibus non relatis, quam de eo, quod civis improbus ut optimus laudatus esset* (where the participial phrase is combined with an equivalent *quod*-clause).

I have noticed about ten examples with *ante*: e.g. Arch. 9 *is qui tot annis ante civitatem datam sedem omnium rerum ac fortunarum suarum Romae conlocavit*; Tusc. 1. 3 *siquidem Homerus fuit et Hesiodus ante Romam conditam*; div. 1. 86 *neque ante philosophiam patefactam, quae nuper inventa est, hac de re communis vita dubitavit.* We may conveniently translate *ante civitatem datam* as 'before the grant of citizenship' and *ante Romam conditam* as 'before the foundation of Rome', but we should note that the English abstract nouns conceal the precision of the participial expression, which carries with it, as an essential part of its meaning, the idea of completed action. *ante civitatem datam* could never be used for *antequam civitas daretur*, but only for *antequam . . . data est.*

No other prepositions are found in this construction in Cicero more than two or three times. The instances, according to my observations, are: *ab* Phil. 3. 9. *ex* fam. 2. 12. 3; off. 1. 56; Brut. 164; nat. deor. 2. 115. *in* Marcell. 3; fam. 10. 6. 3. *praeter* Cluent. 62. *propter* de orat. 3. 135; Sest. 9; fam. 7. 31. 2. *ob* Lael. 25. Madvig saw an example with *sine* in fat. 41 *et nihil vellet sine praepositis causis evenire*,[1] but the participle here is probably to be regarded as attributive.

It will be appropriate, at this point, to quote a few examples which throw light on the relationship between the participle and the gerundive in this construction. fam. 2. 12. 3 *spero me integritatis laudem consecutum; non erat minor ex contemnenda quam est ex conservata provincia. contemnenda* refers to Cicero's attitude before he took up his provincial command, *conservata* to his actual conduct of it. Verr. II. 3. 206 *ut omittam tuos peculatus, ut ob ius dicendum pecunias acceptas*; nat. deor. 3. 74 *repete superiora, Tubuli de pecunia capta ob rem iudicandam.* The gerundive is used, because the money was received *beforehand*, as a bribe.

(2) Non-prepositional uses

More important, for its influence on the economy of sentence-structure, was the development of the *ab urbe condita* construction, independently of prepositions, as a unit of sense equivalent generally to a substantival *quod*-clause, and capable of standing in any position in the sentence which could be occupied by a noun. In Cicero this use, particularly in the nominative, accusative, and genitive, is well established.

(a) Nominative

One example, apart from the XII Tables, is quoted from early Latin: Plaut. Cist. 686 *nulla est* (sc. *cistella*) *neque ego sum usquam. perdita perdidit me.*[2] But if we remember Plautus' taste for animating

---

[1] Adv. Crit. 2. 367, discussing Sen. brev. vit. 10. 1 *sine adiecta virtute.*
[2] Bennett, op. cit. i. 441; Heick, op. cit., pp. 9, 13.

the inanimate,[1] and observe the characteristic paronomasia, we shall conclude that *perdita* is more likely to be a normal predicative participle, qualifying the half-personified *cistella*. The oxymoron contained in *perdita perdidit* finds a close parallel in Cicero, S. Rosc. 33 *eiusdem viri mortem, quae tantum potuit, ut omnes occisus perdiderit et adflixerit*.[2]

The fact that several examples occur in Cicero's early work suggests that the non-prepositional use had begun to appear before his time, but it may be of some significance that, in most of the passages where he uses it, the participial phrase does not itself stand, or does not stand alone, as the subject of a finite verb, but is related to a nominative noun or pronoun in such a way that its syntactical function is clear. Sometimes it is found in correspondence to, or in conjunction with, a pronoun or noun in the nominative, especially an abstract verbal noun: Caecin. 33 *nec aequitati quicquam tam infestum est quam convocati homines et armati*;[3] Cluent. 101 *irridebatur haec illius reconciliatio et persona viri boni suscepta*; Planc. 45 *decuriatio tribulium, descriptio populi, suffragia largitione devincta severitatem senatus . . . excitarunt*; Att. 7. 12. 2 *nec eum rerum prolatio nec senatus magistratuumque discessus nec aerarium clausum tardabit*. Cf. de orat. 3. 206. Combined with verbal nouns in this way, the *ab urbe condita* phrase, like the attributive participle combined with true adjectives (see p. 59 above), can be an effective stylistic device: dom. 146 *non me bonorum direptio, non tectorum excisio, non depopulatio praediorum, non praeda consulum ex meis fortunis crudelissime capta permovet*.

In some instances the participial phrase stands in apposition to the grammatical subject, noun or pronoun: Verr. II. 1. 76 *constituitur in foro Laodiceae spectaculum acerbum et miserum et grave toti Asiae provinciae, grandis natu parens adductus ad supplicium*; Att. 5. 14. 1 *interea tamen haec mihi quae vellem afferebantur, primum otium Parthicum, dein confectae pactiones publicanorum, postremo seditio militum sedata ab Appio stipendiumque eis usque ad Idus Quinctilis persolutum*.

---

[1] Ed. Fraenkel, *Plautinisches im Plautus*, 101–10. See especially p. 104, note 1, where attention is drawn to personification of the *cistella* in Cist. 731.

[2] I accept *occisus*, the reading of *Σ*, as virtually certain.

[3] The reading *convocari . . . armari*, which occurs in two fifteenth-century manuscripts, is no doubt due to Renaissance conjecture.

This appositional use, as the last example shows, enables a series of participial phrases to be used with clarity and elegance, and Cicero employs it several times: e.g. Att. 6. 3. 3 *reliqua plena adhuc et laudis et gratiae, digna iis libris quos dilaudas, conservatae civitates, cumulate publicanis satis factum, offensus contumelia nemo*; Att. 1. 18. 3 *quantum hoc vulnus! facto senatus consulto de ambitu, de iudiciis nulla lex perlata, exagitatus senatus, alienati equites Romani.* Even without a noun or pronoun subject, the parallelism alone, in a series of participial phrases in the nominative, is sufficient to establish the syntactical function of the individual components of the series: Pis. 85 *dubitabat nemo quin violati hospites, legati necati, pacati atque socii nefario bello lacessiti, fana vexata hanc tantam efficerent vastitatem.* This passage is relevant to the remark of Schmalz–Hofmann (p. 609) that Cicero is not prepared to go so far as to say *interfectus Caesar,* instead of *interitus Caesaris,* in a sentence such as Phil. 2. 88 *num etiam tuum de auspiciis iudicium interitus Caesaris sustulit?* We see from *legati necati* that Cicero did not regard this particular manifestation of the construction as inadmissible, though it may be that he would not have used *legati necati* without the shelter and support of the parallel series in which it occurs.

Cicero, however, could dispense with such syntactical support. We cannot exclude the possibility that in the use of double phrases in the following two examples considerations of clarity played some part: Mur. 35 *dies intermissus aut nox interposita saepe perturbat omnia*; nat. deor. 2. 6 *saepe Faunorum voces exauditae, saepe visae formae deorum quemvis non aut hebetem aut impium deos praesentes esse confiteri coegerunt.* But the construction is quite unsupported in Mil. 17 *mors quidem illata per scelus isdem et poenis teneatur et legibus* (where the subject is obviously not *mors,* but *mors . . . illata per scelus*), and it is used in Cluent. 61 with an expansiveness which suggests that Cicero did not feel any need to be particularly circumspect: *tum vero illa iudicia senatoria non falsa invidia, sed vera atque insigni turpitudine notata atque operta dedecore et infamia defensioni locum nullum reliquissent* (the *fact* that they were . . .).

A passage of special interest is Mur. 42: *quid tua sors? tristis, atrox, quaestio peculatus ex altera parte lacrimarum et squaloris, ex altera plena catenarum atque indicum; cogendi iudices inviti, retinendi contra voluntatem; scriba damnatus, ordo totus alienus; Sullana gratificatio reprehensa, multi viri fortes et prope pars civitatis offensa* [*est*]; *lites severe aestimatae; cui placet obliviscitur, cui dolet meminit* (*est* del. Lambinus). If we compare this passage with Att. 6. 3. 3 and, still more, with Att. 1. 18. 3 (quoted p. 91), we can have little doubt that the nominative phrases are here being used in the same pictorial way,[1] that the participles belong to the *ab urbe condita* type, and, therefore, that *est*, as Lambinus saw long ago, is an intrusion. What is even more interesting is that we find, side by side with the participles and in the same construction, the nominative gerundive, a usage which is generally said to begin with Livy 2. 13. 2 *adeo moverat eum et primi periculi casus . . . et subeunda dimicatio totiens, quot coniurati superessent.*[2] If, as I feel convinced, *cogendi iudices . . . retinendi* means 'the *fact* that jurymen had to be collected and retained', Cicero is here breaking new ground, and preparing the way for the later development of the gerundival use.

(b) Accusative

In the accusative the construction is used with as much freedom in Cicero's earlier, as in his later, work; I have noted about eighteen examples in all. A few of these are passages in which the participial phrases, singly or in series, correspond to pronoun or noun: e.g. Verr. I. 11 *quid aliud habet in se nisi Cn. Carbonem spoliatum a quaestore suo pecunia publica, nudatum et proditum consulem, desertum exercitum, relictam provinciam, sortis necessitudinem religionemque violatam?*; Phil. 2. 62 *quid ego istius decreta, quid rapinas, quid hereditatum possessiones datas, quid ereptas proferam?* (cf. Pis. 38, nat. deor. 3. 62). In the majority of Cicero's examples, however, the accusative phrase is governed by a verb expressing what one might describe as 'mental reaction to a situation'. Such verbs are *neglego, relinquo, mitto, queror, (moleste) fero, (pluris) facio*, and *persequor* (used in these passages of a mental attitude, rather than of a physical action). Characteristic passages are: Manil. 11 *illi*

---

[1] For nominatives used in series, without finite verb, see W. Havers, 'Zur Syntax des Nominativs', *Glotta*, 16. 94–127, especially 98–111. E. Löfstedt, *Syntactica*, i². 75 f., quotes a good Ciceronian example: Sest. 74 *clamor senatus, querelae, preces, socer ad pedes abiectus.*

[2] e.g. Schmalz–Hofmann, 609; Riemann, *La Langue et la grammaire de Tite-Live*, 105 note.

libertatem imminutam civium Romanorum non tulerunt; vos ereptam vitam neglegetis? *ius legationis verbo violatum illi persecuti sunt; vos legatum omni supplicio interfectum relinquetis?*; Att. 6. 1. 6 *si praefecturam negotiatori denegatam queretur . . . si equites deductos moleste feret*; Mur. 44 *quid ergo?* *acceptam iniuriam persequi non placet*; Sest. 121 *cum patrem pulsum, patriam adflictam deploraret*; Tusc. 1. 90 *nec pluris nunc facere M. Camillum hoc civile bellum, quam ego illo vivo fecerim Romam captam* (cf. Caecin. 9; Catil. 3. 18; Verr. II. 3. 206; ibid. II. 4. 116; Phil. 9. 7).

(c) Genitive

The construction appears in the genitive far more frequently than in any other case. This is natural enough, when we consider the large number of nouns which are regularly accompanied by a dependent genitive, and the conciseness of expression achieved when a participial phrase is made to depend thus. It must be admitted that, in the genitive, it is not always possible to distinguish this type of participle from the attributive use. But allowing for this difficulty, it is clear that Cicero found it a particularly compact and convenient mode of expression.

Among the governing nouns which lend themselves to the construction are words of cause or result, accusation (blame), and penalty: e.g. Att. 1. 11. 1 *verum ne causam quidem elicere (potui) immutatae voluntatis* (cf. Verr. II. 4. 140); Verr. II. 4. 97 *nihil in religiosissimo fano praeter vestigia violatae religionis nomenque P. Scipionis reliquit*; Cluent. 124 *doce quam pecuniam Cluentius dederit, unde dederit, quem ad modum dederit; unum denique aliquod a Cluentio profectae pecuniae vestigium ostende* (not 'a trace of money which has come from Cluentius', but 'of money-having-come from C.'; this is the only Ciceronian example in which I have noticed a deponent participle used in the *ab urbe condita* construction); Verr. II. 4. 88 *pecuniarum captarum crimen*; Cluent. 4 *infamiam iudici corrupti*; Sest. 63 *macula regni publicati*; orat. 35 *ut si sustinere tantam quaestionem non potuero, iniusti oneris impositi tua culpa sit, mea recepti; in quo tamen iudici nostri errorem laus tibi dati muneris compensabit*; Att. 11. 7. 3 *exitus illius minuit eius officii praetermissi reprehensionem*; leg. 2. 41 *poena vero violatae religionis iustam recusationem non habet.*

Cicero often uses the construction with nouns containing the idea of saying, thinking, or feeling: Att. 16. 4. 4 *primum confectorum ludorum nuntios exspectat* (i.e. 'ludos confectos esse') ; Att. 2. 1. 6 *sibi enim bene gestae, mihi conservatae rei publicae dat testimonium* (cf. Sest. 129; dom. 132; Phil. 2. 2; with *testificatio* Phil. 9. 15) ; Cael. 63 *atque equidem vehementer exspectabam quinam isti viri boni testes huius manifesto deprehensi veneni dicerentur* (= 'hoc venenum manifesto deprehensum esse') ; ad Q. fr. 3. 3. 2 *propter suspicionem pactorum a candidatis praemiorum* (cf. Verr. I. 38; Cluent. 49; fam. 3. 12. 4; Phil. 12. 18) ; Sull. 83 *totiens renovetur memoria per me inventae salutis* (not 'salutis quae per me inventa est', but 'salutem per me inventam esse') ; similarly, *indicium oppressi senatus* (dom. 112), *confessio . . . captae pecuniae* (Cluent. 148), *fides reconciliatae gratiae* (Mil. 21). To the same category we may assign Caecin. 35 *sed dolorem imminutae libertatis iudicio poenaque mitigat* and Planc. 103 *nolite animum meum debilitare cum luctu tum etiam metu commutatae vestrae voluntatis erga me* (= 'ne commutata sit vestra voluntas'). To complete this survey of the range and convenience of this genitive use in Cicero's hands, I add two examples of a more subtle kind: de orat. 3. 158 *imprudentia teli missi brevius propriis verbis exponi non potuit* ('the inadvertent throwing of a missile') ; leg. agr. 2. 41 *auctoritatem senatus exstare hereditatis aditae sentio.* The reference in the last extract is to the bequest of his dominions to the Roman people by Ptolemy Alexander. Cicero's phrase means not the Senate's permission to enter on the inheritance, but the Senate's ratification of a situation already produced by Alexander's act.

(d) **Dative and Ablative**

Examples are very few. In the dative I can only quote Phil. 14. 1 *reditum ad vestitum confectae victoriae reservate. confectio autem huius belli est D. Bruti salus,* where *confectio* sufficiently establishes the nature of the participial phrase, and Brut. 207 (see pp. 11 f. above), a passage which has troubled editors, and which it will be useful now to quote with its surrounding context: *scribebat* (sc. *Aelius*) *tamen orationes, quas alii dicerent; ut Q. Metello† F., ut Q. Caepioni, ut Q. Pompeio Rufo; quamquam is etiam ipse scripsit eas quibus pro se est usus, sed non sine Aelio.* his enim scriptis etiam ipse interfui, *cum essem apud Aelium adulescens eumque audire perstudiose solerem* (*scriptis* om. O¹: *scribendis* Lambinus: *scribentibus* Kraffert). The textual problem involved with Q. *Metello* may, for our present purpose, be ignored. The phrase 'his scriptis interfui' involves two serious difficulties, in that there is no parallel either for the combination of a past participle with *interesse* or for the use of a past participle in the *ab urbe condita* construction to express anything other than completed action. This twofold objection seems to rule out the interpretation of Piderit (ad loc.), who, without discussing the syntactical problem, regards *interfui* as a claim to have witnessed the touching-up of the speeches of Pompeius Rufus at the house of Aelius. With Kraffert's conjecture, *his* would refer to the persons mentioned, and the phrase would mean: 'I myself also was present when these men were writing.' This, as it plainly contradicts *scribebat . . . orationes quas alii dicerent*, must be wrong. *scribendis* would mean that the speeches were actually written in Cicero's presence, which is possible, but unlikely. If we could believe that the first hand of O, which omits *scriptis*, gives the authentic text, we might take 'his interfui' to mean 'I had a share in these things' or (less likely) 'I was one of this group of persons.' But the omission is probably no more than a copyist's slip. I would suggest tentatively that the accepted text might mean 'I was present when these speeches were in fact written ("cum scriptae sunt")'. The passage, however, must be regarded as doubtful.

As has already been observed in connexion with the genitive, it is not always possible to distinguish this idiom with certainty from the attributive use of the participle, and a few dative examples may have been overlooked in this way. The same is true of the ablative, where the cognate absolute construction increases the difficulty of identification. The following two examples probably belong to the *ab urbe condita* type, though in the first the participle might be attributive, and in the second, absolute: Cluent. 194 *neque intellegit pietate et religione et iustis precibus deorum mentes, non contaminata superstitione neque ad scelus perficiendum caesis hostiis posse placari*; Phil. 1. 24 *eas leges . . . quibus latis gloriabatur.*

(3) Impersonal

The construction twice appears in Cicero with impersonal verbs. This use, found in early Latin with *opus est* (see p. 86 above), but not otherwise, is considerably developed by Livy and Tacitus:[1] Att. 6. 3. 3 *reliqua plena adhuc et laudis et gratiae, digna iis libris quos dilaudas, conservatae civitates*, cumulate publicanis satis factum, *offensus contumelia nemo*; part. 114 *haec proprie attingunt eos ipsos qui arguuntur, ut telum, ut vestigium, ut cruor, ut deprehensum aliquid quod ablatum ereptumve videatur*, ut responsum inconstanter, ut haesitatum, ut titubatum . . . *ut tremor, ut scriptum aut obsignatum aut depositum quippiam.* It will be noticed that, in each case, the novel phrase is supported by the parallel series in which it occurs. nat. deor. 3. 74, which Kühner–Stegmann (p. 769) quotes in this connexion, is of a somewhat different character: *reliqua* (sc. *iudicia*) *quae ex empto aut vendito aut conducto aut locato contra fidem fiunt*. The participles are apparently being used with impersonal force, but in fact the verbs are personal. Cicero is using formulary legal language, in which, because it is concerned with a general principle, no noun is expressed. But the noun is present, at least potentially, in the reader's consciousness.

(4) Present participle

Apart from the stereotyped phrase *ante solem exorientem*, early Latin shows no example of the present participle in the *ab urbe condita* construction. The first instances appear in Cicero, and it may be taken as reasonably certain that the use was introduced by him. Attention has already been drawn, in Chapter I, to his progressive exploitation of the potentialities of the present participle. So far as the *ab urbe condita* construction is concerned, the first example occurs in a letter of 60 B.C. (Att. 2. 1. 8), and thereafter the construction is found in about a score of passages, of which more than two-thirds belong to the letters and treatises of Cicero's last years.

Cicero's first example may, at first sight, appear doubtful: Att. 2. 1. 8 *quid impudentius publicanis renuntiantibus?* It seems possible to understand *renuntiantibus* as a normal predicative

<hr>

[1] Schmalz–Hofmann, 457; Kühner–Stegmann, 769.

participle (= 'cum renuntiarent'). But, two lines earlier, Cicero has said: *quid verius, quam in iudicium venire, qui ob rem iudicandam pecuniam acceperit?*, which suggests that *publicanis renuntiantibus* is equivalent to 'quam publicanos renuntiare', and this interpretation is confirmed by a similar example in rep. 1. 52 *virtute vero gubernante rem publicam quid potest esse praeclarius?*, where the participial phrase evidently has the force of a substantival clause.

Two instances in the accusative occur in letters to Quintus of 54 B.C.: ad Q. fr. 2. 14. 1 *quod in istis rebus ego plurimi aestimo, id iam habeo, te scilicet primum tam inservientem communi dignitati, deinde Caesaris tantum in me amorem* (the nature of the participle is established not only by *id*, but by the corresponding *Caesaris amorem*): ibid. 3. 4. 2 *tamen in re publica me a se dissentientem non tulit* ('my disagreeing with him'; this example belongs to the type illustrated on pp. 92 f. above, and is guaranteed by Manil. 11, there quoted). Cf. also div. 1. 111 and 2. 16, quoted on p. 42.

Two clear instances in the nominative appear in letters written after 50 B.C.: Att. 7. 11. 4 (49 B.C.) *fugiens denique Pompeius mirabiliter homines movet*; fam. 6. 6. 8 *in quo vehementer eum consentiens Etruria movebit.* But an earlier example can be quoted from the year 56 B.C., and the fact that this too is from a letter is of no significance, for the letter in question (to Lucceius) is one of the most literary pieces that Cicero ever wrote: fam. 5. 12. 5 *quem enim nostrum* ille moriens apud Mantineam Epaminondas *non cum quadam miseratione delectat?* The subject of *delectat* is not *ille Epaminondas*, but the whole participial phrase; what touches the reader is the *scene* of Epaminondas dying at Mantinea. Cicero describes the scene in the next sentence, and then asks a second question, closely parallel to the first in its thought, but with a characteristically sensitive variation of language: *cuius studium in legendo non erectum* Themistocli fuga† redituque[1] *retinetur?* The participial phrase is replaced by nouns with dependent genitive.

Unlike the past participle, the present offers few examples of the construction in prepositional phrases, and not all, even of those few, can be confidently distinguished from attributive uses. In addition to the two passages quoted on p. 61, I have noticed

---

[1] The textual problem here does not affect the syntax. See Sjögren's apparatus.

the following: div. 2. 128 *is cum languore corporis nec membris uti nec sensibus potest, incidit in visa varia et incerta, ex reliquiis, ut ait Aristoteles,*[1] *inhaerentibus earum rerum, quas vigilans gesserit aut cogitaverit* ('ex eo quod inhaerent reliquiae . . .') ; ibid. 2. 136 *de nostris somniis quid habemus dicere? tu de emerso me et equo ad ripam, ego de Mario cum fascibus laureatis me in suum deduci iubente monumentum* (the two dreams are described in detail in div. 1. 58 f.). Doubt may be felt about har. resp. 10: *reperietis enim ex hoc toto prodigio atque responso nos de istius scelere ac furore ac* de impendentibus periculis maximis *prope iam voce Iovis Optimi Maximi praemoneri.* The participle can be taken as attributive ('quae impendent'), but I believe that Cicero intended the prepositional phrase to be equivalent to 'impendere pericula maxima'. This interpretation finds strong support in a number of genitive examples, in which Cicero seems to have been exploring new ground.

In considering Cicero's treatment of the construction with the past participle, we have noticed a significant number of passages in which the participial phrase in the genitive is made to depend on a noun such as *testimonium, suspicio, indicium,* or *metus* (p. 94). This device is extended to the present participle:[2] Att. 14. 2. 1 *ex priore (epistula) theatrum Publiliumque cognovi; bona signa* consentientis multitudinis (= 'consentire multitudinem') ; div. 1. 124 *neque enim domo egredienti . . . signum sibi ullum, quod consuesset, a deo quasi mali alicuius impendentis datum*; Tusc. 3. 25 *nam et metus opinio magni mali impendentis et aegritudo est opinio magni mali praesentis.* In the last passage both the required sense and analogy with the corresponding past participle idiom are against an interpretation of *impendentis* and *praesentis* as attributive. Attributive participles would tend to imply reality, whereas the object of fear and the cause of *aegritudo* alike may be, and often are, non-existent. The phrases after *opinio* are equivalent to 'magnum

---

[1] Cicero appears to be thinking of Aristotle, *De Insomniis*, ch. 3. If so, *ut ait Aristoteles* probably refers not to the whole phrase *ex reliquiis . . . cogitaverit,* for which there is no obvious parallel in Aristotle, but simply to the word *reliquiae,* which represents ὑπόλοιπος and ὑπόλειμμα in the following two passages: 461ᵃ17–22 οὕτω καὶ ἐν τῷ καθεύδειν τὰ φαντάσματα καὶ αἱ ὑπόλοιποι κινήσεις αἱ συμβαίνουσαι ἀπὸ τῶν αἰσθημάτων ὁτὲ μὲν . . . ἀφανίζονται, ὁτὲ δὲ τεταραγμέναι φαίνονται αἱ ὄψεις καὶ τερατώδεις, καὶ οὐκ εἰρόμενα τὰ ἐνύπνια. 461ᵇ21 ὑπόλειμμα τοῦ ἐν τῇ ἐνεργείᾳ αἰσθήματος.   [2] For other genitive examples see pp. 35 f. above.

malum impendere . . . praesens esse'; cf. Tusc. 3. 61 and 4. 14 *est ergo aegritudo opinio recens mali praesentis*, where Heine's note quotes a definition attributed to Andronicus Rhodius: λύπη μὲν οὖν ἐστι δόξα πρόσφατος κακοῦ παρουσίας. This brings us to the most interesting example of all: Tusc. 4. 14 (est ergo) *metus opinio* impendentis mali, *quod intolerabile esse videatur, libido opinio* venturi boni, *quod sit ex usu iam praesens esse atque adesse*. If the considerations put forward above, and the examples quoted, have any cogency, *impendentis* is not attributive, but stands in the *ab urbe condita* construction, in the sense of 'impendere malum'. Heine quotes the Greek version of the definition from Stobaeus: ecl. 2. 172 φόβον δ᾽ εἶναι ἔκκλισιν ἀπειθῆ λόγῳ, αἴτιον δ᾽ αὐτοῦ τὸ δοξάζειν κακὸν ἐπιφέρεσθαι, οὗ παρόντος κακῶς ἀπαλλάξομεν.[1] But if *impendentis* is not attributive, neither is *venturi*, for it is virtually certain that Cicero is using both participles in the same construction, and therefore *venturi boni* is equivalent to 'venturum esse bonum'. Again the Greek definition, as given by Stobaeus (loc. cit.), is illuminating: τὴν μὲν οὖν ἐπιθυμίαν λέγουσιν ὄρεξιν εἶναι ἀπειθῆ λόγῳ, αἴτιον δ᾽ αὐτῆς τὸ δοξάζειν ἀγαθὸν ἐπιφέρεσθαι, οὗ παρόντος εὖ ἀπαλλάξομεν. If *venturi* is, as I believe, being used, by analogy with *impendentis*, in the *ab urbe condita* construction, it is not only evidence of Cicero's boldness in the use of that construction, but also bears witness to the fact that his contribution to the development of the future participle in Latin was more significant than has yet been recognized.

There is an obvious formal affinity between the *ab urbe condita* construction and the more primitive ablative absolute, with which the next chapter will be concerned. To what extent the one facilitated the development of the other it is impossible to say, but their affinity is strikingly illustrated by fin. 2. 9 *estne quaeso, inquam, sitienti in bibendo voluptas? quis istud possit, inquit, negare? eademne quae* restincta siti? *immo alio genere. restincta enim sitis stabilitatem voluptatis habet, inquit.*

---

[1] Heine ought to have said that the words οὗ . . . ἀπαλλάξομεν are a supplement of Salmasius (see the apparatus of Wachsmuth's edition of Stobaeus). The justification of the supplement, which is not accepted by Wachsmuth, is the corresponding phrase in the definition of ἐπιθυμία, quoted on this page, which in the text of Stobaeus precedes the definition of φόβος.

V

THE ABLATIVE ABSOLUTE[1]

I⊤ has been observed that the ablative absolute construction belongs properly to the syntax of the ablative case, rather than to that of the participle,[2] and indeed a participle is not even necessary, as is shown by such phrases as *Cicerone consule*. Nevertheless the participle plays an important part in the development of the construction as a subordinate clause-equivalent.

It is now generally agreed that the absolute construction grew out of the use of phrases consisting of a noun and attribute (whether adjective or participle) in the ablative, to describe the manner or circumstances of the verbal action. Thus, in the line of Naevius

noctu Troiad exibant capitibus opertis[3]

the last two words doubtless represent a simple adverbial phrase of manner, 'with covered heads'. But if predicative force is given to *opertis*, the phrase acquires greater prominence and detachability, so that in a suitable context it could mean 'when they had covered their heads'. There is much probability in the view of Tammelin (pp. 129 f.) that the absolute construction arose from a tendency to treat the participle in such sociative phrases as predicative. When this happened to a past participle, it was natural that the notion of temporal anteriority should attach itself to the phrase, and thus emerged the ablative absolute in its most characteristic classical form. Even in Cicero, however, the sociative element still remains strong, especially with the present

---

[1] For discussion of the nature and origin of the construction see Weihenmajer, *Zur Geschichte des absoluten Partizips im Lateinischen* (Reutlingen, 1891); Tammelin, 126 ff.; F. Horn, *Zur Geschichte der absol. Partizipial-konstrukt. im Lateinischen* (Lund, 1918); Wackernagel, i. 292 ff.; Schmalz–Hofmann, 445 ff.; E. Flinck-Linkomies, *De ablativo absoluto quaestiones* (Helsingfors, 1929); E. C. Woodcock, *A New Latin Syntax*, 34 f.   [2] For example, by E. Wölfflin, *A.L.L.* 13. 271.
[3] *F.P.L.*, Morel, p. 18.

participle, whose concomitant character is naturally adapted to express accompanying circumstances.

A contributory factor in the emergence of the absolute participle is probably to be seen in the practice, fairly frequent in Plautus and Terence, of combining in a sociative phrase a pronoun and predicative noun-complement: e.g. Most. 916 *me suasore atque impulsore id factum audacter dicito* (cf. Eun. 988, Ad. 560); Stich. 602 f. *non me quidem faciet auctore hodie ut illum decipiat* (cf. Eun. 1013); Trin. 1161 *impetrabit te advocato atque arbitro*; Curc. 434 *quod te praesente isti egi teque interprete*; Persa 580 *atqui aut hoc emptore vendes pulchre aut alio non potis*; Hec. 254 f. *aut ea refellendo aut purgando vobis corrigemus te iudice ipso*; Haut. 969 *satius est quam te ipso herede haec possidere Bacchidem*. In all these passages, except the last, the ablatives are sociative; the nouns used describe a person in the capacity of helper or abettor in an action. In Haut. 969 the exceptional *te ipso herede* is probably to be explained by analogy.[1] This use of a predicative noun-complement in sociative phrases continued through the classical period, though its scope was restricted in comparison with the participle, and confined to a relatively small number of nouns such as *duce* and *auctore*. The *temporal* use of a noun in this kind of phrase (e.g. *consule Tullo, me puero*) is practically unknown in early Latin,[2] and in fact it could only gain currency after the absolute participle had been developed.

A. EARLY LATIN

In Plautus and Terence the absolute past participle with temporal force is already in evidence, though in many of the examples the fundamentally sociative character of the phrase is unmistakable. With the present participle the construction appears rarely and in rudimentary form. The evidence of Plautus suggests that in his day the ablative absolute tended to be confined to formal or official speech.[3] We see it in its most primitive

---

[1] Flinck-Linkomies, op. cit., p. 46.
[2] The only instance known to me is the phrase from the *Boeotia* of Aquilius (Ribbeck, p. 38) *me puero venter erat solarium*.
[3] Weihenmajer, op. cit., p. 29.

form in several passages where Plautus parodies the thanksgiving prayer of a triumphing general:[1]

Persa 753 ff. *hostibus victis, civibus salvis, re placida, pacibus per-fectis, | bello exstincto, re bene gesta, integro exercitu et praesidiis, | quom bene nos, Iuppiter, iuvisti, dique alii omnes caelipotentes, | eas vobis habeo gratis atque ago.* Bacch. 1070 f. *salute nostra atque urbe capta per dolum | domum redduco integrum omnem exercitum* (cf. Amph. 188 f., 654 ff.). We find a similar parody of official language in a letter of Cicero to Atticus: Att. 4. 18. 5 *a Q. fratre et a Caesare accepi a.d. viiii Kal. Nov. litteras datas a litoribus Britanniae proxime a.d. vi Kal. Octobres. confecta Britannia, obsidibus acceptis, nulla praeda, imperata tamen pecunia exercitum ex Britannia reportabant.* In Persa 753 ff. and Bacch. 1070 f. *re placida* and *salute nostra* are clearly sociative, and it is equally clear that the participial phrases are parallel to the adjectival. All express the various circumstances accompanying the triumphant general's return. In *hostibus victis* 'with the enemy conquered' the emphasis is on the present situation resulting from the conquest; the predicative participle coalesces with the noun in the same way as in the *ab urbe condita* construction. (Here, perhaps, we may see more clearly the nature of the link between the two constructions, which was mentioned at the end of the last chapter.) The idea of temporal priority is implicit, but less prominent than that of accompanying circumstance. Neverthe-less, in the ancient prayer-formula, with its series of parallel phrases, the participial phrase is beginning to acquire the de-tachability which enabled it to assume the role of a temporal clause and qualify a whole sentence. In the following Plautine passages the temporal force of the participle is more pronounced: Amph. 390 *non loquar nisi pace facta*; ibid. 967 *qui re divina facta mecum prandeat*; Men. 989 *sed metuo ne sero veniam depugnato proelio*; Merc. 92 *his sic confectis navem solvimus*; Mil. 3 *ut, ubi usus veniat, contra conserta manu, praestringat oculorum aciem in acie hostibus* (where the ablative phrase is as detached from *praestringat* as is the clause *ubi usus veniat*);[2] Capt. 82 *item parasiti rebus prolatis latent in occulto*

---

[1] See E. Fraenkel, *Plautinisches im Plautus*, 236 f., and now the *addendum* in the Italian edition, *Elementi plautini in Plauto* (Florence, 1960), p. 429.

[2] I include this example with some hesitation, accepting the traditional punctua-tion after *veniat*. We cannot, however, exclude the possibility that Plautus intended

miseri (the participial phrase looks back to two temporal clauses, 78 *ubi res prolatae sunt* and 80 *quom caletur*). On the other hand, in many passages the participial phrase is not absolute, but a purely modal expression attached closely to the finite verb: e.g. Amph. 953 *cum ego Amphitryonem* collo *hinc* obstricto *traham* (cf. Poen. 790 *optorto collo*); Amph. 1094 *capite operto* (cf. Curc. 288); Cas. 344 *necessumst* vorsis gladiis *depugnarier* (cf. ibid. 352); Poen. 508 *atque equidem hercle* dedita opera *amicos fugitavi senes* (cf. Cist. 670, Trin. 67). Some of these expressions, especially *dedita opera*, are stereotyped usage in classical Latin.

With the present participle most of the examples in Plautus and Terence—comparatively few in number—are sociative, and describe persons participating in, or interested in, the action of the main verb: e.g. Amph. 747 *egone istuc dixi?—tute istic, etiam astante hoc Sosia*; ibid. 997 f. *faxo probe | iam hic deludetur, spectatores, vobis inspectantibus*; Mil. 144 *et sene sciente hoc feci*; Ad. 507 *non me indicente haec fiunt*; Eun. 956 *conligavit?—atque quidem orante ut ne id faceret Thaide*. This last passage is, to my knowledge, the only instance in early Latin of an absolute participle with verbal construction.

When a participle is used whose intrinsic meaning is not sociative, the phrase acquires a stronger temporal force, and consequently becomes more detached, as in Poen. 322 *nam vigilante Venere si veniant eae*. The same is true of the use of *absente*, by analogy with *praesente*; the meaning of the word changes the force of the ablative phrase from that of accompaniment to that of mere time. Flinck-Linkomies (op. cit., p. 60) draws attention to an instructive instance in Most. 1016 ff. *quid autem?—quod me absente hic tecum filius negoti gessit—mecum ut ille hic gesserit,* dum tu hinc abes, *negoti?* Here *me absente* and *dum tu hinc abes* are equated in sense; the text helps us to understand the way by which the absolute construction developed as a clause-equivalent. The only example in Terence in which the participle has purely temporal force, Hec. 830 *eum haec cognovit Myrrhina in digito modo me habente,* must be regarded as doubtful, since *habente* is a conjecture of Bentley for the manuscripts' *habentem*.

usus veniat to go with *contra conserta manu* in the manner of *usus (opus) est*—'when the need for hand-to-hand fighting comes'. Cf. Asin. 312 (p. 87 above).

B. THE CONSTRUCTION IN CICERO

An examination of Cicero's use of the ablative absolute reveals two things. (1) Though the construction always accounts for an appreciable percentage of his total participles, it shows a slight progressive decline; Cicero seems to have found that it did not lend itself to much development as an element in sentence-structure. The relatively static position of the ablative absolute in Cicero's participial usage can be seen from the following table:

Period	Speeches			Letters			Treatises		
	Past	*Pres.*	*Both*	*Past*	*Pres.*	*Both*	*Past*	*Pres.*	*Both*
I	26·7	8·4	35·1						
II	26·4	10·7	37·1	24·1	12·3	36·4	25·6	8·5	34·1
III	24·8	10·5	35·3	28	7·8	35·8	18·4	5·5	23·9

The decline is slight but perceptible, especially in the present participle; this is in interesting contrast to Cicero's progressive development of the predicative present participle. (2) Whilst the temporal or quasi-temporal sense (i.e. the most fully absolute use) is fairly common with the past participle, the sociative use is still prominent, and with the present participle shows a decisive predominance.

(1) Past participle

Of Cicero's use of the absolute participle it is to be observed, in the first place, that the phrases are frequently short, consisting of no more than two or three words, and including many stereotyped expressions such as *re audita, accepta pecunia, signo dato*. In the following examples the length of the phrases is not typical: rep. 2. 27 *excessit e vita, duabus praeclarissimis ad diuturnitatem rei publicae rebus confirmatis, religione atque clementia*; ac. 2. 13 *horum nominibus tot virorum atque tantorum expositis eorum se institutum sequi dicunt*.

Secondly, the temporal force is sometimes strengthened by the addition of an appropriate adverb. This kind of reinforcement is especially noticeable where, as often, the ablative absolute is used to indicate logical priority, i.e. when proceeding from one stage of an argument to the next: invent. 1. 17 *constitutione causae reperta* statim *placet considerare*; ibid. 1. 18 *considerato genere causae*... deinceps *erit videndum*; off. 2. 16 *qui collectis ceteris causis*... deinde *comparat*; fin. 4. 32 *quo constituto* tum *licebit otiose ista quaerere*. (Cf. off. 2. 52; ac. 2. 37.) The use of *sequor* in the following passages is similar: fin. 3. 41 *his igitur ita positis, inquit, sequitur magna contentio*; Tusc. 5. 50 *quibus positis intellegis quid sequatur* (cf. nat. deor. 2. 75).

The fact that Cicero, whether consciously or not, sometimes reinforces the character of priority in the past participle of an absolute phrase, is evidence that such phrases did not always or necessarily possess that character; and, in fact, in many Ciceronian instances the temporal force of the past participle is quite subordinate, the absolute phrase expressing primarily a circumstance accompanying the action of the finite verb. This is seen at its clearest in such simple examples as the following: Verr. II. 4.24 *quem* obtorta gula *de convivio in vincla atque in tenebras abripi iussit* (cf. Cluent. 59 *collo obtorto*, a stereotyped expression found, as already said, in early Latin); ibid. 5 *quae* manibus sublatis *sacra quaedam . . . in capitibus sustinebant*; Cluent. 187 *nam Stratonem quidem, iudices, in crucem esse actum* exsecta *scitote* lingua ('with tongue cut out', a horrifying circumstance of the execution); Pis. 14 *respondes* altero ad frontem sublato, altero ad mentum depresso supercilio *crudelitatem tibi non placere* ('with one eyebrow raised . . . &c.'—the expression on Piso's face as he speaks; it would be grotesque to give temporal force to the participles); Mil. 29 *cum autem hic de raeda* reiecta paenula *desiluisset . . . illi, qui erant cum Clodio*, gladiis eductis *partim recurrere ad raedam*... &c. (the comma which some editors put after *gladiis eductis* is probably wrong; the meaning is surely not 'having drawn their swords', but 'with drawn swords'; Clodius' desperadoes were unlikely to have put off drawing their swords until this moment).

The sociative character is less obvious when the circumstance described by the ablative phrase is not (as in the passages just quoted) a visible and physical accompaniment of the main action. But in many places a careful reading shows that the essential force of the participle is to express not a past action or event, but the present circumstance resulting from it: e.g. Verr. II. 3. 128 *qui non modo ex agris eiecti sunt, sed etiam ex civitatibus suis, ex provincia denique* bonis fortunisque omnibus ereptis *profugerunt*; ac. 2. 12 *itaque complures dies* adhibito Heraclito doctisque compluribus . . . *multum temporis in ista una disputatione consumpsimus*; Arch. 18 *quotiens (hunc vidi) revocatum eandem rem dicere* commutatis verbis atque sententiis.

Frequently the ablative phrase is instrumental: e.g. Verr. II. 1. 145 *omnes illae columnae* . . . machina adposita *nulla impensa deiectae (sunt)*; Cluent. 136 *cum tribunus pl.* populo concitato *rem paene ad manus revocasset*; leg. agr. 2. 10 *largitio aliqua promulgata, quae . . . re vera fieri nisi* exhausto aerario *nullo pacto potest*; Phil. 2. 21 *nisi se ille in scalas tabernae librariae coniecisset* iisque oppilatis *impetum tuum compressisset*. Cf. ac. 2. 62.

(2) Present Participle

If the past participle ablative absolute in the strict sense—that is to say, a phrase qualifying a whole sentence, and as detachable from it as a subordinate temporal clause—is less common in Cicero than might have been supposed, this is still more true in the case of the present participle. The examples in which the absolute present participle expresses mere contemporaneousness, and is equivalent to a *dum*-clause, are by no means negligible in number, but they form a small proportion in comparison with the vast majority of instances, in which the participle expresses action (or reaction) of a person or persons taking part in, or interested in, the action of the main verb. Cicero, in fact, develops, above all, the type represented in early Latin by such phrases as *astante Sosia* and *vobis inspectantibus*. The latter phrase was indeed stereotyped (in classical Latin the verb is only found in this construction), and occurs very often in Cicero, usually in simple expressions like *omnibus* (or *multis*) *inspectantibus*, occasionally expanded, as in p. red. in sen. 11 *quo inspectante ac sedente legem tribunus plebis tulit.* *audiente* and *audientibus* are similarly used in numerous passages.

The majority of Cicero's examples fall under two main headings, both plainly sociative, in which the ablative phrase describes a person or persons, either as taking a leading part in the main action, or as reacting to it in one way or another.

(a) Chief agent

In a forensic context the chief agent may be the prosecuting or defending counsel or the jury. Examples like the following are frequent, especially in the speeches: Quinct. 34 *queritur priore patrono causam defendente nunquam perorari potuisse*; Verr. II. 1. 52 *posteaque se causam apud Chios cives suos* Samiis accusantibus *publice dixisse* (cf. Sest. 89); Cael. 4 *equitis Romani autem esse filium criminis loco poni ab accusatoribus* neque his iudicantibus *oportuit* neque defendentibus nobis (cf. Verr. I. 47). Similarly, in the political sphere, the agency of a magistrate or of the initiator of a proposal is often expressed by this means: e.g. dom. 11 *concursus est ad templum Concordiae factus* senatum illuc vocante Metello consule; Phil. 3. 9 *senatum etiam reges habebant; nec tamen ut* Antonio senatum habente *in consilio regis versabantur barbari armati;* Mur. 51 *tum igitur his rebus auditis meministis fieri senatus consultum* referente me *ne postero die comitia haberentur* (cf. Phil. 2. 31). So, in general, when the action is influenced by advice, persuasion, compulsion, &c.: Att. 3. 15. 3 *quod profecto cum sua sponte tum* te instante *faciet*; leg. 1. 26 *artes vero innumerabiles repertae sunt* docente natura (cf. orat. 178, Tusc. 1. 29 *natura admonente*; fin. 5. 58 *natura ipsa praeeunte*; nat. deor. 1. 66 *nulla cogente natura*); Phil. 2. 45 *cum tu tamen nocte socia*, hortante libidine, cogente mercede *per tegulas demitterere*; fam. 4. 3. 1 *neque id solum mea sponte (prospexi) sed multo etiam magis* monente et denuntiante te.

To the same general type belong the following: Phil. 2. 92 *mihi vero nullo modo, qui omnia* te gubernante *naufragia timebam*; fam. 15. 21. 2 *deinde quod illa . . . fiunt* narrante te *venustissima*; leg. 1. 5 *sic enim putant*, te illam (sc. *historiam*) tractante *effici posse ut in hoc etiam genere Graeciae nihil cedamus*; Arch. 21 *populus enim Romanus aperuit* Lucullo imperante *Pontum.*

(b) Reaction

A great variety of absolute present participles express reaction to the situation or event described by the finite verb, approval, disapproval, acquiescence, &c.: e.g. Att. 7. 3. 1 *etsi cupidissime expetitum a me est, et te approbante, ne diutius anno in provincia essem* (cf. Pis. 7); div. 2. 104 *qui magno plausu loquitur* adsentiente populo; dom. 14 *cum de mea dignitate* . . . *senatus frequentissimus* uno isto dissentiente *decrevisset*; Mur. 79 *id quod ego* multis repugnantibus *egi atque perfeci*; ad Brut. 4. 2 *mihi etiam, qui* repugnante et irascente Pansa *sententiam dixerim*; Mil. 36 *cum* maerentibus vobis *urbe cessi*; fam. 10. 3. 2 *eaque es adeptus adulescens* multis invidentibus, *quos ingenio industriaque fregisti*; ibid. 12. 25. 2 *quo die primum in spem libertatis ingressus sum, et* cunctantibus ceteris . . . *fundamenta ieci rei publicae*; Phil. 12. 8 *quid enim* revocante et receptui canente senatu *properet dimicare?*; fam. 6. 6. 6 *susceptum bellum est* quiescente me, *depulsum ex Italia* manente me, *quoad potui* (as its correspondence to *quiescente* shows, the participle *manente* expresses not mere time, but Cicero's attitude). Cf. Sest. 55; dom. 49; Att. 4. 18. 3; 10. 8. 6. A natural extension of this use is seen in examples like nat. deor. 1. 79 *deinde nobis, qui* concedentibus philosophis antiquis *adulescentulis delectamur, etiam vitia saepe iucunda sunt.*

The short and simple phrases, in which the construction appears in most of the examples quoted, are typical of the sociative use in Cicero. The comparatively infrequent instances in which the participial phrase involves verbal construction of some extent are represented by the following: Att. 1. 14. 5 *cum decerneretur frequenti senatu*, contra pugnante Pisone, ad pedes omnium singillatim accidente Clodio, *ut consules populum cohortarentur ad rogationem accipiendam*; Brut. 89 L. Libone tribuno plebis populum incitante et rogationem in Galbam privilegii similem ferente . . . *M. Cato legem suadens in Galbam multa dixit*; Pis. 11 *pro Aurelio tribunali* ne conivente quidem te . . . sed etiam hilarioribus oculis quam solitus eras intuente, *dilectus servorum habebatur*; ibid. 25 *et (me) absentem* principe Cn. Pompeio referente et de corpore rei publicae tuorum scelerum tela revellente *revocarunt*; ibid. 76 *me Cn. Pompeius* multis obsistentibus eius erga me studio atque amori *semper dilexit.*[1] When thus extended, the participial phrase tends to be felt less as an adverbial qualification of the main verb, and to acquire more of the independence of a subordinate clause.

(c) Accompanying circumstances

Sometimes the sociative present participle absolute is used not of persons participating directly in the main action, whether as agents or interested parties, but of an accompanying circumstance, less closely involved in the action, but belonging to its context: e.g. Verr. II. 5. 100 *dicere omnes et palam disputare minime esse mirandum, si remigibus militibusque dimissis* . . . praetore tot dies cum mulierculis perpotante *tanta ignominia et calamitas esset accepta*; de orat. 3. 14 *pergamus ad ea solacia, quae non modo sedatis molestiis iucunda, sed etiam* haerentibus *salutaria nobis esse possint*; Sest. 73 *iure iudiciisque sublatis*, magna rerum permutatione impendente *declinasse me paulum*; ac. 2. 63 *Hortensius autem vehementer admirans (quod quidem perpetuo* Lucullo loquente *fecerat* . . .) ; nat. deor. 3. 1 *ego enim* te disputante, *quid contra dicerem, mecum ipse meditabar.* Cf. Mil. 61; Tusc. 4. 84. This sociative type corresponds to the similar past participle usage already illustrated (p. 106), and it will be noticed that in three of the above passages past participle and present participle phrases stand side by side.

(d) Temporal

In a number of the examples just quoted the force of the absolute phrase comes near to that of mere time; and in fact, though the sociative type prevails in Cicero, the merely temporal use, which is foreshadowed in early Latin, is found in all periods of his writing: e.g. Cluent. 41 eadem hac Dinaea testamentum faciente, *cum tabulas prehendisset Oppianicus, qui gener eius fuisset, digito legata delevit*; de orat. 2. 287 *ut M. Lepidus, cum,* ceteris se in campo exercentibus, *ipse in herba recubuisset*; ibid. 3. 17 *tum dedita opera,* quiescentibus aliis *in eam exedram venisse in qua Crassus posito lectulo*

---

[1] It is interesting to observe that three of the most extended examples come from the same speech, perhaps through a subconscious association of ideas. This kind of unconscious grouping, in the case of idioms and constructions (as with metrical patterns in verse), would, I suspect, if thoroughly investigated, prove to be fairly common.

recubuisset; Att. 6. 5. 1 *etsi, ut spero*, te haec legente *aliquantum iam viae processero* (cf. fam. 6. 12. 3) ; Att. 8. 3. 7 *sed ecce nuntii* scribente me haec ipsa noctu in Caleno; Deiot. 13 *domum se contulit*, teque Alexandrinum bellum gerente *utilitatibus tuis paruit*; fam. 5. 12. 9 *ut et ceteri* viventibus nobis *ex libris tuis nos cognoscant et nosmet ipsi vivi gloriola nostra perfruamur.*

(3) Quasi-temporal uses

Like the predicative participium coniunctum, the absolute participle, whether past or present, can in an appropriate context assume causal, conditional, or concessive force, sometimes with the addition, if causal, of *praesertim*, if concessive, of *tamen*. The corresponding use with predicative participles has been fully illustrated (pp. 7 ff. above), and no further illustration is necessary. One idiomatic use, however, deserves special mention: that whereby *nisi* is sometimes followed by a past participle ablative absolute, instead of by a clause. This is an old feature, found in Plaut. Amph. 390 *non loquar nisi pace facta* (cf. Rud. 581), and it was evidently still current in Cicero's day. The sentences in which it appears are always negative: Att. 1. 16. 5 *clamare praeclari Areopagitae se non esse venturos nisi praesidio constituto* (= 'nisi praesidium constitutum esset') ; Sest. 84 *quae fieri nisi armis oppressa re publica nullo modo poterant*; dom. 114 *nonne responderes id nisi eversa civitate accidere non posse?*; ac. 2. 44 *nam concludi argumentum non potest nisi iis, quae ad concludendum sumpta erunt, ita probatis ut . . .* (cf. de orat. 2. 190; fam. 1. 4. 1 ; 16. 1. 1 ; Tusc. 1. 23; fin. 3. 73).

(4) Deponent

Cicero has only a handful of deponent participles in absolute construction, and none of them is used transitively: Sull. 56 *illo profecto*; Tusc. 1. 104 *vel exstincto animo vel elapso*; div. 1. 25 *isdem signis antegressis*; Tusc. 5. 97 *comitibus non consecutis* (cf. Brut. 197 where, however, the existence of the reading *consecutus* leaves an element of doubt) ; Sull. 33 *sine armis, sine exercitu*, quinque hominibus comprehensis atque confessis . . . *interitu rem publicam liberavi* (the v.l. *confossis* is impossible; the conspirators were strangled, and cf. Catil. 3. 10–11) ; Tusc. 5. 80 *nec . . . consistet* (sc. *vita beata*) *virtutibusque omnibus* . . . ad cruciatum profectis *resistet extra fores* . . . *limenque carceris.* The last example is the furthest that Cicero permits himself to go in the way of verbal construction with a deponent absolute participle. It was left for others to take the step of allowing such a participle to govern a direct object or a clause.[1]

(5) Subject a clause

Three times in Cicero a clause is made to stand as subject to an absolute past participle: invent. 2. 34 *hoc loco praeterito et* cur praetereatur *demonstrato*; off. 2. 42 adiuncto *vero*, ut idem etiam prudentes haberentur, *nihil erat quod homines iis auctoribus non posse consequi se arbitrarentur*; fin. 2. 85 perfecto enim et concluso, neque virtutibus neque amicitiis usquam locum esse, *si ad voluptatem omnia referantur, nihil praeterea est magnopere dicendum.* This construction becomes fairly frequent later, especially in Livy. The only pre-Ciceronian example that has been adduced is Claudius Quadrigarius, fr. 12 (Peter) impetrato *prius a consulibus* ut in Gallum . . . pugnare sese permitterent, but the words used by Gellius (9. 11) to introduce the extract in which the passage occurs (*ea res* . . . sic profecto *est in libris annalibus memorata*) do not enable us to feel confident that we have before us the actual language of Claudius, rather than a Gellian paraphrase. A fourth Ciceronian passage, similar in its effect, is ac. 2. 33 quo enim omnia iudicantur, sublato *reliqua se negant tollere*, where the suppression of the pronoun antecedent causes the relative clause to appear as the subject of *sublato*.

If Cicero was the originator of this convenient usage, he does not seem to have developed it out of the old impersonal type (*auspicato, composito, consulto*, &c.). This type, in which the participle is no more than a modal adverb, is restricted by Cicero to a narrow range of words, chiefly *auspicato* and *sortito*.

(6) With relative and interrogative pronouns

Attention has already been drawn to some passages in Cicero's later works, in which a predicative present participle, governing

---

[1] Kühner–Stegmann, 783 f.

a relative or interrogative pronoun, carries the main weight of a clause or sentence, and it was suggested that Cicero was consciously introducing a familiar Greek idiom into Latin syntax (pp. 43 f. above). In a number of places, all, with one exception, found in his later works, Cicero uses absolute participles in just the same way. It is tempting to link the two phenomena, and to regard them both as influenced by the same characteristic feature of Greek syntax. leg. 2. 11 *populis ostendisse ea se scripturos atque laturos* quibus illi adscitis susceptisque *honeste beateque viverent*; Tusc. 3. 72 *sed plures sunt causae suscipiendi doloris. primum illa opinio mali* quo viso atque persuaso *aegritudo insequitur necessario*; ac. 2. 116 *non quaero ex his illa initia mathematicorum*, quibus non concessis *digitum progredi non possunt*; off. 3. 109 *honestius hic quam Q̄. Pompeius*, quo, *cum in eadem causa esset*, deprecante *accepta lex non est*; Verr. II. 3. 185 *tu vero* quibus rebus gestis, quo hoste superato, *contionem donandi causa advocare ausus es?*; off. 2. 67 *sed tamen videmus*, quibus exstinctis oratoribus, *quam in paucis spes, quanto in paucioribus facultas, quam in multis sit audacia*; div. 2. 98 *si ad rem pertinet* quo modo caelo adfecto compositisque sideribus *quodque animal oriatur*.

For other relative examples see Att. 7. 2. 4; Tusc. 1. 96; fin. 2. 23; div. 2. 104; top. 75.

(7) Qualifying parts of a sentence other than finite verb

The ablative absolute is essentially an adverbial phrase, qualifying, at its simplest, a finite verb in a clause or sentence; in more elaborate form, acting as a subordinate clause to a whole sentence. But, possibly because of its inherent detachability and its affinity to the descriptive ablative phrase (see Schmalz–Hofmann, 431), it could be associated with other parts of a sentence, and the extent to which Cicero is prepared to do this has not hitherto been fully recognized.

(a) Participles

I have noticed some half-dozen passages in which an ablative absolute qualifies a participium coniunctum:[1] Att. 4. 15. 5 *quod lacus Velinus a M'. Curio emissus interciso monte in Nar defluit*; Sest.

---

[1] The most elaborate is quoted in the next section, p. 115.

46 *cum vero in hanc rei publicae navem* ereptis senatui gubernaculis fluitantem *in alto tempestatibus seditionum ac discordiarum armatae tot classes . . . incursurae viderentur* (the only satisfactory interpretation here seems to be to take *ereptis . . . gubernaculis* as explanatory of *fluitantem*—'drifting along with the helm wrested from the senate'); fam. 15. 15. 3 *ego qui festinavi, ut Caesarem in Italia viderem . . . eumque* multis honestissimis viris conservatis redeuntem *ad pacem . . . incitarem*; Sest. 85 *tribunum plebis* plus viginti vulneribus acceptis iacentem moribundumque *vidistis*; nat. deor. 1. 67 *an* (sc. *est veritas) in individuis corpusculis tam praeclara opera* nulla moderante natura, nulla ratione fingentibus; ad Brut. 23. 5 *taetrum enim spectaculum* oppressa ab impiis civitas opitulandi potestate praecisa (here it would perhaps be more accurate to say that the ablative absolute qualifies not merely the participle, but *oppressa . . . civitas*, that phrase belonging to the type of *ab urbe condita* construction illustrated on pp. 90 f.).

(b) Adjectives

Verr. II. 5. 120 *hoc ne possis dicere, 'patres enim veniunt* amissis filiis irati'[1] (it might be argued that the ablative absolute belongs to the whole phrase *veniunt irati*, but the required sense and the word-order make it clear that *amissis filiis* is intended to be taken closely with *irati*); Sest. 15 *hunc vir clarissimus mihique* multis repugnantibus amicissimus *Cn. Pompeius omni cautione . . . devinxerat*; off. 2. 76 *imitatus patrem Africanus* nihilo locupletior Carthagine eversa (the auxiliary verb is to be supplied in this sentence, either with *imitatus* or with *locupletior*; but even if *fuit* is to be understood with *locupletior*, it is significant that the qualifying ablative phrase did not prevent Cicero from omitting it); Phil. 11. 28 *cum est in Syriam profectus, alienam provinciam, si homines legibus scriptis uterentur, iis vero oppressis suam lege naturae.* In the last example both *alienam* and *suam* are emphatic, and each is qualified as if it were a verbal phrase, *alienam* (= 'quae aliena erat') by the conditional clause, *suam* (= 'quae sua erat') by the ablative absolute. To this group we should probably add the following passage, in which an adjectival substantive is similarly

---

[1] It seems appropriate to treat *irati* as adjective, rather than participle.

qualified : orat. 25 *quod eorum* vicini non ita lato interiecto mari *Rhodii nunquam probaverunt.*

(c) Nouns

Cicero attaches ablative absolute phrases to nouns more frequently than to either participles or adjectives. In half of the instances noted the noun is a verbal one : leg. 2. 37 *quo in genere severitatem maiorum senatus vetus auctoritas de Bacchanalibus et consulum* exercitu adhibito quaestio animadversioque *declarat*; ibid. 3. 23 *sed est iniqua in omni re accusanda* praetermissis bonis malorum enumeratio *vitiorumque selectio*; off. 2. 75 *tanta* sublatis legibus et iudiciis expilatio direptioque *sociorum*; Tusc. 4. 14 *ut aegritudo sit animi* adversante ratione contractio; fam. 11. 14. 1 *tantam spem attulerat* . . . *tua praeclara Mutina eruptio,* fuga Antoni conciso exercitu, *ut omnium animi relaxati sint.* In all these examples some verbal force can be felt in the noun ; it expresses an activity, with which an adverbial qualification is not incongruous. No activity, however, is implied in the noun in Tusc. 5. 28 *neque ulla alia huic verbo, cum beatum dicimus, subiecta notio est, nisi* secretis malis omnibus cumulata bonorum complexio ; and even if this instance be set aside as unsatisfactory, on the ground that the ablative phrase might be taken primarily with *cumulata* (possible, but unlikely), there remains a number of passages in which the noun is not verbal at all : Verr. II. 3. 150 *quantam igitur illi spem praedae propositam arbitramur fuisse, qui tantum praesens* lucrum nulla opera insumpta *contempserit atque despexerit?* ('an immediate profit involving no expenditure of effort' ; there can be no doubt that the absolute phrase is to be taken with *lucrum*) ; Sest. 9 *et hoc tempore eidem homines* nomine commutato coloni decurionesque . . . *beneficium P. Sesti testimonio declarant*; de orat. 1. 118 *sed, quia de oratore quaerimus, fingendus est nobis oratione nostra* detractis omnibus vitiis orator *atque omni laude cumulatus* (with the accepted text, *detractis* . . . *vitiis* is attached adjectivally, like a descriptive ablative, to *orator,* and is parallel to the attributive participial phrase *omni laude cumulatus*; Mohr's proposal to read *aeque* for *atque* (Act. Soc. Phil. Lips. 2. 485), approved by Ritschl, would enable the absolute phrase to qualify the participle *cumulatus*; but this is both artificial and unnecessary; it is clear that Cicero felt it as easy to attach the ablative absolute to nouns as to participles); fin. 4. 6 *nam quidquid quaeritur, id habet aut generis ipsius* sine personis temporibusque *aut* his adiunctis *facti aut iuris aut nominis* contro- versiam (the absolute and prepositional phrases correspond to one another, and both are adjectival qualifications of *controver- siam*). I add a passage in which the relationship of the absolute phrase is less obvious: Att. 6. 3. 4 *non quo ullum periculum videam stante Pompeio vel etiam sedente*. The ablative absolute here qualifies neither *videam* nor *periculum*, but an implied verb such as 'futurum esse' or 'imminere'.

(8) Absolute participial phrases in combination

In its most ancient manifestation, the triumphal thanksgiving formula, the ablative absolute appears in a series of parallel phrases, and this inherited tendency Cicero shows himself well able to exploit for rhetorical ends. Three typical passages will serve to illustrate his method: Flacc. 93 *his tu igitur epistulis, Deciane, recitatis, his mulierculis productis, illo absente auctore laudato, tantum te crimen probaturum putasti?*; Phil. 1. 30 *quem potes recordari in vita inluxisse tibi diem laetiorem quam cum expiato foro, dissipato con- cursu impiorum, principibus sceleris poena adfectis, urbe incendio et caedis metu liberata te domum recepisti?* The third passage is striking not only for the length of the series, but as the most elaborate in- stance in Cicero of absolute phrases qualifying a participle: p. red. ad Q. 18 *en ego tot testimoniis, Quirites, hac auctoritate senatus, tanta consensione Italiae, tanto studio bonorum omnium, agente P. Len- tulo, consentientibus ceteris magistratibus, deprecante Cn. Pompeio, omni- bus hominibus faventibus, dis denique immortalibus frugum ubertate, copia, vilitate reditum meum comprobantibus, mihi, meis, rei publicae restitutus, tantum vobis, quantum facere possum, Quirites, pollicebor.*

It is normal for absolute phrases to be combined in parallel pairs or series, side by side. Where Cicero abandons this arrange- ment it is either for artistic reasons or because the relationship is a different one. A good example of the first kind occurs in a formal letter to D. Brutus: fam. 11. 18. 2 *etenim cum te incluso spem maximam omnes habuissent in tua virtute* florente Antonio, *quis*

erat qui quicquam timeret profligato illo, te liberato*?* The two absolute phrases in the first half of the sentence are parallel to each
other, as are the second two; but the excessive artificiality of two
exactly corresponding pairs is avoided by separating the first
pair and making the correspondence chiastic: *te incluso—florente
Antonio—profligato illo—te liberato*. Further variety is achieved by
the chiastic arrangement of the words within each pair.

In the following passage are two pairs of absolute phrases, in
neither of which are the phrases parallel, though in the second
they stand side by side: prov. 27 *ego*, quo consule referente (1)
primum decem dierum est supplicatio decreta Cn. Pompeio Mithridate
interfecto et confecto Mithridatico bello (2), *et cuius sententia
primum duplicata est supplicatio consularis—mihi enim estis adsensi cum*,
eiusdem Pompei litteris recitatis (3), confectis omnibus maritimis
terrestribusque bellis (4) *supplicationem dierum decem decrevistis,—
sum Cn. Pompei virtutem et animi magnitudinem admiratus. quo consule
referente* is a natural qualification of *est supplicatio decreta*, as is
litteris recitatis of *decrevistis*. Both these phrases describe circumstances attending the action of the main verb. Phrases (2) and
(4), however, provide a different type of qualification, and give
the grounds upon which the action is taken. Thus, there is
a certain incongruity between phrases (1) and (2), and similarly
between (3) and (4), which prevents them from being felt as
parallel. The explanation is that they are not, in fact, in parallel
relationship to one another. Phrases (2) and (4) are to be attached closely to *supplicatio* and *supplicationem* respectively. Each
phrase gives the reason for which the supplicatio was granted,
and probably forms part of the official language of the decree.

Finally, there are some places in which Cicero seems to have
admitted interdependence between two adjacent absolute phrases.
This appears to be the relationship in top. 75 *multi etiam in res
odiosas imprudentes inciderunt, ut Staieno nuper accidit, qui ea locutus est*
bonis viris subauscultantibus pariete interposito, *quibus patefactis
in iudiciumque prolatis ille rei capitalis iure damnatus est. pariete interposito*, standing, as it does, after *bonis viris subauscultantibus*, might
possibly be a parallel qualification of *locutus est*, but it would be
meaningless without the preceding phrase, whereas, if *bonis viris*

subauscultantibus stood alone, the essential meaning would remain intact. It seems rather to be an explanatory qualification of *subauscultantibus*. Other examples of interdependent ablatives absolute will be considered among complex participial constructions in Chapter VII.

VI

THE FUTURE PARTICIPLE[1]

I T is generally agreed that the Latin future participle developed relatively late, out of an etymologically obscure future infinitive ending in *-urum*. In early Latin the participial form is found frequently in the periphrastic conjugation *-urus est*, but its independent participial use is very rare indeed; according to some scholars it is non-existent. Ussing's conjecture at Plaut. Truc. 149 f. *arationes habituris* (for *si arationes habituris*) is ruled out by Plautine usage. If *habituris* is not a desiderative form of *habes* (found only here), we must accept *habituru's*, the solution adopted by Ritschl and Leo. On Asin. 634 *quas hodie adulescens Diabolus ipsi daturus dixit* Leo remarks: 'verborum constructio in Plauto singularis'; the Renaissance reading *daturum* it at least more consistent with Plautus' usage. A line purporting to come from the *Annals* of Ennius, and accepted as such by Vahlen[2], p. 106,

carbasus alta volat pandam ductura carinam

is now generally regarded as spurious; Caspar von Barth, who produced it from an alleged scholiast on Statius, Achill. 1. 558, is an untrustworthy authority,[2] and *pandus* is not found elsewhere before the Augustan age. In the case of Lucilius 314 and 662 (Marx), the syntax is too fragmentary and uncertain to enable any conclusion to be drawn about the forms *incepturus* and *capturus*. In Lucilius 567,

rausuro tragicus qui carmina perdit Oreste

Marx (Commentary, p. 211) claimed to see the earliest example of the future participle in the ablative absolute construction. But

---

[1] An excellent and concise survey of the development of the future participle is given by Wackernagel, i. 286 f. There is a valuable earlier treatment by G. Landgraf in *A.L.L.* 9. 47 ff.

[2] See J. Sandys, *A History of Classical Scholarship*, ii. 363 f., derived from C. Bursian, *Geschichte der klass. Philologie in Deutschland*, 289 f.

this view has been rejected since E. Wölfflin pointed out (*A.L.L.* 13. 275) that the future use does not appear before the Augustan age (Asinius Pollio *ap.* Sen. suas. 6. 24), and *rausuro* is to be regarded as corrupt.[1] One passage from pre-Ciceronian Latin, the most important of all, remains to be considered. Aulus Gellius (11. 10. 1 = Malcovati[2], p. 188) professes to quote an extract from a speech of Gaius Gracchus, in which occurs the sentence: *qui prodeunt* dissuasuri, *ne hanc legem accipiatis, petunt non honorem a vobis, verum a Nicomede pecuniam.* Here we appear to have an isolated example of a predicative future participle expressing purpose. Two attitudes have been adopted towards it. One, represented by Wackernagel (loc. cit.) and, hesitantly, by Schmalz–Hofmann (607), would regard *dissuasuri* as a post-Augustan substitution for an original supine *dissuasum.* The other, represented by Schmalz (loc. cit.), seeks to explain away the participle by taking *prodeunt dissuasuri* as a modified form of the periphrastic conjugation. '*prodeunt dissuasuri*' declares Schmalz 'ist nicht wesentlich verschieden von *sunt dissuasuri*'. I have tried in vain to grasp the alleged equivalence. That Gaius Gracchus, little more than a generation before Cicero, should have ventured on a bold use of an independent future participle seems to me more comprehensible than that he should have reduced a verb of motion like *prodeunt*, however stereotyped its forensic use, to the role of an auxiliary verb. (The context, moreover, rules out any such possibility, since the verb *prodire* occurs, in different forms, three times in the three preceding sentences, and is the keyword of the whole passage.) Both these attitudes arise from an effort to maintain the view that there are no genuine pre-Ciceronian, or even Ciceronian, instances of the predicative future participle. But if an awkward passage can only be disposed of by arbitrary emendation or by singularly unconvincing explanation, we must ask ourselves whether it may not, in fact, be what it appears to be. It is true that the Gracchus passage is an isolated phenomenon,

---

[1] Cf. J. H. Schmalz, *B.Ph.W.* 31 (1911), 350 f.; H. Sjögren, *Zum Gebrauch des Futurums im Altlateinischen*, 225 f.; F. Leo, *Ausgewählte kleine Schriften*, i. 233, 237 f., 239.

and it would be convenient to have a few more similar examples. But there is no reason why, in a relatively small and fragmentary body of literature, we should think it impossible for a syntactical innovation to be represented by no more than one instance. Moreover, the innovation of Gracchus is supported by an early Ciceronian example : Verr. II. 1. 56 *P. Servilius, vir clarissimus, maximis rebus gestis*, adest *de te sententiam* laturus. One must, in honesty, point out that, whilst this reading has the stronger authority, and is accepted by Peterson (O.C.T.) and by Klotz (Teubner), a group of manuscripts, not all 'deteriores', since they include Parisinus 7776 of the eleventh century, read *laturus est*. This was adopted, in his edition of 1826, by Orelli, who printed a colon after *adest*. Landgraf (loc. cit.), without questioning the accepted reading (as he perhaps might have done, if the worth of Parisinus 7776 had been realized in 1896), explained *adest* as a quasi-auxiliary verb ('eigentlich nur ein verstärktes *est*'), so that the expression was half-way between 'laturus est' and 'venit laturus'. In this he was followed by Schmalz, who, rightly perceiving that the Cicero and the Gracchus passages must stand or fall together, offered the same explanation, as we have seen, for *prodeunt dissuasuri*. But though *adest* shows an obvious formal kinship with *est*, which is lacking in *prodeunt*, I find myself equally unable to see *adest* as a quasi-auxiliary verb. If one merely surveys the instances in Merguet's lexicon of the forensic use of *adsum* in Cicero, one finds that the verb always has its proper sense of being present, and often with distinct emphasis : e.g. Verr. II. 5. 10 *tum potuit a Leonida nummorum aliquid auferre, cum denuntiavit ut adesset*; ibid. 122 *adest Phylarchus Haluntinus . . . adest Centuripinus Phalacrus*. The Gracchus passage and Verr. II. 1. 56 give each other mutual support, and I can see no sufficient reason for refusing to believe that they are genuine innovations, which foreshadow the predicative use of the future participle expressing purpose, later to be freely exploited by Livy and the post-Augustans. Nor does Verr. II. 1. 56 stand entirely alone in Cicero's work as an example of a predicative future participle. An apparent parallel is ad Q. fr. 2. 16. 3 *ego eodem die* (sc. *quo haec scripsi*) *post meridiem Vatinium aderam defensurus*, where *aderam* is given by all the manuscripts, and defended by Sjögren (*Commentationes Tullianae*, 140), mainly on the ground that *aderam* is the proper word for an advocate.[1] But Lambinus, who substituted *eram* (epistolary imperfect), showed his customary sensitiveness to Cicero's language. Cicero is writing in the morning, and contemplating the defence of Vatinius in the afternoon. *eram* is adopted by Watt in his recent Oxford text. There is, however, a striking passage in which, so far as the participles are concerned, no question of textual uncertainty arises: Att. 8. 9. 2 *si quidem etiam vos duo tales ad quintum miliarium* (sc. obviam ituri estis), *quo nunc ipsum unde se recipienti, quid agenti, quid acturo?* It is clear that Greek syntax has influenced Cicero in his use of participles with interrogative pronouns (see pp. 43 f. above), and it is equally clear that the future participle *acturo* is helped by the present *agenti*. The fact remains that here we have an unmistakable, and relatively subtle, use of a predicative future participle expressing purpose, giving additional confirmation of Verr. II. 1. 56. Its very subtlety suggests that Cicero was not attempting something for the first time; he was more likely to begin with a nominative than with an oblique case.

A passage which I believe to be a third instance of predicative use, though of a different kind, is Tusc. 4. 14 (est ergo) *metus opinio impendentis mali, quod intolerabile esse videatur, libido opinio venturi boni, quod sit ex usu iam praesens esse atque adesse*. *venturi* is generally said to be attributive, and a mere variation for *futuri*. But this is less likely than might appear. Apart from this one passage, Cicero confines the attributive future participle to *futurus*; there are many instances of this, in most of which the participle is used as a simple adjective, analogous to *praesens* and *praeteritus*. *venturus*, on the other hand, has no such regular attributive use. I have discussed the passage at some length (p. 99 above), and have given reasons for believing that Cicero is here using the participles in the *ab urbe condita* construction. The future participle is eased by the present (cf. Att. 8. 9. 2 above) and by the fact that *impendens* and *venturus* are almost identical in meaning. We might translate the participial phrases: 'a sense of the imminence of evil . . . of the approach of good'. If with Tusc. 4.

---

[1] See also his apparatus, where he refers also to Schmalz's article.

14 we compare Tusc. 5. 52 *est enim metus futurae aegritudinis sollicita exspectatio*, we may at first feel that the expression is essentially the same as *opinio venturi boni*. There are, however, important differences: (i) *futurus* is almost always attributive in Cicero, whereas *venturi* stands alone; (ii) in Tusc. 4. 14 the noun to which the participle belongs is also qualified by an adjectival relative clause, which makes an attributive use of the participle not impossible, but somewhat less natural; (iii) *exspectatio* is more apt than is *opinio* to be constructed with an objective genitive noun, and therefore the attributive character of *futurae* is strengthened ('the expectation of future sorrow'). Relevant to this discussion is a passage from a letter of Asinius Pollio to Cicero, written in May or June of 43 B.C.: fam. 10. 33. 3 *et ego mehercules longe remotus ab omni suspicione futuri civilis tumultus, penitus in Lusitania legiones in hibernis collocaram*. Pollio is writing from Spain, and he excuses his failure to come to the aid of the Republic by the fact that the distance from Italy—at the end of the letter he complains that it takes six weeks, or more, for news to reach him—prevented him from knowing anything about the approaching clash with Antony, until it was an accomplished fact. He remarks that the battle of Mutina had taken place on the very day on which the sailing season from Gades began. Thus, *remotus ab omni suspicione futuri civilis tumultus* evidently means: 'without any inkling of the civil strife which was (destined) to arise'.

Cicero uses attributive *futurus* frequently. Sometimes its character is confirmed by a corresponding word or phrase: e.g. off. 1. 11 *similitudines comparat, rebusque praesentibus adiungit atque adnectit futuras*; Tusc. 4. 64 *est enim metus, ut aegritudo praesentis, sic ille futuri mali*; leg. 3. 29 *non enim de hoc senatu nec his de hominibus, qui nunc sunt, sed de futuris . . . haec habetur oratio*. Cf. Lael. 11; Att. 5. 13. 3. But in numerous instances Cicero dispenses with such support: e.g. Tusc. 1. 33 *inhaeret in mentibus quasi saeclorum quoddam augurium futurorum*; Lael. 40 *ut nos longe prospicere oporteat futuros casus rei publicae*; div. 2. 23 *ignoratio futurorum malorum utilior est quam scientia*, &c. I have noticed two examples which show verbal construction: fin. 3. 57 *dicuntque, ut liberis consultum velimus, etiamsi postumi futuri sint, propter ipsos, sic* futurae post mortem *famae tamen esse propter rem, etiam detracto usu, consulendum* (the construction is very simple, and is helped by the corresponding notion contained in *postumi*) ; part. 37 *in temporibus autem praesentia praeterita futura cernuntur; in his ipsis vetusta recentia instantia* paulo post aut aliquando futura (a glance at the context will show that the adjectives and participles here are not substantival, but attributive, and agree with *tempora* understood. In the light of the whole sentence the adverbial qualification of *futura* presents no difficulty.).

The substantival use of *futurus* in the neuter (= 'the future') is also common in Cicero's later work, occasionally in the singular, but much more often in the plural: e.g. off. 1. 11 *ad id solum quod adest quodque praesens est se accommodat, paulum admodum sentiens praeteritum aut futurum*; fat. 13 *si vere dicatur de futuro* (ibid. 17 *in futuro*); div. 1. 10 *natura significari futura sine deo possunt*; ibid. 63 *futura providet*; Phil. 4. 10 *sive . . . prodigiis atque portentis di immortales nobis futura praedicunt*; Cato 78 *tanta memoria praeteritorum futurorumque prudentia*; Att. 15. 4 A *tuas igitur* (sc. *litteras*) *exspecto, nec actorum solum sed etiam futurorum*, &c. A passage of great interest, if indeed it exemplifies a substantival future participle, is div. 1. 29 *etenim dirae, sicut cetera auspicia, ut omina, ut signa, non causas adferunt, cur quid eveniat, sed nuntiant* eventura, nisi provideris. If *eventura* is equivalent to 'ea quae eventura sunt', it is noteworthy for two reasons: (1) it is a bold departure from Cicero's practice, which, so far as attributive and substantival future participles are concerned, is otherwise restricted to *futurus*; (2) it involves the dependence of the clause *nisi provideris* in a way for which I can find no parallel in Cicero's use of substantival participles. However, there seems to be no satisfactory alternative to this interpretation, and it is of some interest that Marcus Brutus, in a letter to Cicero, uses a very similar dependent clause with an attributive future participle: ad Brut. 24. 10 *te, Cicero, rogo atque hortor, ne defatigere neu diffidas, semper in praesentibus malis prohibendis* futura quoque, nisi ante sit occursum,[1] *explores, ne se insinuent.*

Cicero twice uses the participle as a predicative adjective

---

[1] Suggestions for transposing this clause (see Sjögren's apparatus) are beside the mark.

(Type 1) : Tusc. 5. 16 *quid, qui non modo ea futura timet, verum etiam fert sustinetque praesentia*; Brut. 329 *sed fortunatus illius exitus, qui ea non vidit cum fierent quae providit futura.* It is possible, in the second passage, to take *futura* as infinitive. But concinnity is at the heart of Cicero's writing, and, in the sense of 'cum futura essent', *futura* provides a balance to *cum fierent* which an infinitive would impair, if not destroy.

Cicero's contribution to the development of the future participle may appear very modest, but we must remember that he took it over when it was not yet emancipated. If Gracchus was indeed the pioneer of its emancipation, we find no trace of his example being followed before Cicero. It was Cicero, we may believe, who laid the foundations for its predicative use, and if he showed conservatism in practically confining other uses to *futurus*, he gave the participle, here too, a measure of verbal freedom. Already before Cicero's death, we find a younger contemporary prepared to go further than Cicero himself. In a letter written by Brutus to Atticus in 43 B.C. occurs the following passage : ad Brut. 25. 2 *quid hoc mihi prodest, si merces Antoni oppressi poscitur in Antoni locum successio, et si vindex illius mali auctor exstitit alterius* fundamentum et radices habituri altiores, *si patiamur?*

VII

COMPLEX PARTICIPIAL
CONSTRUCTIONS

THE development of complex participial constructions in Greek
and Latin formed the subject of a monograph by C. Mugler,
published in 1938.[1] The author regarded as complex all constructions in which a participle was 'amplified' either by another
participle or by a subordinate clause, and attempted to maintain
the thesis that in Latin there was no continuous development of
such constructions, which he considered to be due, in the writers
in whom they occurred, to the influence of Greek syntax. In
particular, he argued that such constructions are almost entirely
lacking in Cicero (p. 132), who deliberately avoided them 'comme
s'il s'agissait d'un moyen d'expression incompatible avec l'esprit
de la langue latine' (p. 120).

The basic assumption from which Mugler sets out is, as
Marouzeau rightly pointed out in a review,[2] untenable. A participle is not 'amplified' by an accompanying subordinate
clause. The two are linked not to one another, but both to the
main clause. The number of parallel subordinating members *of
different types*, which a single Latin period can contain, is limited
only by considerations of symmetry and rhythm. In a period
such as the following, from Caesar, B.G. 2. 11. 1 *ea re constituta,
secunda vigilia magno cum strepitu ac tumultu castris egressi, nullo certo
ordine neque imperio, cum sibi quisque primum itineris locum peteret . . . ,
fecerunt ut consimilis fugae profectio videretur*, the various elements are
held together by their common dependence on the main clause,
and the difference of type ensures that there is no confusion.

But the element of complexity does appear when two participles occur in the same sentence, agreeing with the same noun,

[1] Ch. Mugler, *L'Évolution des constructions participiales complexes en grec et en latin*
(Paris, 1938).   [2] *R.É.L.* 17. 195 ff.

but not co-ordinated either by a conjunction or by asyndeton. Marouzeau (loc. cit.) disposes of such cases too easily when he refers them to the same principle that governs subordinating elements in general. The juxtaposition of two subordinating members grammatically identical has its own interest. Granted that both participles qualify the main sentence, what is their relationship to one another, since it is presumably not one of co-ordination, and how is confusion avoided?

I shall attempt to study the problem by surveying the considerable number of examples to be found in the works of Cicero. In the process it will, I hope, become clear that Mugler, who based his conclusions, so far as Cicero was concerned, on an examination of three works only (*Pro Roscio Amerino, In Catilinam,* and *Laelius*), was wrong in asserting that Cicero deliberately abstained from the usage. A feature which appears at least fifty times cannot be said to have been avoided, and when half of the instances occur, as they do, in the production of his later years, we must assume, if not development, at least no decline.

(1) Participles of different function

In some instances complexity is more apparent than real. The two participles may have recognizably different functions. Thus, an attributive participle is, in most cases, readily distinguishable from a predicative: fam. 1. 7. 3 *virum enim excellentem et tibi tua praestanti in eum liberalitātĕ dēvīnctūm | non nihil suspicantem . . . retinuisti.* The attributive character of *devinctum* is unmistakable (see pp. 57 f. and 69 above), and the clearness of the clause-ending at this word[1] makes confusion impossible. The following examples are similar: leg. agr. 2. 97 *nedum isti ab Rullo et Rulli similibus conquisiti et electī cŏlōnī | Capuae in domicilio superbiae atque in sedibus luxuriosis conlocati non statim conquisituri sint aliquid sceleris et flagiti;* fam. 1. 9. 13 *illud quidem certe nostrum consilium iure laudandum est, qui meos cives et a me conservatos et me servārĕ cŭpĭēntēs | spoliatos ducibus servis armatis obici noluerim.* It will be observed, in fam. 1. 9. 13,

---

[1] Ed. Fraenkel in 'Kolon und Satz', i (*Nachrichten der Gött. Ges. d. Wiss.* 1932) illustrates, from apparent instances of *enjambement* in Latin elegiacs, the fact that participial phrases can stand as separate syntactical members, no less than subordinate clauses. See especially pp. 202, 213; also 'Kolon und Satz', ii (1933), 348 f.

how the duplication of the attributive participles, and particularly their combination by *et . . . et*, emphasizes the colon. Sometimes one of the two participles is of the predicative adjective type (pp. 9 f.): Mur. 32 *quem L. Murena, pater huiusce, vehementissime vigilantissimēquĕ vēxātūm | repressum magna ex parte, non oppressum reliquit* ('after he had been incessantly harried, left him considerably curbed, but not crushed'; *vexatum* is a normal predicative participle; the partial antithesis *repressum . . . oppressum* makes clearer the division at *vexatum*); dom. 23 *homini taeterrimo . . . L. Pisoni nonne nominatim populos liberos, multis senatus consultis, etiam recenti lege generi ipsius lībĕrātōs, vinctos et constrictos tradidisti?* (*liberatos* could be read either as a predicative or as an attributive participle; *vinctos . . . tradidisti*—'handed over bound and shackled'; the duplication of the predicative adjective participles strengthens the colon at *liberatos*); Mil. 40 *cum M. Antonius . . . illam beluam iudicii laqueos declinantem | iam inretitam teneret* (the distinction of function is naturally enhanced by tense-difference).

If the second participle is completive (pp. 50 f.), its close association with the main verb is even more marked than that of the predicative adjective type. Cato 54 *at Homerus, qui multis, ut mihi videtur, ante saeculis fuit, Laertem lenientem desiderium, quod capiebat e filio, colentem agrum et eum stercorantem facit* (*lenientem* is normal predicative: 'depicts Laertes, while (by way of) assuaging the longing . . . as tilling his land and manuring it'); nat. deor. 1. 106 *ut Ti. Gracchum cum videor contionantem in Capitolio videre de M. Octavio deferentem sitellam, tum eum motum animi dico esse inanem* (*contionantem*—'in the middle of his speech'; as in the previous example, the more remote predicative participle comes first). In these passages colon-division is not prominent; the two participles are separated, in the first case, by a relative clause, in the second, by the main verb. Seyffert–Mueller, *Laelius*, p. 366, quotes, as a passage in which predicative and completive participles are combined, div. 1. 56 *qui cum ignotum quendam proiectum mortuum vidisset*. *mortuum* is here taken as predicative (appositive), *proiectum* as completive with *vidisset*. The order of words, however, is against this analysis; we should expect to find next to the verb the participle which is naturally the more closely attached to it, i.e. the completive. It is better to regard both participles as completing *vidisset*; either could be removed, and still leave the clause both grammatical and intelligible, but together they give the full picture intended. A similar example of two completive participles combined is fin. 3. 7 *quo cum venissem, M. Catonem, quem ibi esse nescieram, vidi in bibliotheca sedentem multis circumfusum Stoicorum libris.*

(2) Participles not distinguished by function

The largest and most interesting group, however, consists of passages in which two predicative participles are combined. Sest. 117 *cum vero ipse qui ludos faciebat consul assedit, stantes ei manibus passis* gratias agentes et lacrimantes gaudio *suam erga me benevolentiam ac misericordiam declaraverunt.* ibid. 118 *in eo homine cui tum* petenti iam aedilitatem *ne histriones quidem* coram sedenti *pepercerunt.* On Sest. 117 Holden[1] suggests that *stantes* is subordinate to *gratias agentes et lacrimantes.* Reid[2] proposes to insert *et* after *stantes*, remarking that 'the asyndeton *stantes . . . agentes* is entirely unlike Cicero. The case of *petenti . . . sedenti* is rendered quite different by the *ne . . . quidem'.* It is difficult to see how *ne . . . quidem* can possibly affect the participles. The two examples are entirely comparable, and involve neither inter-subordination nor asyndeton. In both these instances, and in many others which I shall presently quote, the first participle gives the remoter or more general background of the verbal action, the second qualifies the verb more closely. The two passages from the *Pro Sestio* should be translated thus: 117 '. . . standing up with arms outstretched[3] they manifested their goodwill and pity for me with expressions of gratitude and tears of joy'; 118 'in the case of that man whom, when he was actually a candidate for the aedileship, not even the actors spared as he sat in the audience'.

The pattern of the sentence is, in fact, precisely that which Nägelsbach, p. 632, gives as a characteristic form of the period in Latin: a: (b:A). In this pattern the subordinate clause (b)

---

[1] Edition of *Pro Sestio*, p. 224.
[2] In a note added after Holden's, loc. cit.
[3] The fact that the physical gesture of *manibus passis* goes more naturally with *stantes* is itself an argument against Reid's proposed insertion.

affects only the main clause (A), whilst the subordinate clause (a) depends on the complex (b:A). Nägelsbach quotes, as a typical example, de orat. 2. 279 *ut, cum Cato percussus esset ab eo qui arcam ferebat* (a), *cum ille diceret 'cave'* (b), *rogavit num quid aliud ferret praeter arcam* (A). It will be seen that the respective functions of the participles in the two passages from the *Pro Sestio* correspond exactly to those of the subordinate clauses in the extract from the *De Oratore*.

In considering the remaining Ciceronian instances of participial complexity, it may be possible to isolate certain features which help to mitigate or to avoid possible confusion.

(a) Subject interposed

In both the instances from the *Pro Sestio* quoted above the subject of the main verb is placed between the two participles: in Sest. 117 *ei*, in 118 *ne histriones quidem*, where the emphatic *ne . . . quidem* enhances the separative force of the noun. Other examples of this kind are: Mil. 43 *hunc igitur diem campi speratum atque exoptatum sibi proponens* | Milo *cruentis manibus scelus et facinus prae se ferens et confitens ad illa augusta centuriarum auspicia veniebat?* (when he had hopes of the consulship (background), was Milo likely to come to the assembly flaunting the crime of murder?); de orat. 2. 106 *ut eidem Carboni tribuno plebis alia tum mente rem publicam capessenti* | P. Africanus *de Ti. Graccho interroganti responderat iure caesum videri*; Phil. 2. 63 *in coetu vero populi Romani negotium publicum gerens* | magister equitum, *cui ructare turpe esset*, is *vomens frustis esculentis vinum redolentibus gremium suum et totum tribunal implevit* (by interposing not merely the subject, but also the relative clause and the resumptive *is*, Cicero succeeds in giving to *vomens* just the distasteful prominence at which he aims). In the last two passages we notice again that the more remote, or 'background', participle, which qualifies the whole sentence, comes first. Our earlier detailed analysis of the predicative present participle enables us to recognize distinctions not of function, but of type. Thus, in Phil. 2. 63 *gerens* is concomitant, *vomens* modal; in de orat. 2. 106 both participles are concomitant, but the second is of the 'reciprocal' variety.

(b) Main verb or clause interposed

In a number of passages either the main verb or the whole main clause[1] comes between the two participles: Att. 11. 9. 2 *illi ad me statim ardentes dolore* venerunt *scelus hominis clamantes* (*ardentes dolore* expresses the state of mind, *clamantes* the manner of its expression); rep. 6. 18 *nam terra nona immobilis manens* una sede semper haeret *complexa medium mundi locum*; Sest. 147 (*di immortales*) *qui me suis templis advenientem* receperunt *stipatum ab his viris et P. Lentulo consule*; dom. 63 *omnemque impetum discordiarum, omnem diu collectam vim improborum, quae inveterata compresso odio atque tacito* iam erumpebat *nancta tam audaces duces, excepi meo corpore* (*nancta . . . duces* gives the immediate occasion for *erumpebat, inveterata* the pre-existing condition); fin. 5. 74 *qua impulsi* multa faciunt *nullam quaerentes voluptatem* (*qua impulsi* in this stereotyped use (p. 5) is hardly felt as a participial phrase); Tusc. 5. 69 *cum totius mundi motus conversionesque perspexerit sideraque viderit innumerabilia caelo inhaerentia* cum eius ipsius motu congruere *certis infixa sedibus*; Att. 9. 2a. 3 *vixdum epistulam tuam legeram, cum ad me, currens ad illum*, Postumius Curtius venit *nihil nisi classes loquens et exercitus* (*currens*—concomitant, *loquens*—modal); Pis. 89 *quod inde te recipiens* in villa Euhadiae, quae fuit uxor Execesti, iacuisti *maerens aliquot dies* (*recipiens*—concomitant 'during your withdrawal', *maerens*—modal).

(c) Subordinate clause interposed

(i) *Relative*: fin. 4. 45 *mihi autem aequius videbatur Zenonem cum Polemone disceptantem*, a quo quae essent principia naturae acceperat, *a communibus initiis progredientem videre ubi primum insisteret et unde causa controversiae nasceretur, non stantem cum iis qui ne dicerent quidem sua summa bona esse a natura profecta, uti isdem argumentis quibus illi uterentur, isdemque sententiis.* The framework of this elaborate passage is *aequius videbatur Zenonem . . . videre . . . non uti . . .* &c. *disceptantem* is concomitant, 'in his discussion with Polemo'; *progredientem* and *stantem*, both modal, closely qualify *videre* and *uti* respectively. The separative effect of the relative clause (which itself contains an indirect question) is enhanced by

[1] With 'main' I include any clause which is qualified by both the participles.

the fact that it is an indicative clause inserted in a passage of oblique statement.

(ii) *Indirect interrogative*: fin. 1. 33 *at vero eos et accusamus et iusto odio dignissimos ducimus, qui blanditiis praesentium voluptatum deleniti atque corrupti*, quos dolores et quas molestias excepturi sint, *obcaecati cupiditate non provident*.

(iii) *Ablative absolute*: invent. 1. 102 *quintus locus est per quem ostendimus ceteras res perperam constitutas* intellecta veritate *commutatas corrigi posse; hanc esse rem quae si sit semel iudicata, neque alio commutari iudicio neque ulla potestate corrigi possit*. The almost adverbial force of *commutatas* has been noticed on p. 16 above.

(iv) Cum-*clause*: Tusc. 5. 64 (Archimedes) *cuius ego quaestor ignoratum ab Syracusanis*, cum esse omnino negarent, *saeptum undique et vestitum vepribus et dumetis indagavi sepulcrum*.

A similar separative influence is seen in the correlative prepositional phrases in Brut. 320 *longius autem procedens* | ut in ceteris eloquentiae partibus tum maxime in celeritate et continuatione verborum *adhaerescens sui dissimilior videbatur fieri cotidie*, where the construction of these phrases with *adhaerescens* is made clearer by the colon-end at *procedens*, and vice versa. Mutual disjunction of the same kind is to be seen in Planc. 33 *ubi illa antiqua libertas, quae malis oppressa civilibus* | extollere iam caput et aliquando *recreata se erigere debebat?* The interposition of the first of the two coordinate infinitives not only separates the participles, but by its dependence on *debebat* reinforces the break at *civilibus*.

The passages which we have just been examining enable us to interpret with confidence nat. deor. 1. 41 *quem Diogenes Babylŏnĭŭs cōnsĕquēns* | in eo libro, qui inscribitur de Minerva, partum Iovis ortumque virginis ad physiologiam traducens diiungit a fabula. There is a colon-end at *consequens*, the 'background' participle ('following his example') ; *in eo libro . . . Minerva* is therefore to be taken with the main verb *diiungit*, of which *ad physiologiam traducens* is a modal qualification.

(d) Distinction made chiefly by colon

In most of the examples considered so far the participial colon has been a factor in distinguishing the two participles. In many instances it is the main factor, though there is usually present some other feature to enhance the distinction and emphasize the break. Cato 56 *cuius dictatoris iussu magister equitum C. Servilius Ahala Sp. Maelium* regnum adpetentem | occupatum interemit; Tusc. 2. 23 *has igitur* poenas pendens | adfixus ad Caucasum *dicit haec.* In both these examples the colon, which alone separates the participles, is assisted by the formal difference of tense. In both examples the first participle is more general than the second; in Tusc. 2. 23 *poenas pendens* refers to Prometheus' general situation, *adfixus ad Caucasum* to the particular circumstances of *dicit.*

Phil. 2. 45 *recordare tempus illud, cum pater Curio maerens iacebat in lecto, filius* se ad pedes meos prosternens | lacrimans *te mihi commendabat.* Both *prosternens* and *lacrimans* are modal, but *lacrimans,* more stereotyped as a simple adverb, attaches itself closely to the verb, and thus emphasizes the clause-division. The same is true of *flens* in Flacc. 102, where, again, both participles are modal: *cum ego te, Flacce,* caelum noctemque contestans | flens flentem *obtestabar;* here, however, the separative effect of the colon is further enhanced by the use of the colloquial figura etymologica *flens flentem.*

fam. 15. 15. 3 *ego qui festinavi, ut Caesarem in Italia viderem . . . eumque multis honestissimis viris conservatis* redeuntem | ad pacem currentem, *ut aiunt, incitarem, ab illo longissime et absum et afui.* The ablative absolute qualifying the participle *redeuntem* has been noticed in an earlier chapter. For our present purpose, it is to be observed how the two present participles are effectively separated, and the colon ending at *redeuntem* (or possibly at *pacem*) strengthened, by the use of the proverbial phrase *currentem incitare.*

div. 2. 145 *parere quaedam matrona* cupiens | dubitans essetne praegnans, *visa est in quiete obsignatam habere naturam. cupiens* expresses the general state of mind, *dubitans* the particular state in which the dream occurred. The indirect interrogative clause introduced by *dubitans* tends to detach that participle from *cupiens.*

In several passages the duplication of the second participle, either by co-ordination or by antithesis, serves to emphasize the colon: div. 1. 58 (*narravi*) *me, cum Asiae pro consule praeessem,*

vidisse in quiete, cum tu equo advectus ad quandam magni fluminis ripam |
provectus subito atque delapsus in flumen *nusquam apparuisses*; de
orat. 1. 36 *quis enim tibi hoc concesserit* . . . *initio genus hominum in
montibus ac silvis dissipatum* | non prudentium consiliis compulsum
potius quam disertorum oratione delenitum *se oppidis moenibusque
saepsisse?*; Sest. 64 *qui me civem nullo meo crimine patriae nomine
laborantem* | non modo stantem non defenderunt sed ne iacentem
quidem protexerunt. Rarely, the first participle is duplicated
with similar effect. One instance, in fam. 1. 9. 13, has already
been noted (pp. 126 f.). To this we may add Sull. 17 *ille* relictus
intus, exspectatus foris, | *Lentuli poena compressus convertit se ali-
quando ad timorem*. The antithesis between *intus* and *foris* makes it
clear that the essential colon-division is at *foris*. An unusual
arrangement is seen in Tusc. 5. 37 *itaque et arbores et vites et ea
quae sunt humiliora neque se tollere a terra altius possunt, alia semper
virent, alia* hieme *nudata* | verno tempore *tepefacta frondescunt*. The
arrangement is unusual, because it sets up an antithesis between
two participles which are not in the same relationship to the main
verb. In effect, the antithesis is between *nudata* and the phrase
tepefacta frondescunt; that is to say, by emphasizing the indivisibility
of the latter phrase, it strengthens the colon ending at *nudata*.

(3) Some doubtful passages

Three passages in which the complexity is more difficult to
analyse must be discussed at greater length. har. resp. 22 *vis enim
innumerabilis incitata ex omnibus vicis collecta servorum ab hoc aedile
religioso repente e fornicibus ostiisque omnibus in scaenam signo dato
inmissa inrupit*. The problems here centre round *incitata*[1] and some
unexpected features in the word-order. In particular, what is the
relationship, if any, of *incitata* to *collecta*, why is *servorum* so far removed from its governing noun (*vis*), and with which past participle is *ab hoc aedile* to be taken, *collecta* or *immissa*? The Loeb
translator's version of the first half of the sentence is: 'For innumerable bands of slaves that had been mustered by this
scrupulous aedile from every quarter of the city and had been
incited for the occasion . . . .' Without dwelling on the slovenly

---

[1] Ernesti had doubts about the genuineness of the word.

and inaccurate 'innumerable bands', we must observe that the translation 'and had been incited for the occasion' (note the gratuitous addition) implies that the translator understood *incitata* as a predicative participle dependent on the predicative participle *collecta*. Dependence of this kind is quite foreign to Cicero, nor is it easy to see in what way *incitata* and *collecta* could be taken as parallel predicative participles, co-ordinate with one another. *incitata*, therefore, must be attributive. It is used here, in fact, as a simple attributive adjective, attached, without conjunction, to *vis innumerabilis*, in which phrase noun and attribute form virtually a single idea.[1] If Cicero had chosen a more ordinary quantitative adjective than *innumerabilis*, if, for instance, he had said *vis magna incitata*, the attributive character of *incitata* would have been easily recognizable.

We might have expected *servorum* to be placed immediately after *incitata*. This would have had the added result of bringing together *collecta* and *ab hoc aedile*. The interposition of such an alien word as *servorum* between the participle and the ablative phrase seems to have been done deliberately to dissociate them from one another, and the belief that this is so is confirmed by the sarcastic epithet *religioso*, which is much more relevant to Clodius' actual disturbance of the games than to his previous assembling of a troop of slaves. Furthermore, *cōllēctă sērvōrŭm* exhibits the most characteristic of all Cicero's clausula rhythms.

The colon, therefore, ends at *servorum*. The ablative phrase *ab hoc religioso aedile* is placed at the head of its clause for emphasis; *inmissa*, the participle with which that phrase is constructed, is in close juxtaposition with the main verb to express the swift succession of events (see pp. 15 f.). Every word in the sentence stands *suo loco*, and the participial pattern reveals itself once more as a:(b:A). 'For a countless excited mob of slaves, gathered together from all quarters of the city, was by the act of this scrupulous aedile, from all archways and entrances, suddenly, at a given signal, let loose, and burst upon the stage.'[2]

---

[1] See Kühner–Stegmann, 240.

[2] Professor Fraenkel suspects *servorum* to be a gloss (from *servorum eludentium multitudini*, a few lines later), and observes that the clausula -*cis collecta* would then be the same as -*missa inrupit* at the end of the period ($- \smile - \smile$).

About the other two passages I feel less confidence in the solution which I have to offer. They are, so far as I am aware, the only two places in Cicero where the question of interdependence between two participia coniuncta can possibly arise. Tusc. 3. 39 *huiusne vitae propositio et cogitatio aut Thyesten levare poterit aut Aeetam, de quo paulo ante dixi, aut Telamonem* pulsum patria exulantem atque egentem? The participles do not seem to be co-ordinate, and one is tempted to translate 'living in exile and penury after being driven from his country'. A similar interpretation of the participles appears to be called for in the second, and more perplexing, passage. div. 2. 85 *is est hodie locus saeptus religiose propter Iovis pueri, qui lactens* cum Iunone Fortunae in gremio sedens, mammam appetens, *castissime colitur a matribus* (? 'reaching for the breast of Fortune as he sits in her lap'). With *Iovis pueri* we must supply a noun such as *sacellum* or *statuam*. *lactens* has been condemned as a gloss by some editors, but it may be used here substantivally, like *infans*, 'as a suckling'. Rath[1] proposed to delete *est* and to read *sedet* for *sedens*. This solution has not found acceptance, and it is certainly a somewhat drastic cutting of the knot. It deserves mention, however, because, apart from removing a difficult combination of participles, it produces a sense which seems to me better suited to the context. The subject of *colitur* is now not *qui* (i.e. *Iuppiter puer*), but *locus*, and Juno is no longer so pointedly ignored.

But if we cannot avail ourselves of this escape-route, is there any way of explaining the relationship between the participles in this and the preceding passage, other than by assuming an interdependence which is not to be found elsewhere in Cicero? A. S. Pease in his commentary (Illinois, 1920, p. 492) refers the reader, for a discussion of the participles, to T. Wopkens, *Lectiones Tullianae* (1829), pp. 193 ff.[2] Wopkens, in fact, is not very helpful. He explains the passage as an instance of participles in asyndeton, and quotes parallels, but his Ciceronian 'parallels' do not suggest a real understanding of the problem. Tusc. 1. 1 *quae retenta*

---

[1] I derive this information from Orelli's apparatus.
[2] I have only been able to consult the edition of 1730, in which the reference is to p. 138.

animo, remissa temporibus, longo intervallo intermissa revocavi, where the asyndeton is obviously rhetorical (see Pohlenz ad loc.), is not comparable; nor are nat. deor. 1. 41 (a:(b:A) pattern, p. 131 above) and ibid. 106 (participles of different function, p. 106). The only passage which seems to be really relevant is Tusc. 2. 19 *itaque exclamat auxilium expetens, mori cupiens*, and here, perhaps, we can see some light. If we look at our three instances together, Tusc. 3. 39, div. 2. 85, and Tusc. 2. 19, we find that they have one feature in common, in that all three occur in, as it were, pictorial descriptions. div. 2. 85 describes a sculptured group; the two extracts from the Tusculans describe characters in tragedies. In each case the second participle amplifies and completes the picture given by the first. This kind of amplification is analogous to that which we have already seen (p. 128), with two completive participles, in fin. 3. 7 *M. Catonem . . . vidi in bibliotheca sedentem multis circumfusum Stoicorum libris*. Tentative as this explanation is, I find it easier to accept than interdependence.

(4) Absolute participles in complex construction

Although, generally speaking, Cicero does not exploit the subordinating power of the absolute participle as he does that of the participium coniunctum, there are a few passages in which the arrangement of absolute phrases seems to correspond to the a:(b:A) pattern: Sull. 56 *tum autem illo profecto, Sulla procurante eius rem et gerente, plurimis et pulcherrimis P. Sitti praediis venditis aes alienum eiusdem dissolutum est* (the first two phrases give the background circumstances; the third, *plurimis . . . venditis* closely qualifies the main verb); dom. 79 *consulari homini P. Clodius eversa re publica civitatem adimere potuit concilio advocato, conductis operis non solum egentium, sed etiam servorum* (*eversa re publica*, which corresponds to *re publica recuperata* in the previous sentence, is certainly the background phrase; *concilio advocato* and *conductis operis* belong more closely to *adimere potuit*, which is interposed); post red. ad Q. 15 *eodemque P. Lentulo auctore et pariter referente collega frequentissimus senatus uno dissentiente, nullo intercedente dignitatem meam quibus potuit verbis amplissimis ornavit* (*auctore* and *referente* are logically and temporally prior to the other two phrases; the subject of the main verb is interposed).

It cannot be said that in any of these passages the relationship between the absolute phrases is as clear as in many of the examples in which participia coniuncta have been observed in the a:(b:A) pattern, but in each case a distinction seems to be discernible between remoter and more immediately qualifying phrases.

Interdependence, however, of which, between participia coniuncta, Cicero offers no clear instance, appears several times in his treatment of absolute participles. A probable example has been quoted in an earlier chapter (pp. 116 f.): the following seem to be certain:[1] fam. 9. 18. 1 *ex quibus intellexi probari tibi meum consilium, quod, ut Dionysius tyrannus, cum Syracusis pulsus esset, Corinthi dicitur ludum aperuisse,* sic ego sublatis iudiciis amisso regno forensi *ludum quasi habere coeperim* (Cicero is making an explicit comparison, and the whole phrase *sublatis . . . forensi* is intended to correspond to *cum Syracusis pulsus esset*; *sublatis iudiciis* explains *amisso regno forensi*); Pis. 26 *an tum eras consul cum in Palatio mea domus ardebat non casu aliquo, sed* ignibus iniectis instigante te? (again, what corresponds to *casu aliquo* is the whole phrase *ignibus . . . te*); Att. 4. 3. 2 *deinde inflammata (domus est)* iussu Clodi, inspectante urbe coniectis ignibus, *magna querela et gemitu non dicam bonorum . . . sed plane hominum omnium* (no conceivable punctuation could make it natural to take *inspectante urbe* otherwise than as qualifying *coniectis ignibus*).

That Cicero was prepared to allow interdependence between absolute participles is in keeping with the adaptability of the ablative absolute phrase to be attached to other parts of the sentence than a finite verb (see pp. 112 ff.). If an absolute participle can qualify a participium coniunctum, especially when used as in ad Brut. 23. 5 *oppressa ab impiis civitas opitulandi potestate praecisa*, its attachment to another absolute participle presents little difficulty.

Complex participial structure of the kind which we have been

---

[1] Kühner–Stegmann, 782 f., in illustrating this feature, has no instance from Cicero.

examining in Cicero is not found in early Latin. There are certainly passages in Plautus and Terence which contain two or more participles combined without conjunction: e.g. Aul. 727 *quinam homo hic ante aedes nostras eiulans conqueritur maerens*; Curc. 124 *nam tibi amantes propitiantes vinum potantes danunt omnes*; Pseud. 1271 *illos accubantis, potantis, amantis cum scortis reliqui*; Rud. 560 f. *Veneris signum flentes amplexae tenent nescioquem metuentes miserae*; Haut. 182 *advenientem e navi egredientem ilico abduxi ad cenam*. But in these and other passages the participles are accumulated, without any attempt to distinguish their status (in Aul. 727 and Rud. 560 f. the remoter participle follows a more immediately adverbial one). There is as yet no pattern in their arrangement.

Indeed, the deliberate use of complex participial construction could only begin when the participle had acquired the power to represent a clause, since this use is based upon clause-structure, and presupposes a state of the language in which subordinate clauses were well developed. That stage was not reached before the time of Cicero, and it is very probable that these artistic ways of combining participles all grew up in Cicero's lifetime, if they were not all initiated by him. The bulk of Cicero's examples, and the most subtle ones, come from his latest period. In his early works instances are infrequent, and sometimes seem to lack something of the clarity and sureness of touch which we find later. In Verr. II. 4. 84 *quid? a Tyndaritanis non eiusdem Scipionis beneficio positum simulacrum Mercuri pulcherrime factum sustulisti?*, it is not clear whether the first participle is predicative or attributive. If the latter, this is the only instance known to me of two attributive participles being attached to a noun in this way (the case of a definition such as we find at Phil. 11. 28[1] is different). If the former, one would expect a colon either at *positum* or at *Mercuri*, and at neither place is such a break admissible. Verr. II. 5. 142 *sic ille adfectus illim tum pro mortuo sublatus perbrevi postea est mortuus* seems to exhibit the incipient a:(b:A) pattern, but the distinction of status between the participles is not well marked, and one would expect a stronger colon ending at *adfectus*. In both these

---

[1] *est enim lex nihil aliud nisi recta et a numine deorum tracta ratio, imperans honesta, prohibens contraria.* See pp. 53 f. above.

passages one suspects that Cicero is handling a technical problem which has yet to be satisfactorily solved. That he did solve it is evidenced by the number and elegance of the examples of participial complexity which are to be found in the works written during the last twelve years of his life.[1]

[1] I have found one good example of the a :(b :A) pattern among Cicero's correspondents, in a letter written by Lentulus in 43 B.C. fam. 12. 14. 4 *exclusus enim ab Antiochia Dolabella et in oppugnando male acceptus | nulla alia confisus urbe Laodiceam . . . se contulit.*

VIII

THE PARTICIPLE IN DIFFERENT GENRES

ONE of the most interesting features of Cicero's use of participles is that they are not evenly distributed through his writing, and this unevenness is too pronounced to be explained merely by the fact that mechanical regularity is not to be expected when we are dealing with linguistic phenomena. In a given work the average incidence of participles may be two or three to a page, but the actual distribution is such that, whilst some pages contain as many as eight or nine participles, there may be stretches of two or more pages without a single occurrence. It may be possible to explain this inequality, and to see in what contexts and for what purposes Cicero found participles specially convenient, if we survey works in different genres, written at or about the same time. I have chosen for consideration a cross-section of Cicero's latest production: the Philippics, the *De Officiis* and (because of its different subject-matter) the somewhat earlier *Orator*, and the letters of 44–43 B.C.

(1) The Philippics

The average incidence of participles is just over two per Teubner page, but there is considerable discrepancy between individual speeches. The lowest average, in the Seventh, is less than one; the highest, in the Ninth, is three. If we look at the distribution throughout a particular speech, we notice a strong tendency for the participles to be concentrated in groups. The Third Philippic, for instance, gives the result facing.

Even more noteworthy is the short Sixth speech, in which nine of the seventeen participles occur in the first three sections, yet not one in sections 4–8. Nor is this the longest such gap. In the Seventh speech there are seven consecutive sections (20–26,

2½ pages) without a participle; in the Eighth a stretch of fourteen sections (7–20, 5½ pages) contains only one commonplace ablative absolute. It cannot be said that the sections without participles represent a flatter or less elevated style; sometimes, indeed, they show Cicero at his most eloquent.

The most promising line of inquiry seems to be to examine some of the passages which exhibit the highest concentration of participles. Let us begin with 6. 1–3 (already mentioned) and 3. 30–33 (see table below). Cicero begins his Sixth Philippic (to the people) by describing the events leading up to the Senate's

Sections	Participles	Sections	Participles	Sections	Participles
1–3	2	15	2	26, 27	4
4	3	16–18	none	28, 29	none
5–7	2	19, 20	4	30–33	14
8, 9	8	21, 22	none	34, 35	1
10–12	3	23	1	36	4
13, 14	none	24, 25	6	37–39	none

decision to send envoys to Antony. He refers to his own speech of 20 December and the popular support for his policy: 2 *hoc vestro iudicio tanto tamque praeclaro excitatus ita Kalendis Ianuariis veni in senatum, ut meminissem quam personam impositam a vobis sustinerem.* The recent Senate debate has resulted in a decision disappointing to Cicero himself: *hodierno autem die spe nescio qua eis obiecta remissior senatus fuit,* and he gives reasons why he believes the decision must be unwelcome to his hearers: 3 *ad quem enim legatos? ad eumne qui pecunia publica dissipata atque effusa, per vim . . . impositis rei publicae legibus, fugata contione, obsesso senatu ad opprimendam rem publicam Brundisio legiones accersierit, ab iis relictus cum latronum manu in Galliam inruperit, Brutum oppugnet, Mutinam circumsedeat?* He then proceeds, in the remainder of the speech, to enlarge on the uselessness of negotiation with Antony.

In sections 30–33 of the Third speech Cicero shows how intolerable is the prospect of Antony in power, in view of his past behaviour (30–31, 7 participles); the circumstances will never be more favourable for resisting him: 32 *non tempore oblato, ducibus paratis, animis militum incitatis, populo Romano conspirante, Italia tota ad libertatem reciperandam excitata*[1] *deorum immortalium beneficio utemini? nullum erit tempus hoc amisso . . . magna vis est, magnum numen unum et idem sentientis senatus . . .* 33 *hunc ego diem exspectans M. Antoni scelerata arma vitavi, tum cum ille in me absentem invehens non intellegebat, quod ad tempus me et meas vires reservarem. si enim tum illi caedis a me initium quaerenti respondere voluissem, nunc rei publicae consulere non possem. hanc vero nactus facultatem nullum tempus, patres conscripti, dimittam neque diurnum neque nocturnum . . .* &c.

From these two passages it seems possible to discern two separate motives for the concentration of participles; first, to avoid diffuseness in the description of a succession of events or of the various factors in a given situation, and secondly, to ensure that such factors or events receive the desired prominence. Perhaps we shall be able to recognize the presence of one or both of these motives in other passages. Cicero begins his First Philippic by explaining his reasons for withdrawing from Rome and for his unpremeditated return. Having devoted six sections (2 pages) to his withdrawal, Cicero evidently felt that it would be inappropriate to deal with his return at equal length: 7 *exposui, p.c., profectionis consilium: nunc reversionis, quae plus admirationis habet, breviter exponam.* He does so in three sections (1 page) containing six participles. Similar considerations seem to have influenced him in 12. 7–10, where eleven participles occur in the space of 1½ pages. He is arguing against the sending of peace proposals to Antony, and in these sections he describes the probable reaction of various groups to such a course. Diffuse treatment here would not only have been tedious, but would have destroyed the cumulative forcefulness of the passage.

The motive of forcefulness seems to predominate in the following illustrations. In 2. 64 he describes the infamous auction of Pompey's property, for which Antony was the only bidder: *hasta posita pro aede Iovis Statoris bona Cn. Pompei—miserum me! consumptis enim lacrimis tamen infixus animo haeret dolor—bona, inquam, Cn. Pompei Magni voci acerbissimae subiecta praeconis. una in illa re servitutis oblita civitas ingemuit servientibusque animis, cum omnia metu*

---

[1] Here, as often, the participles lend themselves to the principle of expansion ('wachsende Glieder', see E. Lindholm, *Stilistische Studien*, Lund, 1931, p. 16) which pervades Cicero's writing.

tenerentur, gemitus tamen populi Romani liber fuit. exspectantibus omnibus quisnam esset tam impius, tam demens, tam dis hominibusque hostis qui ad illud scelus sectionis auderet accedere, inventus est nemo praeter Antonium. Dolabella's murder of Trebonius is vividly sketched in six lines containing five participles: 11. 5 *consularem hominem consulari imperio provinciam Asiam obtinentem Samiario exsuli tradidit: interficere captum statim noluit, ne nimis, credo, in victoria liberalis videretur. cum verborum contumeliis optimum virum incesto ore lacerasset, tum verberibus ac tormentis quaestionem habuit pecuniae publicae, idque per biduum. post cervicibus fractis caput abscidit, idque adfixum gestari iussit in pilo; reliquum corpus tractum atque laniatum abiecit in mare.* In the last sentence especially we should notice the stark concentration of detail achieved by the use of participles. A similar kind of effect (though the context is quite different) is produced in the Ninth speech—Cicero's tribute to Servius Sulpicius—at the end of his peroration, where, after nearly a page without a participle, Cicero concludes with three in close succession. I quote the latter part of the passage: 9. 14 *maiores quidem nostri statuas multis decreverunt, sepulcra paucis. sed statuae intereunt tempestate, vi, vetustate: sepulcrorum autem sanctitas in ipso solo est, quod nulla vi moveri neque deleri potest, atque ut cetera exstinguuntur sic sepulcra sanctiora fiunt vetustate. augeatur igitur isto honore etiam is vir, cui nullus honos tribui non debitus potest; grati simus in eius morte decoranda, cui nullam iam aliam gratiam referre possumus. notetur etiam M. Antoni nefarium bellum gerentis scelerata audacia. his enim honoribus habitis Ser. Sulpicio repudiatae reiectaeque legationis ab Antonio manebit testificatio sempiterna.* In three lines Cicero succinctly reminds his hearers of what, although he is speaking of Sulpicius, he is most concerned to emphasize; the fact that Antony is a public enemy, whose conduct makes it impossible to have dealings with him.

Not all groups of participles are to be explained in this way. Concinnity is the reason for many smaller groups, not merely for simple pairs such as 2. 37 *propter vitae cupiditatem, quae me manens conficeret angoribus, dimissa molestiis omnibus liberaret,* or 12. 4 *si iacens vobiscum aliquid ageret, audirem fortasse:* . . . *stanti resistendum est aut concedenda una cum dignitate libertas,* but for such passages as 3. 8–9 *neque enim* Tarquinio expulso *maioribus nostris tam fuit optata libertas quam est* depulso Antonio *retinenda nobis. illi regibus parere iam* a condita urbe *didicerant: nos* post reges exactos *servitutis oblivio ceperat.* The use of ablatives absolute in series is an inherited feature, as has already been observed, and typical examples are to be seen in 1. 30 or 3. 32 (quoted pp. 115, 141 f.).

Occasionally, where there is no question of concinnity, Cicero uses, in close succession, two or more participles of the same type. In 2. 92, for example, three absolute present participles (*te gubernante . . . inspectantibus vobis . . . stante re publica*), quite unrelated to one another, occur in the space of eight lines. Similarly, in 5. 17 *post conditam urbem* is followed, three lines later, by *post civitatem a L. Bruto liberatam.* 12. 18 shows three examples of the *ab urbe condita* construction in close proximity: *non quo ita sit aut esse possit, sed mentio a te facta pacis suspicionem multis attulit inmutatae voluntatis. inter has personas me interiectum amici Antoni moleste ferunt.* It seems possible that these and similar groupings have come about by subconscious syntactical repetition (see p. 109 note).

Though Cicero always handles his participles with artistry, it is comparatively seldom that he introduces them purely for artistic effect. We have seen that certain participial usages lent themselves to rhetorical exploitation, and examples are certainly not lacking in the Philippics: e.g. 1. 19 *quae lex melior, utilior,* optima etiam in re publica saepius flagitata; 9. 6 *at ille* properans, festinans, mandata vestra conficere cupiens, *in hac constantia morbo adversante perseveravit*; 10. 6 *quod verbum tibi non excidit, ut saepe fit, fortuito:* scriptum, meditatum, cogitatum *attulisti.* But if stylistic effectiveness had been a main consideration, we should expect to find participles most abundant in the most elevated passages, whereas, in fact, some of Cicero's most eloquent pages are almost or entirely devoid of participial usages. The reader need only be referred, for instance, to the last two pages (sections 11–16) of the Fourth speech or to the last three (sections 20–27) of the Fifth, in order to be convinced that this is so. When Cicero was free to enlarge on a given topic, to spread his wings and bring his rhetorical art to bear on the feelings of his audience, he had no need of participles, except for such commonplace uses as were current in everyday speech. As an orator, he found participles valuable chiefly as a means, adaptable to any sentence-pattern, of introducing relevant information or significant detail, without interrupting or retarding the flow of his utterance. He used them to achieve not conciseness of form, but fullness and pregnancy of content.

(2) The *De Officiis* and the *Orator*

In the treatises the distribution of participles is noticeably more even than in the speeches; there are neither such striking concentrations of participles nor such long intervals without any participial use. This, indeed, is to be expected in what Cicero himself calls (off. 1. 3) 'hoc . . . aequabile et temperatum orationis genus'. In the two works under consideration groupings analogous to those found in the Philippics occur only at two places, both in the third book of the *De Officiis*. The first is in the introductory sections 1–4 (1½ pages), which contain eight participles. Cicero is explaining how the unhappy political situation at Rome has driven him from public life and provided him with leisure to devote himself to literary and philosophical pursuits. Diffuseness here would have been out of taste and inappropriate to his present theme. The second is in sections 112–14 (nine participles in two pages), where Cicero gives in succession three illustrative anecdotes from Roman history.

The most interesting feature about the treatises, however, is not the distribution of participles, but the difference in the relative proportions of the types of participle used. In the Philippics predicative and absolute participles account for 71 per cent. of the total; in the *De Officiis* the figure is 58 per cent. On the other hand, in the case of attributive and substantival uses the situation is reversed; in the Philippics 14·5 per cent. and 3·5 per cent., in the *De Officiis* 22 per cent. and 10 per cent. respectively. That is to say, in the *De Officiis* these uses are almost twice as frequent. The reason is not far to seek. In the Philippics participles are used mainly in the description of actual events and circumstances, and therefore they naturally tend to be either predicative or absolute. In the *De Officiis* such participles find their place in factual and illustrative passages, but the main argument of the work is concerned with human beings, qualities, and actions, conceived not individually, but as types or classes, for which the attributive and substantival uses of the participle often provide the neatest modes of expression. A few examples will make this clear: off. 1. 13 *ut nemini parere animus bene informatus a natura velit nisi praecipienti aut docenti aut utilitatis causa iuste et legitime imperanti*; ibid. 1. 81 *haec sunt opera magni animi et excelsi et prudentia consilioque fidentis*; ibid. 1. 88 *ne si irascamur aut intempestive accedentibus aut impudenter rogantibus in morositatem . . . incidamus*; 2. 6 *hominum est parum considerate loquentium atque in maximis rebus errantium*.

The same is essentially true of the *Orator*, where the proportion of attributive and substantival participles is very nearly the same as in the *De Officiis* (attributive 23%; substantival 9·5%). Much of the discussion is abstract, in that it deals with features of style and with the qualities of the hypothetical *summus orator*. It will suffice to quote two passages which well illustrate the characteristic exploitation of attributive and substantival participles. In the first (20–21) Cicero is describing the three oratorical styles: 20 *nam et grandiloqui, ut ita dicam, fuerunt . . . vehementes varii, copiosi graves, ad permovendos et convertendos animos instructi et parati—quod ipsum alii aspera tristi horrida oratione neque perfecta atque conclusa ⟨consequebantur⟩,*[1] *alii levi et structa et terminata—et contra tenues, acuti, omnia docentes et dilucidiora, non ampliora facientes, subtili quadam et pressa oratione limati; in eodemque genere alii callidi . . ., alii in eadem ieiunitate concinniores . . ., florentes etiam et leviter ornati. est autem quidam interiectus inter hos medius et quasi temperatus nec acumine posteriorum nec fulmine utens superiorum, vicinus amborum, in neutro excellens . . . isque uno tenore, ut aiunt, in dicendo fluit nihil adferens praeter facultatem et aequalitatem.* All the participles here, except the last, are attributive. The second illustration, in which Cicero is summing up the virtues of the orator, is worth quoting in full, in spite of its length, because it strikingly exhibits the way in which Cicero invokes both these types of participle in the treatises: 227 *et nec sententia ulla est quae fructum oratori ferat, nisi apte exposita atque absolute, nec verborum lumen apparet nisi diligenter conlocatorum. et horum utrumque numerus inlustrat; numerus autem—saepe*

[1] add. Piderit.

enim hoc testandum est—non modo non poetice vinctus, verum etiam fugiens illum eique omnium dissimillimus; non quin idem sint numeri non modo oratorum et poetarum, verum omnino loquentium, denique etiam sonantium omnium quae metiri auribus possumus, sed ordo pedum facit, ut id quod pronuntiatur aut orationis aut poematis simile videatur. hanc igitur sive compositionem sive perfectionem sive numerum vocari placet, adhibere necesse est, si ornate velis dicere, non solum, quod ait Aristoteles et Theophrastus, ne infinite feratur ut flumen oratio, quae non aut spiritu pronuntiantis aut interductu librarii, sed numero coacta debet insistere, verum etiam quod multo maiorem habent apta vim quam soluta.

Prominent enough in the *De Officiis* to deserve mention is the use of the adverbial present participle agreeing with the subject. Since in this, as in other treatises, Cicero is much concerned with describing human behaviour, the comparative frequency of the use is natural, and helps to account for the marked development of adverbial participles in Cicero's last period (p. 45). Often the subject is unspecified: e.g. 1. 80 *fortis vero animi et constantis est non perturbari . . . nec tumultuantem de gradu deici*; 2. 67 *licet tamen opera prodesse multis beneficia petentem, commendantem iudicibus, magistratibus, vigilantem pro re alterius, eos ipsos, qui aut consuluntur aut defendunt, rogantem*; 3. 25 *magis est secundum naturam . . . maximos labores molestiasque suscipere imitantem Herculem illum . . . quam vivere in solitudine . . . abundantem omnibus copiis* (cf. 1. 92, 124; 2. 64; 3. 24, 63). The participle is also found attached to a first person plural (1. 17), to an indefinite second person (1. 111), and to the *sapiens, bonus, fortis vir* (3. 31). The subject-matter of the *Orator* offers fewer opportunities for a similar use of this type of participle, but I have noted a number of instances where it is applied to the practice of the ideal orator (59, 85, 122, 138, 231).

(3) The correspondence of 44–43 B.C.

In describing Cicero's letters as a genre we must beware of thinking that they exhibit a single style which can be called 'colloquial'. It is true that many are informal documents, which reflect the *sermo cotidianus*. But there are many letters in which the writing is as elaborate and elevated as anything in the speeches, and often in a single letter Cicero will pass from one manner to another, as his mood changes or as his theme prompts him. This point is well emphasized in a recent remark of Eduard Fraenkel: 'With a stylist as consummate as Cicero, to whom it had become second nature to express every thought and every shade of feeling in the form most adequate to a particular content, the sentence structure and, depending on it, the rhythm of his letters were no longer a matter of deliberate choice—let alone a dress to be put on at will—but were on the contrary the natural and necessary outcome of that frame of mind in which he happened to be at the time of writing.'[1] We must bear this in mind in considering the use Cicero makes of participles in the letters which he wrote between May 44 and July 43 B.C.

We may begin with one of the most informal parts of this correspondence, the letters written to Atticus between mid-May and mid-November 44 B.C., and contained in Books 15 and 16. At the beginning of the series we find Cicero in retirement and in a state of uncertainty and despondency. Many of the letters in Book 15 are short, and most are written in an informal and desultory manner. Often Cicero has nothing to say, except to comment on points in the letter to which he is replying. Participles are few and mostly commonplace, such as might readily occur unsought in ordinary conversation. An exception to the general tenor is letter 11, in which Cicero records a conversation which he has had with Brutus and Cassius at Antium. He has something to write about, and he is obviously in better spirits. The style, though informal, is not desultory, and there is a visible liveliness (e.g. sect. 1 *hoc loco fortibus sane oculis Cassius (Martem spirare diceres) se in Siciliam non iturum*). There are seven participles in two pages, and one feels that they have not happened by chance, but are an integral part of the description. One, for instance, occurs in a metaphor of the ship of state: 11. 3 *prorsus dissolutum offendi navigium vel potius dissipatum*; another is used in an antithesis: ibid. 4 *etenim erat absurdum, quae si stetisset res publica vovissem, ea me eversa illa vota dissolvere.*

The letters of Book 16 fall into two groups. The first seven were written between early July and mid-August. Cicero has made up his mind to depart for Greece; he is less uncertain, less depressed, and his letters become more fluent. In letter 3 he jokes with Atticus about a manuscript which he is sending him: 3. 1 *hunc tu tralatum in macrocollum lege in arcano convivis tuis sed, si me amas, hilaris et bene acceptis, ne in me stomachum erumpant cum sint tibi irati.* He can reflect, with a certain wry detachment, on his proposed journey: ibid. 4 *movet etiam navigationis labor alienus non ab aetate solum nostra verum etiam a dignitate tempusque discessus subabsurdum. relinquimus enim pacem ut ad bellum revertamur, quodque temporis in praediolis nostris et belle aedificatis et satis amoenis consumi potuit in peregrinatione consumimus.* In letter 5 he becomes eloquent on the subject of the young Quintus Cicero, whom he has recently seen and found a reformed character, a fact which has been recognized by Brutus: 16. 5. 2 *duxi enim mecum adulescentem ad Brutum. sic ei probatum est quod ad te scribo ut ipse crediderit, me sponsorem accipere noluerit eumque laudans amicissime mentionem tui fecerit, complexus osculatusque dimiserit.* In letter 7 Cicero describes how, after setting sail, he was driven back by contrary winds, and received news which made him decide to return to Rome. In these seven letters, particularly in 3, 5, and 7, Cicero frequently passes from the desultory, staccato manner which prevails when he is commenting on day-to-day matters or answering points in Atticus' letters, to a more 'literary' style, with longer and more complex sentences. In these seven letters are found two-thirds of the participles contained in Book 16. The second half of the book shows a marked contrast. Letter 8 is written at the beginning of November. The First Philippic has been delivered, but Cicero does not yet feel able to challenge Antony's power. He has withdrawn to Puteoli, there to busy himself with the Second Philippic and the *De Officiis*, and to wait on events. He does not know how far the young Octavian is to be trusted, nor what is his own best course of action, to stay in retirement, to withdraw further away, or to return to Rome: *numquam in maiore ἀπορίᾳ fui.* This mood persists. A week later, in letter 10, written on the way to Arpinum, he is again asking Atticus for advice: *tria sunt autem, maneamne Arpini an propius accedam an veniam Romam. quod censueris faciam. sed quam primum*; and, again, in letter 13 from Aquinum he repeats the question. Letter 14 begins with a complaint about the lack of news. In all these letters the writing is conversational and desultory. Only in 15 does he find something to write about—his breach with Dolabella, and on this subject he expresses himself fluently and in longer, constructed sentences. In the latter half of Book 16, written when Cicero was in a state of doubt and with little to stimulate his pen, and in which the prevailing manner is conversational and disconnected, there are only nine participles, most of them commonplace absolute or predicative uses.

We thus reach the plain, if not surprising, conclusion that in his letters to Atticus Cicero's use of participles tends to increase in proportion as his writing becomes more connected and literary. Where he is most colloquial, participles are few, and virtually confined to an occasional ablative absolute and such stereotyped epistolary uses as *mane proficiscens has litteras dedi* or *epistolam . . . sibi a nescio quo missam.*

When we turn to his correspondence with others, we are often able to see both sides, and we find that, generally speaking, his correspondents are prepared to use participles as freely as Cicero himself, if not more so. This is most evident in certain letters from provincial commanders, reporting on activities and events in their provinces. For instance, two successive letters from Asinius Pollio, governor of Further Spain, contain 16 participles in little more than 4 pages (fam. 10. 31 and 10. 32). Even more striking is an official dispatch from Lentulus to the Senate (fam. 12. 15) containing 25 participles in $3\frac{1}{2}$ pages, whereas his preceding 3-page letter to Cicero himself has only 4. It was indeed natural that an account of events to be contained in the moderate compass of a letter should make free use of participles, and Cicero himself, writing in similar circumstances to Cato from Cilicia in 50 B.C. (fam. 15. 4), had used 32 participles in less than 7 pages.

I propose to look, in some detail, at three exchanges of correspondence during the chosen period, the letters to and from Munatius Plancus, Decimus Brutus, and Marcus Brutus.

In 44–43 B.C. Plancus was governor of Northern Gaul and consul designate for the year 42. His adherence to the senatorial cause was obviously vital, particularly after the siege of Mutina had begun. Throughout the series of letters (fam. 10. 1–24) Cicero's efforts are directed towards confirming and maintaining his loyalty; in vain, as it happened, since in the end Plancus joined Antony. Cicero writes with the dignity proper to an elder statesman addressing a person almost a generation younger, combined with the respect due to one who held important office, and whose goodwill was essential. Concinnity is prominent, even in the shorter notes towards the end of the series. The writing never loses its air of carefulness, and the letters in which he is most earnestly exhorting Plancus become more elaborate in construction and lend themselves to the use of participles: e.g. fam. 10. 3. 2 *ego, Plance, necessitudinem constitutam habui cum domo vestra ante aliquanto quam tu natus es, amorem autem erga te ab ineunte pueritia tua, confirmata iam aetate familiaritatem cum studio meo tum iudicio tuo constitutam*; ibid. 6. 3 *talem igitur te esse oportet, qui primum te ab impiorum civium tui dissimillimorum societate seiungas, deinde te senatui bonisque omnibus auctorem, principem, ducem praebeas, postremo ut pacem esse iudices non in armis positis sed in abiecto armorum et servitutis metu* (we should observe the chiastic arrangement of the two *ab urbe condita* phrases and their effectiveness in giving weight both of sound and of sense to the third colon); ibid. 12. 1 . . . *qui et te nossem et tuarum litterarum ad me missarum promissa meminissem et haberem a Furnio nostro tua penitus consilia cognita.*

The letters from Plancus are elegantly written and polite; while the issue remains undecided, Cicero is to be treated with every respect. Participles are most evident where he is giving situation reports, especially in letters 15, 18, and 21. The following passage illustrates not only his readiness to use participles as subordinating elements in a complex sentence, but also the comparative clumsiness of the result: fam. 10. 18. 2 *sciebam enim, etsi cautius illud erat consilium exspectare me ad Isaram dum Brutus traiceret exercitum, et cum conlega consentiente, exercitu concordi ac bene de re p. sentiente, sicut milites faciunt, hostibus obviam ire, tamen, si quid Lepidus bene sentiens detrimenti cepisset, hoc omne adsignatum iri aut pertinaciae meae aut timori videbam, si aut hominem offensum mihi, coniunctum cum re p. non sublevassem aut ipse a certamine belli tam necessari me removissem.*

The correspondence with Decimus Brutus (fam. 11. 4–26)

extends from the beginning of November 44 to June 43. Decimus
Brutus was governor of Cisalpine Gaul and consul designate for
42. As one of the conspirators his loyalty to the Senate and
opposition to Antony could be relied upon, and Cicero has no
such misgivings about him as he obviously feels about Plancus.
Of Decimus' letters to Cicero all except the first (11. 4) were
written after the battle of Mutina. Most are short and couched in
a style which is economical, not to say terse, and in marked
contrast to the elaborate manner of Plancus: e.g. 11. 4. 2 *cum
omnium bellicosissimis bellum gessi; multa castella cepi, multa vastavi.
non sine causa ad senatum litteras misi.*[1] The text of his letters,
amounting to about seven pages, contains eighteen participles,
but most of these are commonplace absolute phrases.

Cicero's letters to Decimus are written in a plainer and less
expansive style than he adopts towards Plancus. Not only are
there no complimentary passages expressed in elaborate sentences with prominent concinnity, but even where Cicero writes
to the two men on the same topics, his manner with Brutus is
simpler and more direct. On 29 May 43 B.C. he writes thus to
Plancus: fam. 10. 20. 2 *sin ut scripsisti ad collegam, ita se res habet,
omni cura liberati sumus nec tamen erimus prius quam ita esse tu nos
feceris certiores. mea quidem, ut ad te saepius scripsi, haec sententia est, qui
reliquias huius belli oppresserit, eum totius belli confectorem fore; quem te
et opto esse et confido futurum.* To Decimus, on the same day, thus:
11. 14. 3 *id si ita est, omnia faciliora; sin aliter, magnum negotium, cuius
exitum non extimesco. tuae partes sunt; ego plus quam feci facere non
possum. te tamen, id quod spero, omnium maximum et clarissimum videre
cupio.* To Decimus, towards the end of June, he writes: 11. 15. 1
*coniunctio tua cum conlega concordiaque vestra, quae litteris communibus
declarata est, senatui populoque Romano gratissima accidit.* For Plancus
the language is enhanced: 10. 22. 1 *concordia vestra, quae senatui
declarata litteris vestris est, mirifice et senatus et cuncta civitas delectata
est.* In each case Cicero's style seems to match that of his corre-
spondent. A small cross-section of the letters, written at a time
when Cicero was preoccupied with the struggle against Antony,

---

[1] For an illuminating discussion of this style see E. Fraenkel, 'Eine Form römischer
Kriegsbulletins', in *Eranos* 54 (1956), 189 ff.

does not permit any conclusion. But if we were to examine the whole of the *Epistulae ad familiares* with this in view, we might well find clear evidence that Cicero's manner tended unconsciously to adapt itself to that of the person to whom he was writing. So far as participles are concerned, it is worth observing that, whereas in the letters to Plancus the average frequency is 2·5 per page, in the letters to Decimus the figure falls to 1·5.

The few participles in these letters include several interesting examples, such as are not to be found in Cicero's correspondents. In 11. 14. 1 an absolute phrase is attached to a noun (*fuga Antoni conciso exercitu*); in 11. 16. 1 an attributive participle produces balance without mechanical concinnity: *nam quem ad modum coram qui ad nos intempestive adeunt molesti saepe sunt, sic epistulae offendunt non loco redditae*; in 11. 18. 2, a passage discussed on pp. 115 f., four absolute phrases are carefully arranged to produce a double antithesis without banality.

What remains of the correspondence between Cicero and Marcus Brutus covers the period from early April to late July 43 B.C. Cicero could rely completely on Brutus; his only misgiving was lest Brutus might be too ready to come to terms with Antony and his supporters. For Cicero this was a serious divergence of outlook. Brutus, for his part, became increasingly concerned about what seemed to him the excessive respect shown by Cicero for the young Octavian.

The first three letters from Cicero were written when the situation at Mutina was critical; the writing is plain, the tone subdued. The third (ad Brut. 4), a reply to a letter from Brutus, is written in haste ('hoc paululum exaravi ipsa in turba matutinae salutationis'). Apart from two stereotyped epistolary uses and one absolute phrase, these letters have no participle. Letter 5 was written on 14 April, the day after letters from Brutus and from Antony had been read in the Senate. Cicero has been troubled by what he considers the dangerously placatory attitude of Brutus towards Antony, and in the first part of the letter he is at pains to explain his own policy ('illud necesse me ad te scribere, quid sentirem tota de constitutione huius belli et quo iudicio essem quaque sententia'). The page in which he does this contains three participles, the rest of the letter ($1\frac{1}{2}$ pages), none. Letters 6, 7, 8, 9, 10, 13, and 17 are short and plain, though 17—a message of condolence on the death of Brutus' wife—is expressed with grace and dignity; in these letters participles are very few. In 18 Cicero, having no letter from Brutus to answer and no news of his movements, takes occasion to give him a full account of the existing situation and the events leading up to it. The two-page letter contains seven participles, six of them in the first page. Even more striking is 23, a long letter in which Cicero justifies the position which he has adopted ('quid ego autem secutus hoc bello sim in sententiis dicendis aperire non alienum puto'). In the first part of his apologia he summarizes the events between the Ides of March and his return to Rome in August 44 B.C. This account is necessary because he wishes to show the consistency of his own attitude; but the events themselves were well known to Brutus, who had taken part in them, so that brevity is essential. The passage, very elaborate in style, deserves to be quoted at length, because it well illustrates the compression of sense achieved by the use of participles, of which there are here seven in half a page: ad Brut. 23. 4 *post interitum Caesaris et vestras memorabilis Idus Martias, Brute, quid ego praetermissum a vobis quantamque impendere rei publicae tempestatem dixerim non es oblitus: magna pestis erat depulsa per vos, magna populi Romani macula deleta, vobis vero parta divina gloria, sed instrumentum regni delatum ad Lepidum et Antonium, quorum alter inconstantior, alter impurior, uterque pacem metuens, inimicus otio. his ardentibus perturbandae rei publicae cupiditate quod opponi posset praesidium non habebamus; erexerat enim se civitas in retinenda libertate consentiens, nos tum nimis acres, vos fortasse sapientius excessistis urbe ea quam liberaratis, Italiae sua vobis studia profitenti remisistis. itaque cum teneri urbem a parricidis viderem nec te in ea nec Cassium tuto esse posse eamque armis oppressam ab Antonio, mihi quoque ipsi excedendum putavi; taetrum enim spectaculum oppressa ab impiis civitas opitulandi potestate praecisa. sed animus idem qui semper infixus in patriae caritate discessum ab eius periculis ferre non potuit.*

The seven letters from Brutus reveal a strikingly similar tendency; participles are infrequent except in two letters, in both of which Brutus is writing about the subject which most preoccupies him—Cicero's attitude to Octavian. In 12, the letter in which this anxiety first appears, there are 7 participles in little more than a page. Later Brutus devotes to the theme a whole letter (24), the five pages of which contain 20 participles. Atticus had sent him part of a letter from Cicero to Octavian, and he has been deeply offended by a phrase in which Cicero had commended to Octavian the welfare (there is no adequate equivalent of *salus*) of Brutus and Cassius: ad Brut. 24. 1 *sic enim illi gratias agis de re publica, tam suppliciter ac demisse—quid scribam? pudet condicionis ac fortunae, sed tamen scribendum est: commendas nostram salutem illi, quae morte qua non perniciosior? ut prorsus prae te feras non sublatam dominationem sed dominum commutatum esse.* To Brutus it seemed intolerable that Cicero should behave as a relentless enemy to Caesar's lieutenant, but show servility to Caesar's adopted son and heir—a mere boy at that; it was still more intolerable that he should show servility on Brutus' behalf. Tyrrell and Purser, staunch champions of Cicero, can see no merit in this devastatingly critical letter. They speak of it as 'ponderous and laboured', they stigmatize its 'studied and elaborate style' and its 'poverty of thought'. Shuckburgh describes it as 'querulous, poor, ill-expressed and tautological'. I cannot share these views. The letter seems to me to be carefully written, but by no means laboured. It is a piece of sustained and passionate argumentation by one who saw the actual situation perhaps more clearly than Cicero, or who at least could be excused for misinterpreting Cicero's behaviour. His own pride is certainly involved, but he is genuinely convinced of the falsity of Cicero's position, and tries every means to demonstrate it. It is this concentration of thought which is reflected in the style of the letter, and particularly in the large number of participles, which, incidentally, Brutus uses more effectively than any other of Cicero's correspondents. I quote a few further extracts from the letter, if only to show that it does not altogether deserve the contempt with which it has been treated:

24. 4 *tu quidem, consularis et tantorum scelerum vindex, quibus oppressis vereor ne in breve tempus dilata sit abs te pernicies, qui potes intueri quae gesseris, simul et ista vel probare vel ita demisse ac facile pati ut probantis speciem habeas?*

24. 6 *hanc ego civitatem videre velim aut putem ullam, quae ne traditam quidem atque inculcatam libertatem recipere possit, plusque timeat in puero nomen sublati regis quam confidat sibi, cum illum ipsum qui maximas opes habuerit paucorum virtute sublatum videat?*

24. 9 *quid enim est melius quam memoria recte factorum et libertate contentum neglegere humana? sed certe non succumbam succumbentibus nec vincar ab iis qui se vinci volunt, experiarque et temptabo omnia neque desistam abstrahere a servitio civitatem nostram.*

We have observed, in the letters both of Cicero and of his correspondents, that in the informal, day-to-day communications participles tend to be few or non-existent. Such instances as occur are either the stereotyped epistolary uses already mentioned or commonplace absolute or predicative participles. It is when the writing becomes 'literary' that participles are used as an integral element, and then they tend to appear not in isolation, but in groups. We find them where the language is specially elaborate and the sentence-structure complex, as in some of the letters to Plancus; we find them above all when it is a matter of succinctly describing or explaining a series of events or a situation, and in passages of close argumentation. Cicero's practice differs from that of his correspondents only in the greater skill which he shows in incorporating participles in his sentence-structure.

These findings confirm what was observed in the speeches, where participles tend to be grouped not necessarily in the most eloquent places, but where there is a concentration of fact or thought which requires brief or forceful expression.

The treatises, consisting of continuous argumentation, interspersed with illustrative anecdotes, show a more even distribution of participles, and their subject-matter entails a development of substantival and attributive types.

Summing up, we may say that participles enable Cicero to achieve sometimes a concise antithesis, sometimes a satisfying expansion (this is particularly true of the attributive type), sometimes variety within concinnity. But more important for him seems to have been their ability to produce compression of sense, permitting factual information or detailed argument to be communicated briefly and effectively.

GENERAL INDEX

(See also List of Contents)

a: (b:A)pattern in complex participial constructions, 128 f.

ab urbe condita construction, affinity with abl. absol., 99, 102.

— affinity with gerundive construction, 87, 89.

— frequently used in genitive, 93 f.

— in apposition to noun or pronoun, 90.

— in parallel series, 91, 96.

— not always distinguishable from attrib. use, 60 ff., 93, 95, 97 f.

— not derived from Greek, 84 ff.

— rare in early Latin, 86.

— use with present part. introduced by Cicero, 96 f.

— with future participle, 99, 121.

ablative absolute, relatively static in Cicero, 104.

— sociative origin of, 100 f.

absolute phrases, combined otherwise than in parallel, 115 f.

— interdependence between, 116 f., 137.

adsum, forensic use of, 120.

antithetic phrases, predicative participle in, 15.

— substantival participle in, 78.

arrival and departure, verbs of, 38 ff.

attributive *futurus* frequent in Cicero, 122 f.

'au sens d'équivalence', type of modal participle, 25.

'background' participle in complex constructions, 128, 129.

Bennett, C. E., 1 f.

Cicero's correspondents, 19 n. 1, 30, 38, 40, 123, 124, 139 n., 150 ff.

complex participial structure not found in early Latin, 138.

'conative' present participle, 40 f.

concentration of participles, 140 f.

— motives for, 142, 156.

different styles adopted towards different correspondents, 152 f.

distribution of participles uneven, 140.

emphatic predic. part. not always distinguishable from attrib., 48, 65 f.

expansion, attributive part. lends itself to, 58, 59.

— with absolute phrases, 115, 142 n.

figura etymologica, 17 ff., 132.

Fraenkel, E., 44 n. 1, 90 n. 1, 102 n. 1, 126 n. 1, 134 n. 2, 148, 152 n.

frequentative present participle, 42.

genitive, predicative participle in, 60.

genitive present part., substantival bias in, 34 f.

— very rare in early Latin, 34.

Greek, influence of, 38, 43 ff., 53 f., 112.

ille, frequently associated with attributive participles, 56.

Lebreton, J., 25, 26, 28.

letters of Cicero exhibit no single style, 147 f.

logical subject, adverbial participle agreeing with, 30, 31.

Marouzeau, J., 19 f., 24, 27 f., 31 f., 39, 41, 42, 125.

Mugler, C., 125, 126.

past part. originally purely adjectival, 2 f.

philosophical terminology, use of participles in, 63, 78 f.

predicative adjectives, two types of, 1.

predicative part. agreeing with unspecified subject in O.O., not to be confused with substantival use, 76.

prepositional phrases, predicative participle in, 60.

present part., adverbial uses progressively developed by Cicero, 22 f.

quidam, frequently associated with attributive participle, 56.

'reciprocal' present participle, 36 ff.

PASSAGES DISCUSSED

PRINTED IN GREAT BRITAIN
AT THE UNIVERSITY PRESS, OXFORD
BY VIVIAN RIDLER
PRINTER TO THE UNIVERSITY